The Social Thought of
Max Weber

SAGE was founded in 1965 by Sara Miller McCune to support the dissemination of usable knowledge by publishing innovative and high-quality research and teaching content. Today, we publish over 900 journals, including those of more than 400 learned societies, more than 800 new books per year, and a growing range of library products including archives, data, case studies, reports, and video. SAGE remains majority-owned by our founder, and after Sara's lifetime will become owned by a charitable trust that secures our continued independence.

Los Angeles | London | New Delhi | Singapore | Washington DC | Melbourne

And why then did capitalist interests not call forth this stratum of jurists and this type of law in China or India? How did it happen that scientific, artistic, and economic development, as well as state-building, were not directed in China and India into those tracks of *rationalization* specific to the West? (Weber, 2011, p. 245; emphasis in original)

The origin of economic rationalism depends not only on an advanced development of technology and law but also on the capacity and disposition of persons to organize their lives in a practical-rational manner. Wherever magical and religious forces have inhibited the unfolding of this organized life, the development of an organized life oriented systematically toward *economic* activity has confronted broad-ranging internal resistance. (Weber, 2011, p. 246; emphasis in original)

Behind the [varieties of belief was] a stand regarding something in the actual world which was experienced as specifically "senseless." Thus, the demand has been implied that the world order in its totality is, could, and should somehow be a meaningful "cosmos." (Weber, 2011, p. 242)

[Weber] revealed to us things we had not seen before in such contexts. What he elucidated, what he left to us as his legacy, has today become part and parcel of our political, social, and scientific thinking to a far greater extent than we ourselves could possibly have realized half a century ago. (Loewenstein, 1966, p. 104)

Social Thinkers Series

Series Editor
A. Javier Treviño
Wheaton College, Norton, MA

Published
The Social Thought of Georg Simmel
By Horst J. Helle

The Social Thought of Karl Marx
By Justin P. Holt

The Social Thought of Erving Goffman
By Michael Hviid Jacobsen and Søren Kristiansen

The Social Thought of Émile Durkheim
By Alexander Riley

The Social Thought of Talcott Parsons
By Helmut Staubmann

The Social Thought of C. Wright Mills
By A. Javier Treviño

The Social Thought of Max Weber

Stephen Kalberg

Boston University

Los Angeles | London | New Delhi
Singapore | Washington DC | Melbourne

FOR INFORMATION:

SAGE Publications, Inc.
2455 Teller Road
Thousand Oaks, California 91320
E-mail: order@sagepub.com

SAGE Publications Ltd.
1 Oliver's Yard
55 City Road
London, EC1Y 1SP
United Kingdom

SAGE Publications India Pvt. Ltd.
B 1/I 1 Mohan Cooperative Industrial Area
Mathura Road, New Delhi 110 044
India

SAGE Publications Asia-Pacific Pte. Ltd.
3 Church Street
#10-04 Samsung Hub
Singapore 049483

Acquisitions Editor: Jeff Lasser
Editorial Assistant: Alexandra Croell
Production Editor: Libby Larson
Copy Editor: Deanna Noga
Typesetter: C&M Digitals (P) Ltd.
Proofreader: Allison Syring
Indexer: Kathy Paparchontis
Cover Designer: Candice Harman
Marketing Manager: Jennifer Jones

Printed in the United States of America

Library of Congress Cataloging-in-Publication Data

Names: Kalberg, Stephen, author.

Title: The social thought of Max Weber / Stephen Kalberg, Boston University, USA.

Description: Los Angeles : SAGE, [2017] | Includes bibliographical references and index.

Identifiers: LCCN 2015045994 | ISBN 9781483371498 (pbk. : alk. paper)

Subjects: LCSH: Weber, Max, 1864-1920. | Sociology—Germany—History.

Classification: LCC HM479.W42 K3724 2017 | DDC 301.092—dc23 LC record available at http://lccn.loc.gov/2015045994

This book is printed on acid-free paper.

16 17 18 19 20 10 9 8 7 6 5 4 3 2 1

Contents

Detailed Contents

Series Editor's Foreword

The SAGE Social Thinkers series is dedicated to making available compact, reader-friendly paperbacks that examine the thought of major figures from within and beyond sociology. The books in this series provide concise introductions to the work, life, and influences of the most prominent social thinkers. Written in accessible and provocative prose, these books are designed for advanced undergraduate and graduate students of sociology, politics, economics, and social philosophy, as well as for scholars and socially curious general readers.

The first few volumes in the series are devoted to the "classical" thinkers—Karl Marx, Emile Durkheim, Max Weber, Georg Simmel, George Hebert Mead, Talcott Parsons, and C. Wright Mills—who, through their seminal writings, laid the foundation for much of current social thought. Subsequent books will feature more "contemporary" scholars as well as those not yet adequately represented in the canon: Jane Addams, Charlotte Perkins Gilman, Harold Garfinkel, Norbert Elias, Jean Baudrillard, and Pierre Bourdieu. Particular attention is paid to those aspects of the social thinker's personal background and intellectual influences that most impacted his or her approach in better understanding individuals and society.

Consistent with SAGE's distinguished track record of publishing high-quality textbooks in sociology, the carefully assembled volumes in the Social Thinkers series are authored by respected scholars committed to disseminating the discipline's rich heritage of social thought and to helping students comprehend key concepts. The information offered in these books will be invaluable for making sense of the complexities of contemporary social life and various issues that have become central concerns of the human condition: inequality, social order, social control, deviance, the social self, rationality, reflexivity, and so on.

These books in the series can be used as self-contained volumes or in conjunction with textbooks in sociological theory. Each volume concludes with a Further Readings chapter intended to facilitate additional study and research. As a collection, the Social Thinkers series will stand as a testament to the robustness of contemporary social thought. Our hope is that these books on the great social thinkers will give students a deeper understanding of modern and postmodern Western social thought and encourage them to engage in sociological dialogue.

Premised on Newton's aphorism, "If I have seen farther, it is by standing on the shoulders of giants" (an aphorism, incidentally, that was introduced into sociology by Robert K. Merton, himself a towering figure in the discipline), the Social Thinkers series aims to place its readers on the shoulders of the giants of 19th- and 20th-century social thought.

Acknowledgments

When this volume began is not easy to say. Perhaps its gestation occurred long ago when students in the United States were protesting against the anonymity and power characteristic of modern-day bureaucracies. Weber's insightful essay on the nature of these large organizations became widely read. Or perhaps this study originated from a reading of *The Protestant Ethic and the Spirit of Capitalism* in the 1970s. Weber's message struck a chord: Sociology's task also involves investigation of how world views and values influence our activities. Or perhaps decisive were his masterful insights on the multiple ways in which the past clandestinely – or overtly – intrudes into the present. Or perhaps this volume developed from the strong impression left by the last chapter of Weber's *Religion of China*; vividly portrayed here are the ways in which the values taught by Confucius are different from those held by seventeenth-century Puritans in the West. Or, finally, perhaps at the source of this study are the questions my students formulated in my first classical sociological theory seminar. They have challenged me over many years to render Weber's often obtuse writings in an understandable manner.

I am deeply indebted to Robert J. Antonio, Hinnerk Bruhns, Donald Nielsen, and Javier Trevino for their insightful and helpful comments upon this volume's early drafts. I am especially thankful to Javier, as the "Sage Social Thought" series editor, for inviting me to write this volume.

Several publishers have graciously provided permission to re-publish material in this volume. They are acknowledged now with gratitude:

Oxford Publishing Limited:

FROM MAX WEBER translated by H. H. Gerth & C. Wright Mills (1946): "Politics as a Vocation," pp. 95, 114–17, 120–8; "Science as a Vocation," pp. 145–53 © 1946, 1958, 1973 by Gerth and Mills.

Oxford University Press:

Extract (c.14400w) from Part 4, pp. 319–348. 'Introduction' from "Max Weber: *The Protestant Ethic and the Spirit of Capitalism with Other Writings on the Rise of the West.*" Translated and edited by Stephen Kalberg (2009).

American Sociological Association:

Kalberg, Stephen. "On the Neglect of Weber's Protestant Ethic as a Theoretical Treatise: Demarcating the Parameters of Postwar American Sociological Theory." *Sociological Theory*, Vol. 14, No. 1 (Mar., 1996), p. 63.

John Wiley & Sons:

Max Weber: Readings and Commentary on Modernity. Edited by Stephen Kalberg. Wiley-Blackwell: February 2005. Pp. xv–xix.

Kalberg, Stephen. "Max Weber." *The Wiley-Blackwell Companion to Major Social Theorists: Classical Social Theorists, Volume I.* Eds. George Ritzer and Jeffrey Stepnisky. Malden, MA: Wiley-Blackwell, 2011. Pp. 330–345

To the memory of my teacher,
Lewis A. Coser

Introduction

The religion of brotherliness has always clashed with the orders and values of this world, and the more consistently its demands have been carried through, the sharper the clash has been. The split has usually become wider the more the values of the world have been rationalized and sublimated in terms of their own laws. And that is what matters here.

(Weber, 1946b, p. 330)

The broad-ranging questions and concerns of Max Weber (1864–1920) still speak to us nearly 100 years after his death. Those who seek to understand the internal workings and dynamics of modern and premodern societies alike appreciate and learn even today from his concepts and theories. In all corners of the globe, social scientists and historians stand under a strong obligation to become acquainted with the central dimensions of *Weberian* sociology.

Weber has been acclaimed universally as a sociologist of sweeping scope, insight, and conceptual powers. He is today best known in most regions of the world for his attempts to define the uniqueness of the modern West and to provide rigorous causal explanations for its singular historical development. However, far from offering a justification for Western industrial societies, his sociological and political writings evidence a profound ambivalence toward them. Although impressed by their capacity to sustain high standards of living, Weber feared that many fundamental features of modern societies opposed values and ideals he held dear: ethical action, the individual's autonomy, the personality unified by reference to a constellation of noble values, and a universal ideal of compassion.

His quest to comprehend the particular features of Western modernity and the causes at the source of the West's long-range trajectory pushed him to pursue an extraordinarily comparative research agenda. Extensive cross-civilizational investigations alone, he was convinced, would reveal the West's uniqueness and the roots of its specific development.

1

Thus, his urgent questions led him to a series of massive works. Remarkably, his inquiries spanned the histories of China, India, and the civilizations of Western antiquity. With full sovereignty, they traversed as well across each century of the West's 2,600-year development. In detailed investigations, he explored, for example, Old Testament prophecy and the Bible; the salvation doctrines of Buddhism, Hinduism, ancient Judaism, early Christianity, Islam, medieval Catholicism, Lutheranism, and ascetic Protestantism; the decline of the Roman Empire, the accounting practices of medieval trading companies; the possibilities for democracy in Russia; and the causes behind the rise of the caste system in India, Confucianism in China, and monotheism in ancient Israel.

To Weber, all these studies related—some more directly than others—to his overarching concern to define the uniqueness of the West and the causes behind its particular pathway. His approach abjured a focus on single factors, such as economic *or* religious forces. It sought instead to offer multidimensional and multicausal analyses that rigorously evaluated—through precise comparisons—the causal weight in particular of economic and political interests, values and ideals, longstanding conventions and customs, new innovations and new knowledge, and charismatic figures. Weber was particularly concerned to identify the configurations of groups that facilitated—or hindered—the origin and expansion of an ethos of compassion and *ethical* action generally. Will constellations of binding values remain in the modern era? Will a firm foundation for ethical decisions continue to exist?

At the dawning of the 20th century, Weber posed burning questions: "How shall we live with dignity in this new era?" "Where are we headed?" He worried that our society might become a "steel-hard casing" of impersonal and instrumental relationships incapable of nourishing values, ideals, and compassion. His cross-civilizational explorations can be also comprehended as a manifestation of his quest to demarcate realistic parameters for substantial social change. The West, he believed, stood at the precipice of a potentially debilitating crisis.

Weber sought to conduct his comparative investigations *impartially*. He attempted to do so even though the activities of peoples across the globe at times appeared to him, from the point of view of his own values, odd and even bizarre. His research remains valid today in part owing to his unwillingness to evaluate civilizations, unlike most of his colleagues, in reference to an unquestioned hierarchy of Western values. On behalf of an understanding of Weber's overarching themes on the one hand and his distinct research procedures on the other hand, this volume seeks to fulfill two large goals.

First, it strives to define his main themes by reference to the intellectual, social, and political contexts within which he lived and wrote. Intense debates on the origins and character of the modern world and the appropriate methodology for social science research surrounded Weber even during his student years. They influenced him significantly and entered deeply into the formation of his "interpretive" (*verstehende*) and highly comparative-historical sociology. In addition, his writings responded directly to the secularization, industrialization, and urbanization transformations occurring on a wide scale throughout the West. *His* generation reacted vigorously to this monumental social metamorphosis.

Second, Weber's central studies—*The Protestant Ethic and the Spirit of Capitalism* (*PE*; 2009, 2011), *Economy and Society* (*E&S*; 1968), and the Economic Ethics of the World Religions series (EEWR; 1946b, 1946c, 1951, 1952, 1958)—are addressed in this volume, in opposition to almost all the commentary on his works, in a *synthetic* manner. Its focus is on the ways in which his queries regarding the singularity of the West and its causes extend *throughout* his main works. This orientation diverges from the present-day discussions on Weber. How is this the case?

Max Weber has contributed more to the intellectual capital of the modern-day social sciences than any other founder. His classic definitions—for example, of a "Protestant ethic," the bureaucracy, charismatic leadership, status groups, the state, the nation, the city, feudalism, power, and authority—have become institutionalized in various disciplines. Perhaps just the clarity, precision, and usefulness of his constructs and typologies stand at the source of the recent revitalization in the United Kingdom and northern America of an earlier Weber reception that focused on the "correct" definition of his "major concepts." As a consequence of his skill as a classifier, he is today widely perceived in these regions mainly as a superior taxonomist and as an ahistorical theorist who formulated an invaluable lexicon for sociology.

This "concepts interpretation" neglects a great deal. Indeed, omitted are the most interesting and profound components of Weber's sociology—namely, a discussion of the broad themes we have noted that run prominently throughout his works and connect his many studies: the modern West's singular contours and the causes behind its particular historical trajectory. This volume's task is now clear: It seeks to provide an accessible articulation of these themes, one that offers an accurate portrait of Weber's overarching concerns and mode of conducting research. In doing so, this study introduces Weber's *sociology of civilizations* in a detailed manner. Finally, it maintains that a frequent stigma attached to Weber—"His writings are fragmented and lacking in coherence"—must be understood as a further enduring misperception. The remainder of this chapter outlines the steps to be taken.

An Overview

Chapter 1 examines aspects of Weber's life and the intellectual context within which his works originated. His thematic concerns and research agenda were influenced on the one hand by an eventful and civic-oriented personal history and on the other hand by the dominant intellectual currents established by the great European scholars of the 19th century. His rejection of all attempts, on the basis of social science research, to construct generally applicable and "true" values, general laws, and "objective facts" is discussed in this chapter. Weber's aim to formulate a particular type of comparative-historical sociology that places *subjective meaning (subjektive Sinnbedeutung)* at its core is also addressed.

Chapter 2 focuses on *The Protestant Ethic and the Spirit of Capitalism (PE)*, Weber's most famous and accessible book. It argues that the "Protestant ethic thesis," correctly understood, refers both to a pivotal argument in *PE* (believers must testify through their conduct to their salvation "before God") and to a central argument in his "Sect essays" (believers must testify through their conduct to their salvation "before men").

This classic study also best illustrates central features of Weber's methodology; for example, his emphasis on the significance of subjective meaning in a sociological analysis, the capacity of an "interpretive understanding" approach to facilitate access by researchers to the varying motives of people, the influence of religious belief on conduct, and the capacity of religions to leave important secular legacies.

Having examined *PE*'s argument and the ways in which it illustrates major aspects of Weber's mode of research, Chapter 3 turns directly to his methodology. Several background ideas and presuppositions first capture our attention. Weber's opposition to a view widespread among his colleagues—modern social science should be defined as involving a search for true values, general laws, and objective facts—is addressed. His fundamental rejection of organic holism is as important for comprehension of his research procedures.

Weber also opposed vehemently the predominant Eurocentrism of his times. This foundational position allowed him to develop his methodology forcefully in the direction of a rigorous comparative-historical sociology of "subjective meaning" *(subjektive Sinnbedeutung)* and "an empirical science of concrete reality."

Chapter 3 as well defines the basic research tools and terms of Weber's sociology. What exactly does "interpretive understanding" imply? And "subjective meaning"? His unwavering commitment to *multicausal* modes of explanation is also explored, as are the ways in which he connects subjective meaning both to "four types of social action" and to his foundational research construct: the "ideal type."

Finally, Weber's notions of "value-freedom," "value-relevance," and "objectivity," all of which are indispensable components of the impartial research process he advocates, are defined in Chapter 3, as is the *goal* of his sociology: to offer causal analyses of specific cases and developments. Discussions of basic features of Weber's procedures, such as his perpetual intertwining of the past with the present and his elevation of hypothesis-forming models to a central position in his sociology, run as red threads throughout this chapter. As will become apparent, many of the key heuristic concepts, modes of analysis, and building blocks for Weber's sociology of civilizations are illuminated in this chapter.

Chapter 4 examines his analytic treatise, the three-volume *Economy and Society*. One of the most unusual studies in the history of sociology, and surely the most ambitious, Weber offers here "a sociologist's world history . . . [that] raises some of the big questions [regarding] the modern world" (Roth, 1968, p. xxix). Indeed, he takes *most* of written human history as his broad palette, ranging with great command freely across the ancient, middle, and modern periods in China, India, and Europe. However, far from a narrative attempt to capture history's flow in its entirety, he aims here—as a sociologist—to construct arrays of models. Nonetheless, Weber insists that every construct must be based on a wealth of empirical knowledge. A back-and-forth movement in *E&S* between empirical detail and analytic generalization (especially in the longer Part II) tries the patience of every reader.

Fortunately, Weber's strong interest in the unique features of Western history and the singular causes of its particular trajectory continuously reappears, thereby endowing this enormous opus with a degree of unity. *E&S*'s innumerable models also serve this interest. He provides further direction and order by organizing these volumes largely by reference to four major "societal spheres" (*Lebensordnungen, Lebensbereiche, Lebenssphaeren*) and their "rationalization"—or systematization—processes: the economy, law, rulership, and religion domains. As is discussed, within each arena arrays of salient ideal types—arranged as "developmental form" constructs—chart out separate rationalization models.

These concepts form hypotheses on every page. For example, rationalization occurs in the law arena along an analytic pathway from primitive law to traditional law to natural law and then to "logical-formal" law. What causes *in a particular empirical case* appeared in such a manner that rationalization actually took place? And did its pathway conform to the pathway articulated by the developmental form model? Which civilizations conformed somewhat to the developmental models in the rulership, economy, religion, and law spheres? Which did so to a certain degree? Which hardly at all? What accounts for the diverging pathways?

Weber's empirical analyses, as noted, were built on a foundation of knowledge that encompassed a broad comparative terrain. His constructs, he hopes, will offer helpful means of orientation (*Orientierungsmittel*) and clear guidance to researchers engaged in empirical projects and searching for causes. However, they must be prepared to recognize history's perpetual irregularities and switchbacks, Weber insists—for issues of power and domination enter ubiquitously into rationalization and other social change processes. How strong and entrenched, he queries constantly, were the groups that "carried" a particular set of values or sets of economic and political interests? And how cohesive and powerful were other carrier groups that defended stability and tradition? Weber's *multicausality* assumes complex forms that take cognizance of a wide range of "driving forces."

All these issues find their way onto every page of *E&S*. Last but not least, Weber contends throughout these volumes—as well as throughout his oeuvre—that developments in the past very often, when they acquire constellations of strong carrier groups in amenable configurations, live on and permeate into the present to a significant degree. An unceasing interweaving of past and present occurs in all regions, he holds.

Chapter 5 turns in a different direction. It examines the social and political context of Weber's time, thereby offering to the reader a respite from *E&S*'s mixture of empirical detail, models-based hypotheses, and a broad-based multicausality. Here his sociological works are explored from a different angle: namely, against the backdrop of Imperial Germany's (1871–1918) major contours. Severe ruptures came to the surface as this nation attempted to adjust to four simultaneous processes: secularization, democratization, urbanization, and industrialization. The positions Weber supports in responding to this upheaval are summarized.

In particular, his analysis of, and proposals to address, the crisis of democracy confronted by Germany are scrutinized in Chapter 5. In this respect, Weber calls for greater societal dynamism. No less noteworthy in this regard is his firm view that the social sciences should not be expected, despite secularization, to respond by offering a new, quasi-religious world view. Rather, he contends, they appropriately fulfill modest tasks only.

Chapter 5 also presents examples of how Weber calls on deep sociological insight and a command of long-term historical developments to formulate viable analyses of immediate social ills. It charts the fields of Weber's peripatetic engagement and citizen activism.

Chapter 6 commences this volume's shift to Weber's sociology of civilizations. It first addresses his often-neglected three-volume Economic Ethics of the World Religion series. This massive tome asks whether an "economic ethic" existed in Confucianism, Taoism, Hinduism, Buddhism, Jainism, and ancient Judaism. If so, did it place a push into motion toward the development of modern capitalism similar to the Protestant ethic? Hence, we see in these volumes again Weber's search to identify the uniqueness of the West. He now sought to do so through EEWR's large-scale—though precisely designed—comparisons across the "world religions."

However, EEWR moves beyond *PE* in a highly significant way: It avoids a presentation of only "one side of the causal nexus"—namely, a monocausal methodology rooted exclusively in values and ideas. Instead, all EEWR investigations scrutinize "both sides" (see 2011, pp. 178–179). Weber's studies again become broadly multicausal.

In the volumes on China and India, for example, EEWR analyzes the development of the economy and the types of law. It also compares China, India, ancient Israel, and the medieval and modern West in regard to stratification configurations and rulership dynamics. Finally, the EEWR studies address as well the "strength of the family" and the major features of cities in highly comparative terms.

Indeed, EEWR's broad multicausality allows Weber not only to isolate more clearly unique aspects of the West and the modern West, and to identify more precisely the twists and turns of its 2,000-year development, but also to offer causal explanations for the developmental route followed in the West. Moreover, he argues in both EEWR and *E&S* that *each* civilization's singularity—its "civilizational rationalism"—can be charted. Thus, he repeatedly refers to the "rationalism" of China, India, ancient Israel, the medieval West, and the modern West. His works now articulate a highly comparative sociology of civilizations.

Chapter 7 takes the reader a large step farther into this sociology: It reconstructs Weber—in the sense of drawing on highly scattered texts—on the uniqueness of the West and the singularity of its long-range development to the 20th century. It also reconstructs his complex, multicausal analysis of the origins of "Western rationalism" and "modern Western rationalism." Among other major differences, the West called forth, Weber holds, a "structural heterogeneity" in the 17th and 18th centuries that widely introduced competing powers and an unusual degree of dynamism. Both these developments assisted significantly in creating sets of preconditions that in the end, he maintains, had the effect of constructing conducive pathways toward the growth of capitalism and the advent of modern capitalism.

Weber's long-term agenda to identify the uniqueness of the West and the causes behind its particularity would seem, at this point, to reach its conclusion. However, two additional building blocks in his sociology of civilizations should be examined: Chinese rationalism and the rationalism of India. Both chapters further indicate *how* he shaped and molded his vast macro comparisons to isolate and explain the West's uniqueness. Moreover, they construct the contours and parameters of Weber's sociology of civilizations more clearly. Finally, they offer further testimony to its analytic power and expansive reach.

Chapter 8 reconstructs the rationalism of ancient, medieval, and early modern China (see Weber, 1951). In the course of doing so, Weber's comparisons to the West are frequently noted.

His analysis emphasizes the high social prestige of the educated *literati* stratum in China and its role as a strong social carrier of Confucianism, the support of Confucianism by the dominant patrimonial rulership, the upholding of the firmness of the highly extended family—the clan—by Confucianism, the support of emperors and patrimonial administrators for the Examination system (which evaluated a candidate's knowledge of Confucianism), the pervasive expansion throughout the peasantry of magic and ancestor worship, and the small size of the merchant and entrepreneurial class. A traditional agrarian economy grounded deeply in the single relationship of trust—within the clan—prevailed and remained unchallenged. Groups capable of standing against the clan quickly died out. Neither Confucianism nor Taoism introduced an economic ethic. Finally, even though the literati, as a highly educated stratum, opposed magic and ancestor worship, it tolerated their existence on behalf of social stability.

Hence, Weber saw in China a high overlapping of groups. Indeed, the symmetry of China's rationalism placed strong barriers, he concluded, against competing groups, a dynamic economy, and the expansion of social trust beyond the clan.

The rationalism of ancient, medieval, and early modern India (see Weber, 1958) is reconstructed in Chapter 9. Dominated by the caste system, Brahmin priests, and Hinduism, inequality became institutionalized and legitimated. Neither the rulership sphere—dominated by feudalism and patrimonialism—nor India's traditional form of law and caste-based traditionalism in the economy arena allowed oppositional groups to form widely and to place confrontational powers into motion.

According to Weber, the caste order's "traditional spirit" upheld Hinduism's traditional economic ethic. And severe restrictions by both the caste system and rulership powers insured that the development of cities would be limited. Thus, the rationalism of India—another independent and autonomous civilizational rationalism—offered to Weber a further highly differentiated model. It provided a distinct contrast to the West.

We shift away from his sociology of civilizations in Chapter 10. Another major component in Weber's agenda is here illuminated: his aim to offer a type of sociology that charts a clear approach and demarcates guidelines for its *application*. Weber wishes his concepts and his research procedures to be *useful* to researchers.

This chapter demonstrates how his approach can be applied. It does so by reconstructing Weber's incomplete analysis of how, in the American political culture, a civic *sphere* with powerful religious roots congealed in the 17th and 18th centuries. With significant secularization, the religious dimension indigenous to this sphere weakened, he notes. However, instead of vanishing from the American political culture, legacies endured into the 19th century in a forceful manner—though now in largely secular manifestations as *civic associations*.

According to Weber, the American civic sphere served as a causal impulse that *called forth* an abundance of civic associations. The reconstruction offered here applies many of Weber's concepts and research procedures. It also offers suggestions for the utilization of his approach in a variety of ways.

Chapter 11 concludes this presentation of Weber. In a succinct manner, it seeks to assess Weber's *distinct* "interpretive understanding" approach and his comparative-historical agenda. His overall project must be held up to the light.

Weber proposes a singular sociology, one anchored in multicausal procedures, a variety of ideal type models, a rigorous comparative methodology, a severe empiricism, and a firm interweaving of the past and the present. He advocates a consistent orientation by researchers to the subjective meaning of persons in groups and its interpretive understanding. Several weaknesses and dilemmas, as formed by his many critics, must be examined. An array of strengths are also scrutinized.

This volume adds a Glossary, a Chronology of Weber's life, and a Further Readings chapter. The latter (a) calls attention to insightful commentary on various aspect of Weber's works and (b) reprints pivotal sections from his famous and widely read lectures, "Politics as a Vocation" and "Science as a Vocation." Finally, at the end of every chapter several "study questions" are formulated. They seek to highlight major themes and to assist reflection and understanding.

Our next task is to introduce Weber. Chapter 1 turns first to his personal biography and then to major features of his encompassing intellectual milieu.

1

The Person and
the Intellectual Context

The Person

Max Weber was born in Erfurt, Germany, into a distinguished and cosmopolitan family of entrepreneurs, scholars, politicians, and strong women. Most of his younger years were spent in Berlin. He attended a series of excellent schools that required a strenuous regimen of study.

Recognized early on as an exceptional student, he developed a precocious love of learning and a particular fondness for philosophy, literature, and ancient and medieval history. His teenage essays and letters comment on, among many others, the merits of Goethe, Kant, Hegel, Spinoza, and Schopenhauer. They analyze in depth the societies of the Renaissance and ancient Rome. They also demonstrate, as the eldest child, an abiding affection for his many siblings and a concern for his overworked, devout mother. Although influenced strongly by his father, a central figure in the city government of Berlin and the state government of Prussia, and an elected member of the German parliament (*Reichstag*), he deplored his patriarchal ways and insensitive treatment of his wife.

Weber studied economic history, law, and philosophy at the universities of Heidelberg, Berlin, and Göttingen. In Berlin, he became the protégé of the legal historian Levin Goldschmidt (1829–1897) and the Roman historian Theodor Mommsen (1817–1903). At an unusually young age he was appointed to a chair in commercial law at Berlin's Humboldt University.

He accepted in 1894 a chair in economics and finance in Freiburg and in 1896 he received an appointment in economics at the University of Heidelberg.

At the age of 33 in 1897, having recently married a distant cousin, Marianne Schnitger, Weber evicted from their Heidelberg home his visiting father, who had mistreated his mother. His father's death soon afterward seemed to have served as the catalyst for a paralyzing mental illness that endured for more than five years. During much of this time, Weber traveled and passively pondered the fate of persons living in the new world of secularism, urbanism, and capitalism.

A 10-week trip to the United States in the autumn of 1904 played a significant part in his recovery. Journeying across much of the east, south, and Midwest, he gained an appreciation for America's dynamism, energy, and uniqueness, as well as for the widespread self-reliance and distrust of authority among its citizens. His most famous work, *The Protestant Ethic and the Spirit of Capitalism* (2011), was completed soon after his return to Germany. Although unable to teach until 1918, Weber began once again to publish on a vast array of topics.

His interest in the "ascetic Protestantism" of the American Calvinist (Presbyterian), Methodist, Baptist, Quaker, and Mennonite churches derived in part from the religiosity of his Huguenot mother, Helene, and her sister, Ida Baumgarten. These Christian social activists and admirers of 19th-century American Unitarianism and English progressive theology transmitted to the young Weber a heightened sensitivity to moral questions, an appreciation of the ways in which the life of dignity and meaning must be guided by ethical standards, and a respect for the worth and uniqueness of every person. While Marianne reaffirmed these values, they opposed the lessons taught by Max's father: the necessity to avoid "naïve idealism," to confront the ways of the world in a pragmatic, even amoral, fashion, and to avoid personal sacrifice.

Nonetheless, Weber waged impassioned battles throughout his life on behalf of ethical positions and scolded relentlessly all who lacked a rigorous sense of justice and social responsibility. As his student Paul Honigsheim reports, he became a man possessed whenever threats to the autonomy of the individual were discussed (see Honigsheim, 1968, pp. 6, 43)—whether to mothers seeking custody of their children, women students at German universities, or bohemian social outcasts and political rebels.

Not surprisingly, his concerns for the fate of the German nation and the future of Western civilization drove him perpetually into the arena of politics. Vigorously opposed to the definition of this realm as one of "sober realism," or wheeling and dealing (*Realpolitik*), he called vehemently for politicians to act by reference to a stern moral code: an "ethic of responsibility" (*Verantwortungsethik*). (On Weber's life, see the sources listed in Chapter 12.)

The Intellectual Context

Long before Weber formulated his sociological concepts and research procedures, many 17th- and 18th-century thinkers in the West had sought to discover, through the systematic investigation of the natural and social worlds, proof of the existence of an all-powerful supernatural Being. If the centipede's 100 legs moved in a coordinated fashion, this extraordinary achievement must itself indicate the intelligence of a superior Being as its creator (see 2005, p. 325).[1] Moreover, the "hand of God" must be at work as well in the social world's "natural laws," it was believed.

Once proven, God's existence implied the necessity for "His children" to follow His Commandments. Hence, the investigation of the natural and social worlds held out the promise of embattled Christianity's renascence. The "divine order" would appear on Earth. Soon thereafter, the triumph of Christian compassion and universal love would banish the danger of a Hobbesian "war of all against all."

Although the 19th century brought these hopeful and optimistic investigations to a close, social thinkers in the West only grudgingly set aside an idea prominent in all salvation religions: All history and all activities of the human species possess a higher meaning and direction. Even as openly theological explanations for the purpose of life and history waned, the notion remained that a component more majestic than everyday activity was bestowed on human life. Whether Utilitarians in England at the beginning of the century or Spencerian Social Darwinists at its end; whether Hegelians or Marxists in Germany; whether followers of Saint Simon or Comte in France: All these schools of thought, although otherwise so different, articulated the idea that history moved in a lawful manner and in an evolutionary direction.

It thus contained a meaning all its own. In his expansive studies, the distinguished mid-century historian Leopold von Ranke (1795–1886) discovered the values of Christian Humanism at work through the ages, and the idealist philosopher Georg Wilhelm Friedrich Hegel (1770–1831) charted the history of the West as a progressive realization of the idea of freedom. Even thoroughly secularized German intellectuals at the end of the century—the philosopher Heinrich Rickert (1863–1936), for example—argued that history offered evidence for a firm hierarchy of true values, indeed ones capable of guiding our lives today. The economic historian Gustav Schmoller (1838–1917) sought to discover, through historical research, the underlying moral justification for the development of modern capitalism.

For all these thinkers, history retained a teleology and an "objective meaning." Conformity with its unified value system would ensure progress, as well as the just ordering of society, it was believed. Throughout the 19th century, and despite the turning by Marx of ethereal Hegelian thought "on its head," a rearguard reluctance to abandon the notion of a transcendental guiding force—now manifest in impersonal forms rather than understood as the direct will of a monotheistic and anthropomorphic God—prevailed.

Even Marx's "scientific socialism" formulated "dialectical laws of history." The present must be understood as only one of many historical stages, he argued, all of which lead along a predetermined route toward more advanced societies. Protestant Christianity's optimistic view regarding man's capacity to master his sinful human nature and to improve earthly existence constituted the facilitating cultural background for a flourishing of the secular ideas of Progress, Reason, and Freedom, as well as for all ideals of natural justice and all value hierarchies.

Max Weber's works stand directly antagonistic to these ideas of the 17th, 18th, and 19th centuries. With his sociology, a new *position* for the human species crystallized, one steadfastly opposed to the notion that history possessed an independent meaning: *Persons* now existed as the unequivocal makers of their destinies and as the cause of their activities. At the dawning of the 20th century, Weber insisted that meaning could arise only out of struggles to mold "meaningful lives" and the choices people made on this behalf:

> Every single important activity and ultimately life as a whole, if it is not to be permitted to run on as an event in nature but is instead to be consciously guided, is a series of ultimate decisions through which the soul . . . *chooses* its own destiny; that is, the meaning of its activity and existence. (1949, p. 18; translation altered; original emphasis; see also p. 81; 2005, pp. 331, 334–335)

Several currents of thought that placed the individual in the forefront came here to a synthesis: The Enlightenment's individual endowed with Reason and Rationality, the creative and introspective individual of the German Romantics (mainly Johann Wolfgang von Goethe [1749–1832] and Friedrich von Schiller [1759–1805]), and ascetic Protestantism's activity-oriented individual.[2]

The same antagonism to the notion that the flow of history contained a transcendental meaning accounts as well for Weber's opposition to the grounding of knowledge and activity beyond the empirical realm. With the prominent exception of the philosopher Friedrich Nietzsche (1844–1900), he saw more acutely than his contemporaries that, once the axial turn from theocentrism and quasi-theocentrism to anthropocentrism had been taken, a unifying set of quasi-religious values, the "course of history" and the "idea of progress" could no longer erect a firm foundation for the social sciences. The study of the *meaning-seeking person* must now move to the forefront and must be firmly rooted in reality. To Weber, "[t]he type of social science in which we are interested is an *empirical science of concrete reality*" (*Wirklichkeitswissenschaft*) (1949, p. 72; original emphasis).

The formation of this central tenet of Weber's sociology was directly influenced by the secular and industrial character of German society, as Weber himself acknowledged. Nonetheless, it must not be concluded that his research is empowered to investigate exclusively those few epochs and civilizations in which individualism has come to the fore and unified con-stellations of values have vanished. On the contrary, as noted, a highly comparative and historical horizon characterizes his investigations.

Weber knew well that subjective meaning may be created in a *vast* variety of ways. Indeed, his research revealed that the overriding beacon of light and guiding force for persons for millennia had originated from *diverse* orientations to the supernatural realm (see 2005, p. 331). Even though the notion of subjective meaning stands at the core of Weber's sociology, and hence the individualism dominant in his own epoch's "value ideas" (*Wertideen*) is apparent in its fundamental axioms, Weber's methodology emphatically leaves open—to be studied empirically on a case-by-case basis—the extent to which the formation of subjective meaning is influenced by the mundane world or the supernatural realm.

This monumental shift to a radically empirical sociology rooted in an identification of the subjective meaning of persons in groups must be acknowledged as foundational to Weber's entire sociology. Recognition of this turn allows its central features to become more easily comprehensible. They can be best discussed and illustrated by an examination of Weber's volume, *The Protestant Ethic and the Spirit of Capitalism* (PE). This study is the subject of the next chapter. Having investigated its argument and major methodological tools, Weber's concepts and research procedures become more accessible. In the subsequent chapter (Chapter 3), his meth-odology captures our attention in more detail.

Study Questions and Thoughts to Ponder

1. The author has argued that the secular ideas of Progress and Evolution had their roots in the realm of religion. Summarize and evaluate his argument.

2. Please review the foundational tenet of Weber's sociology: the endeavor to study the subjective meaning of persons.

3. Weber's sociology takes an "empirical turn." Please explain.

4. Why was the proof of God's existence so important to 17th- and 18th-century thinkers?

5. Nineteenth-century thinkers saw a "higher meaning and direction" in all history and human activity. Trace the sources of this notion.

6. What foundational axiom in Weber's methodology opposed strictly the idea that "history possessed an independent meaning"?

7. Is the "formation of subjective meaning" influenced only by the mundane world? Only by the supernatural realm? By both?

Notes

1. Unless otherwise noted, all references are to Weber.

2. That these major currents of thought remained otherwise so difficult to render into a unity laid the foundation for tensions that run throughout Weber's sociology. This will become apparent.

2

The Protestant Ethic and the Spirit of Capitalism and the "Sect Essays"

"The Protestant Ethic Thesis" I: *The Protestant Ethic and the Spirit of Capitalism*

Weber wrote the latter half of *PE* (1904–1905) after returning from his 10-week sojourn in the United States. Its thesis regarding the important role played by values in the development of modern capitalism set off an intense debate that has, remarkably, continued to this day. PE's methodology exemplifies a variety of foundational procedures utilized throughout his sociology even though Weber here comes prominently to the fore as a theorist who attends exclusively to values and ideas.

The Background

A number of historians and economists in Weber's time emphasized the importance for economic development of technological advances, the influx of precious metals, and population increases. Others were convinced that the greed, economic interests, and "desire for riches" of all—but especially of great "economic supermen" (the Carnegies, Rockefellers, and Vanderbilts, for example) and the bourgeoisie in general—pushed economic development past the agrarian and feudal stages to mercantilism and *modern* capitalism. Disagreeing with all these explanations, evolutionists argued that the expansion of production, trade, banking, and commerce could best be understood as the clear manifestation of a general, societal-wide unfolding of "progress."

Weber insists that none of these forces offered an explanation for that which distinguished modern capitalism from capitalism as it had existed throughout the ages: relatively free market exchange, a separation of business accounting from the household's accounting, sophisticated bookkeeping, formally free labor, *and* a specific "economic ethos." This ethos stood behind the rigorous organization of work, the methodical approach to labor, and the systematic pursuit of profit typical of *this* form of capitalism, he holds. It was constituted from an "idea of the *duty* of the individual to increase his wealth, which is assumed to be a self-defined interest in itself" (2009, p. 71); the notion that "labor [must be] performed as if it were an absolute end in itself" (p. 78); the idea that "the acquisition of money, and more and more money, takes place . . . simultaneously with the strictest avoidance of all spontaneous enjoyment of it" (p. 72); the view that the "acquisition of money . . . is . . . the result and the expression of competence and proficiency *in a calling*" (p. 73; original emphasis); and "the frame of mind . . . that strives systematically and rationally *in a calling* for legitimate profit (p. 80; original emphasis).

Embodied in these ideas was a *spirit* of capitalism. Weber argues vehemently that a full understanding of the origins of *modern* capitalism must, first, take cognizance of the causal push placed into motion by this "modern economic ethos" and, second, identify its sources (pp. 73, 97).

Hence, an investigation of the specific ancestry of this "spirit" rather than the sources in general of either capitalism or modern capitalism was *PE*'s modest project (see 2001, pp. 105–109; 2009, pp. 71, 73–74, 87–88, 96–97). After citing numerous passages from the writings of Benjamin Franklin, whose values represent to Weber the "spirit" of capitalism in a pure form, he asserts that he has here discovered an *ethos*, "the violation of [which] is treated not as foolishness but as forgetfulness of *duty*" (2009, p. 71; original emphasis).[1] However, in seeking to unravel the causal origins of this new *set of values* and "organization of life" (*Lebensführung*), this "positive critique of historical materialism" rejects the view that capitalism's dominant class gave birth to this spirit (see, for example, 2009, pp. 70–88, 215–216). It opposes as well the argument that social structures stand at its origin (see 1946c, p. 292; 2009, pp. 88, 103–139). Instead, against strong opponents, Weber wishes to explore the "idealist side" (see, for example, 2009, pp. 158–159) *and* the subjective meaning of several groups of devout believers.

The Argument

After observing various ways in which Protestants seemed attracted to business-oriented occupations and organized their daily lives in an especially rigorous fashion, Weber began to explore Protestant doctrine. He discovered a "world-oriented ethos" in the Westminster Confession (1647) and the sermons of a 17th-century Puritan successor of John Calvin (1509–64), the activist minister Richard Baxter (1615–1691) in England.

For Weber, the revisions of Calvin's teachings by Baxter and other leading "Puritan Divines" sought above all to banish the bleak conclusions rationally implied by Calvin's "Doctrine of Predestination": If the question of salvation constituted *the* burning question to believers (see 2009, pp. 110–111), if the "salvation status" of the faithful was predestined from the very beginning, and if God had selected only a tiny minority to be saved, massive fatalism, despair, loneliness, and anxiety *logically* followed among the devout (see pp. 103–105; 108–118; 500, n. 76). Recognizing that the harshness of this decree precluded its continued endorsement by most believers (see p. 110), Baxter undertook doctrinal alterations that, according to Weber, launched the Protestant ethic.

Along with Calvin, Baxter acknowledged that the mortal and weak devout cannot know the reasons behind God's decision making; the motives of this majestic, distant, and all-mighty Deity of the Old Testament remain incomprehensible to lowly terrestrial inhabitants (2009, pp. 106–108). However, Baxter emphasized that "the world exists to serve the glorification of God" (pp. 108–109) and that God wishes His Kingdom to be one of wealth, equality, and prosperity—for abundance among "His children" would surely serve to praise His goodness and justice (see pp. 109–110; 142–143; 532, n. 39).

Understood as a means toward the creation of God's affluent community on Earth, regular and dedicated labor—work in a "calling"—now acquired a *religious* significance among the devout. Believers comprehended their worldly economic activity as *in service to* a demanding God and thus *sacrosanct*, and they viewed themselves as noble instruments—or tools (2009, p. 120)—of His Commandments and His Divine Plan: "Work in the service of all impersonal social usefulness [promotes] the glory of God—and hence [is] to be recognized as desired by Him" (p. 109; see pp. 144–147; 155–156; 532, n. 39; 547, n. 122). Indeed, believers *capable* of systematic work could convince themselves that the enormous strength required to labor methodically *must* have emanated from the favoring Hand of their omnipotent and omniscient Deity—*and*, the faithful could further conclude, their God would favor only those He had chosen to be among the predestined (see pp. 151–152).

Moreover, continuous and systematic work possesses an undeniable virtue for the good Christian, according to Baxter: It *tames* the creaturely and base side of human nature and thereby facilitates the concentration of the mind upon God and the "uplifting" of the soul" (2009, pp. 143–144). Finally, "intense worldly activity" also effectively counteracts the penetrating doubt, anxiety, and sense of unworthiness induced by the Predestination Doctrine and instills the self-confidence that allows believers *to consider* themselves among the chosen (see pp. 111–112). In this manner, methodical work, as well as the "systematic rational formation of the believer's ethical life" (p. 121), became providential.

Nonetheless, the singular power of the Protestant ethic to banish the deeply rooted "traditional economic ethic" originated not simply in these ways, Weber argues. In addition, and if one wishes to understand fully its capacity to call forth among Puritans an "uninterrupted self-control" and "planned regulation of one's own life" (2009, p. 121; see p. 122), a further adjustment undertaken by Baxter must be noted.

According to the Predestination Doctrine, believers could never *know* their salvation status. However, in light of God's desire to see the creation of an earthly Kingdom of abundance to serve His glory, they could logically conclude that the production of great wealth could be viewed as a *sign* that God favored this individual. In effect, personal wealth itself became to the faithful *evidence* of their salvation. In His universe, nothing happened by chance. Omnipotent and omniscient, God surely would never allow one of the condemned to praise His glory: "The acquisition of wealth, when it was the *fruit* of work in a vocational calling, [was viewed] as God's blessing" (2009, pp. 151–152; original emphasis).

Thus, and although the devout could never be absolutely certain of their membership among the saved, more business-oriented believers could seek to *produce* the evidence—literally, wealth and profit (see 2009, p. 146)— that enabled them to convince themselves of their salvation. In view of the unbearable anxiety provoked by the central religious question—"am I among the saved?"—in 16th- and 17th-century England, a *psychological certainty* of a favorable salvation status was the crucial issue, Weber emphasizes. Baxter's revisions allowed the faithful to comprehend their successful accumulation of wealth, and its reinvestment for the betterment of God's Community, as tangible testimony to their membership among the predestined elect (see pp. 154; 545–546, n. 115). Uniquely, riches now acquired among believers a positive *religious* significance: Because wealth constituted a sign that indicated one's membership among the foreordained elect, it lost its traditionally suspect character and became endowed with a "psychological reward." And the most adequate means toward great wealth—methodical work—was further intensified.

In this manner, a set of labor-oriented values heretofore scorned (see 2009, pp. 74–75, 85–86) became of utmost centrality in the lives of the devout. Neither the age-old desire for riches alone nor the efficient adaptation to technological innovations, but only work motivated "from within" by an "internally binding" set of religious values was empowered to introduce, Weber argues, a "systematization of life organized around ethical principles" (p. 119) and a "planned regulation of one's own life" on behalf of work and the pursuit of wealth (p. 121; see also pp. 120–123). Only this *ethically ordered life anchored in values* was endowed with the methodicalness and intensity requisite for an uprooting and banishing of the traditional economic ethic. *PE*'s last chapter outlines the distinct frame of mind and Puritan style of life at the foundation of this Protestant ethic.

The Puritan Style of Life

People engaged in business and oriented to profit were in Puritan regions now no longer scorned as calculating, greedy, and self-interested actors; rather, they became perceived as honest employers engaged in a task given by God. A good conscience was bestowed upon them, even those engaged in hard competition (2009, pp. 146, 154–155). Similarly, the reinvestment of profit and surplus income signified loyalty to God's grand design and an acknowledgment that all riches emanated from the hand of this omnipotent deity. Because believers viewed themselves as merely the earthly trustees of goods awarded by their divinity, all wealth had to be utilized on behalf of *His* purposes only—that is, to build the affluent kingdom that would praise His glory (pp. 150–153).

Hence, the devout practiced frugality, restricted consumption (especially of luxury goods), and saved and invested in large quantities (2009, pp. 150–151). A preference to live modestly characterized the Puritan outlook, for to indulge desires would weaken the required focus on God's will, the faithful knew. Indeed, and although wealth was now created on a large scale, its enjoyment became "morally reprehensible." The pursuit of an ostentatious mode of living became perceived as obstructing the goal of creating the righteous kingdom on Earth in His honor. As self-idolatry, the search for riches as an end in itself, and all avarice and covetousness, became strictly prohibited (pp. 142, 151–152).

Furthermore, these modest living habits must be accompanied by the appropriate demeanor: reserve, self-control, respectability, and dignity. All deep affectual ties to others, which would only compete with the more important allegiance to God, must be avoided. After all, the emotions were of no relevance to the all-important "certainty of salvation" question, the Puritans knew (see Kalberg, 2012, pp. 291–300). On the contrary, an alert and cerebral monitoring and directing of action proved indispensable. Continuous activity—not leisure and enjoyment—increased the majesty of God. And an unwillingness to work, or a lapse into begging, assumed now a providential meaning,[2] as did the believer's use of time—for "every hour not spent at work is an hour lost in service to God's greater glory" (2009, p. 143). "Time is money" and it must not be "wasted." The "responsible" person of "good moral character" now appeared (pp. 142–144, 150).

Finally, the Puritans perceived feudalism's aristocracy severely: lacking an orientation to God and thus as decadent. For this reason, the purchase of noble titles and all imitation of the manorial lifestyle, as commonly occurred among the *nouveaux riches* could not appeal to these sincere believers. This "feudalization of wealth" also precluded the reinvestment of profits and further pulled the devout away from an orientation to God. Property, the Puritans knew, must be used alone for purposes of production and to increase wealth (1968, p. 1200; 2009, pp. 146, 152–153).

Taken together, these features constitute the Puritan life outlook and style of life of the 17th century (see 1968, p. 1200). When combined with the methodical-rational organization of life rooted in this-worldly asceticism, this conduct comprised the Protestant ethic's uniqueness, Weber maintained. A new "type of human being" now vigorously appeared on the stage of Western history (2009, p. 447). This "modern ethos"—a "Protestant ethic"—directly opposed economic traditionalism and served as a significant disrupting force, he contends. It stood at the source of the spirit of capitalism.

Carried by ascetic sects and churches (mainly, the Presbyterians, Methodists, Baptists, and Quakers), this ethic spread throughout several New England, Dutch, and English communities in the 16th and 17th centuries. Both the wealth that followed from a steadfast adherence to its religious values and disciplined, hard labor in a calling marked a person as "chosen." One century later, in Benjamin Franklin's more secularized America, this Protestant ethic had spread beyond churches and sects and into entire communities. As it did so, its specifically religious component became weakened and "routinized" into a "utilitarian-colored ethos" (2009, pp. 71–72, 153–155, 157)—namely, a spirit of capitalism.[3] Adherents of this ethos such as Franklin, rather than believed to be among the "chosen elect," were viewed simply as respectable, hard-working, and community-oriented citizens of good moral character.

The Protestant Ethic Thesis II:
The Protestant Sects and Ethical Action

After returning from his whirlwind tour of the United States in November, 1904, Weber finished *PE* and wrote two short essays on the Protestant sects in America (see 2009, pp. 185–204). His "Protestant ethic thesis" must be understood as constituted from *PE and* these essays.

The process of testifying to one's salvation status assumed significant new contours in the course of the 18th century. It moved away from the English Puritan engaged in a lonely attempt to orient his activities to God and to create "evidence" of his salvation, Weber holds, and toward believers in America situated deeply within a *social* milieu—namely, in *Protestant sects*. Hence, he now expands his analysis beyond *PE*'s question of how the faithful prove their devoutness *before God* to an investigation of how the devout testify to their sincere belief *in sects before men* (2009, p. 198).

Although believers drew upon an internal strength to lead "the moral life" and retain a focus on God, the sect's strict monitoring of behavior and unrelenting pressure to conform significantly influenced members' ethical conduct. This cohesive group, Weber argues, confirmed the beliefs and psychological rewards enunciated by Puritan doctrine and conveyed them *systematically* to the faithful. The sect, in doing so, sustained the ethical action originally expected by the Puritan Divines and contributed mightily to the formation of a Protestant ethic.

The sect's strong grounding of ethical action and influence on the unfolding of a methodically organized life became manifest in several ways, Weber maintains. First, as a consequence of selective admission procedures, sect membership itself legitimized and guaranteed one's good character. This "certificate of moral qualification," combined with the believer's focus on God, clearly defined every transgression: A "fall from grace" had occurred rather than a random and forgivable lapse. The Protestant sect, however, having banished Catholicism's mechanism—the Confession—to address sinfulness, lacked institutionalized means to relieve internal distress (2009, p. 198). A qualitative strengthening of the necessity for the faithful *continuously* to act in a righteous manner resulted, according to Weber.

Second, the sect's self-governing feature also enhanced its capacity to call forth ethical activity. The exercise of discipline and authority in this group was distinct from the exercise of discipline and authority in churches, Weber maintains: Although less centralized and authoritarian because now in the hands of laymen, it became for this reason more thorough and encompassing (2009, pp. 195–196). Any misstep would surely be revealed.[4]

Third, the definition of the American sect as an exclusive organization of pure and "certified" believers implied that expulsion would follow immediately upon any exposure of "poor character." This harsh treatment involved an intolerable situation for the expelled, Weber emphasized: Through its innumerable activities (church suppers, Sunday school, charitable activities, team sports, bible study groups, etc.), the sect not only shaped members efficiently and hence provided a guarantee of appropriate socialization, but also monopolized the believer's social life.

Those excluded for "dishonorable conduct" immediately "[suffered] . . . a kind of social boycott" and a collapse of their entire social existence (Weber, 2005, pp. 287–288; see 1968, p. 1206; 2009, pp. 196, 198). The necessity to "hold one's own" under the watchful eyes of peers—to testify unceasingly through ethical conduct to one's membership among the elect—now became intensified. The sect's capacity to mold action increased accordingly: "The most powerful individual interest of social self-esteem [was put] in the service of this breeding of traits" (Weber, 2009, pp. 198–199).[5]

Fourth, Weber refers to a related social-psychological dynamic to explain further the unique capacity of the Protestant sects to cultivate and sustain ethical activity. The faithful, as a consequence of the sect's selection of members on the basis of moral qualities, were viewed within their geographical regions as persons of great integrity and even trustworthiness. As the sect—largely for this reason—acquired social prestige, members became subject to enhanced conformity pressures to uphold "good moral character" standards. Thus, supervision and monitoring among the devout became further intensified. The sect's favorable reputation in its region must be maintained.

A shaping of an ethical posture took place also in this manner, Weber contends. Indeed, by engaging the entire person and bestowing both social honor and esteem,[6] the sect had the effect, especially in contrast to the authoritarianism of churches, of disciplining believers on behalf of ethical action to a unique degree of intensity: "According to all experience there is no stronger means of breeding traits than through the necessity of holding one's own in the circle of one's associates" (2009, p. 198; see pp. 195–197; 1968, p. 1206). Weber saw here a source of American initiative taking and the American notion of self-respect.

Fifth, and finally, the sect constituted a functional and "impersonal" (*sachliche*) group: It was oriented above all *to tasks* in service to God's greater glory and to the construction of His kingdom. By promoting "the precise ordering of the individual into the instrumental task pursued by the group," this "mechanism for the achievement of . . . material and ideal *goals*" circumscribed affect- and tradition-laden relationships among the faithful (Weber, 2005, p. 286; see 2009, p. 492, n. 34).

Hence, an emotion-based mode of interaction never prevailed in the sect.[7] In addition, a halo never encompassed the sect—one into which the faithful could merge amid a sacred glow: All residues were banished of any "mystical total essence floating above [the believer] and enveloping him" (2005, p. 286).[8] Finally, a sentimental, warm, and comfortable mode of interaction rooted in familiar and longstanding traditions was also excluded.[9] Instead, an orientation by the devout to tasks in service to God and high standards of ethical conduct reigned. Stalwart believers, evaluated exclusively by reference to the "religious qualities evident in [their] conduct," constantly attended to the necessity of holding their own (2005, pp. 284–286). Despite the typically intense interaction among sect members, "association" and "sociability" (*Vergesellschaftung*) characterized interaction, Weber maintains (see Scaff, 1998), rather than a cultivation of deep emotional ties or an immersion into the group. A "type of human being" now appears *located* in principle *primarily* outside the "universal organizations": the family, clan, and tribe. Moreover, far from random or temporary, this new location is legitimized by religious beliefs central to the believer.

In sum, sects juxtaposed an unceasing, means-end rational orientation to activities and tasks, intense conformity pressures, and a hold-your-own individualism oriented to ethical values. In doing so, these cohesive groups pulled the devout away from emotion-oriented relationships, tradition-oriented sentimentality, and all inclinations to attribute a sacred aura to groups. However, sects never abandoned believers either to an interest-oriented, "practical-rational" flux and flow or to an endless nihilistic drift. Instead, this organization immediately took firm hold of the faithful and bound them tightly within its own social-psychological dynamic—one that actively cultivated and sustained ethical action.

For Weber, the *methodical-rational* organization of life typically found among ascetic Protestants arose not only from the individual's lonely quest to create "evidence" of his salvation and the psychological rewards placed on ethical action by the Puritan Divine ministers, as charted in *PE*, but also from the Protestant sect's efficient "implementation" of this highly organized life. Indeed, the requirement of this group—to insure that only the morally qualified participate in communion—can be understood as itself placing into motion a major thrust toward the congregation's many social activities, for they enabled the indispensable monitoring of members' conduct.[10] Weber perceives this capacity of the sect as central for the development of ascetic Protestantism's economic ethic:

> Unqualified integrity, evidenced by, for example, a system of fixed prices in retail trade, strong management of credit, avoidance of all "worldly" consumption

and every kind of debauchery, in short, life-long sober diligence in one's "calling," appears as the specific, indeed, really the *only* form by which persons can demonstrate their qualification as Christians and therewith their moral legitimation for membership in the sect. (1985, p. 8; emphasis in original)

To Weber: "The sect and its derivations are one of [America's] unwritten but vital constitutional elements, since they shape the individual more than any other influence" (1968, p. 1207).

For all these reasons, high *standards* of conduct accompanied methodical work and the search for wealth and profit. Rewards were apparent—as were punishments. Sect members in search of bank loans and financial opportunities of various sorts were viewed as creditworthy,[11] and the devout became perceived as honest merchants who could be trusted even with the customer's money. A halo of respectability replaced the traditional view of the businessperson as an unethical and manipulative figure.[12] And this aura *must* be maintained, because otherwise potential customers would abandon their preference to conduct business with sect members and a boycott would ensue (see Weber, 1985, p. 9; 2009, pp. 186–188, 193–194; 1968, pp. 1204–1206). Highly intertwined, both the believer's "social existence" and business reputation were at stake. Specifically American forms of social trust and respectability developed.

In this manner, the impact of the Protestant sect on the Protestant ethic proved significant, Weber argues. The sect remained a functional and impersonal organization that subordinated the faithful to its overarching tasks and coordination of labor. Formal legal equality, abstract norms, and bureaucratization, as well as modern capitalism's purposeful mode of utilizing persons and the "lifestyle in [its] . . . middle classes," were all here foreshadowed: "[T]his-worldly asceticism . . . and the specific discipline of the sects bred the capitalist frame of mind and the rational 'professional' (*Berufsmensch*) who was needed by capitalism" (Weber, 1968, pp. 1209–1210; see 2005, p. 286; 2009, p. 492, n. 34).

Thus, the sects played a crucial role in Weber's argument. They conveyed an intense economic ethic *into the worlds* of labor and commerce far more efficiently than the admonitions of Baxter and other Puritan Divines. Moreover, albeit transformed, the sects formulated legacies that endured: Manifest in the 18th and 19th centuries in secular form, their economic ethic penetrated directly into nation-wide arrays of associations, clubs, and societies. These new carrier groups cast the values of the direct successor of the Protestant ethic—the spirit of capitalism—widely through generations and even into the 20th century. Weber's full "Protestant ethic thesis" is captured only if the complimentary character of *PE* and the sect essays is acknowledged.

He investigated the "causal origins" of the spirit of capitalism in these ways. The subjective meaning of devout believers, as captured through religious sources and values rather than by reference to social structural factors, rational choices, economic interests, domination and power, specific classes, or evolutionary progress, remains central throughout. This spirit, Weber held, gave a decisive, although in the end unquantifiable, push to modern capitalism's development.

Nonetheless, Weber calls attention to an altogether different dynamic when he turns briefly in *PE*'s last pages to the present era. Once the spirit of capitalism had assisted the growth of modern capitalism and once this type of economy becomes firmly entrenched amid massive industrialism, it sustains itself on the basis alone of *means-end rational* action carried out in reference to pragmatic necessities, he argues. If present at all, "the idea of an 'obligation to search for and then accept a vocational calling' now wanders around in our lives as the ghost of past religious beliefs." The Puritan "*wanted* to be a person with a vocational calling; we *must* be" (2009, pp. 157–158; original emphasis). Diagram 2.1 captures the *four* stages of Weber's argument.

As a case study of the spirit of capitalism's origins, *PE* stands as a powerful demonstration of the ways in which social action may be influenced by non-economic forces. Sociological analysis must not focus exclusively on material interests, power, structural forces, and "economic forms" to the neglect of action-orientations toward religion and "economic ethics," Weber insists. However, sociologists must also reject a focus alone on "ideas." "*Both* sides" must be given their due and a "single formula" must always be avoided:

> of course it cannot be the intention here to set a one-sided spiritualistic analysis of the causes of culture and history in place of an equally one-sided "materialistic" analysis. *Both* are *equally possible*. Historical truth, however, is served equally little if either of these analyses claims to be the conclusion of an investigation rather than its preparatory stage. (2009, p. 159; original emphasis)

Hence, and although *PE* demonstrates the ways in which values influence the playing out of economic interests and provide the "content" for social structures, Weber recognized that a full understanding of the origins of modern capitalism requires a series of broad-ranging, *multicausal and comparative* investigations. Values *and* mundane economic and political interests must be scrutinized. Furthermore, if the spirit of capitalism is to have a substantial impact on the development of modern capitalism, then constellations of patterns of action oriented to the rulership, economy, law, status honor, family, and clan must congeal to formulate a conducive context, he was convinced (see 2009, pp. 159; 543–544, n. 96; Marshall, 1980).

Diagram 2.1   Four Stages of Weber's Argument

	Period	Organization	Types of Action	Religious Belief
I. **Calvin:** Fatalism as a result of doctrine of predestination	16th cen.	small sects	value-rational	yes
II. **Baxter:** The Protestant ethic (The Puritans; Ascetic Protestantism)	17th cen.	churches and sects	value-rational (methodical this-worldly activity)	yes
III. **Franklin:** The spirit of capitalism	18th cen.	communities	value-rational[36] (methodical this-worldly activity)	no
IV. The **"specialist":** capitalism as a "cosmos"	20th cen.	industrial society	means-end rational	no

"Powerful Lever"

"Elective Affinity"

"Adequacy"

Adapted from Kalberg, "On the Neglect of Weber's *Protestant Ethic* as a Theoretical Treatise" (*Sociological Theory*; 1996, p. 63), with permission from the American Sociological Association.

PE comprised simply the first step in Weber's grand scheme to investigate the causal origins of modern capitalism. EEWR took up this theme and, indeed, extended it to encompass the question of the origins of "modern Western rationalism."

This is our subject in Chapters 6–9. However, an examination of the basic foundations of Weber's methodology, as well as its specific components, is indispensable before moving to this large and central theme. This is our focus in the following chapter. Equally indispensable in this regard is an investigation of the major axes of Weber's analytic opus, *E&S*. Chapter 4 examines this three-volume treatise.

Study Questions and Thoughts to Ponder

1. Did the introduction by the Protestant ethic of a "new organization of life" require *both* sermons from the pulpit and sects?

2. Why did the Puritans, given the doctrine of Predestination, not simply withdraw from all activity?

3. The logical consequence of the doctrine of Predestination for believers was clinical depression. Why did this not occur among Puritans?

4. Why, according to Weber, was the universal "desire for wealth" unable to shatter the traditional economic ethic?

5. Members of the Protestant sect must "hold their own" against all conformity pressures. Please explain why.

6. The Puritan believer must "prove" himself before God *and* before men. Explain this statement.

7. Did the Puritan Divines or the Protestant sects play the most important part in Weber's "Protestant ethic thesis?"

Notes

1. Weber makes this point even more vividly in a later essay: "The origin of economic rationalism, [of the type which, since the 16th and 17th centuries, has come to dominate the West], depends not only on an advanced development of technology and law, but also on the capacity and disposition of persons to *organize their lives* in a practical-rational manner (2009, p. 216; see 1946c, p. 293).

2. The devout could understand an unwillingness to work as a sign that one is not among the saved. Those living in poverty could not possibly be among the saved (see 2009, p. 109). Being poor now indicated not only laziness, but also a poor *moral* character.

3. Rather than a "determinative" relationship, Weber sees an "elective affinity" (*Wahlverwandtschaft*) between the Protestant ethic and the spirit of capitalism (2009, pp. 97, 157). Along these lines, Weber notes further, "It should here be ascertained only whether, and to what extent, religious influences *co*-participated in the qualitative formation and quantitative expansion of [the spirit of capitalism] across the globe" (2009, p. 97; original emphasis). Furthermore: "Our analysis should have demonstrated that one of the constitutive components of the modern capitalist spirit and, moreover, generally of modern civilization, was the rational organization of life on the basis of the *idea of the calling*. It was born out of the spirit of *Christian asceticism*" (2009, p. 157; emphasis in original).

4. This feature of the sect in particular, Weber contends, lends to it a monitoring capacity that rivals that of the monastic order (2009, pp. 195–198).

5. "Hold one's own" is the usual translation of *sich behaupten*. It implies, within a constituted group, a maintenance and defense of an individual's social—and ethical—standing vis-à-vis one's peers. "Prove your mettle" conveys today the same idea, as does the notion that persons should "measure up" to the task at hand. While *within* a group, members do not "lose themselves" to, or "dissolve" into, the group; rather, and despite interaction of a degree of intensity that otherwise would ensure an orientation exclusively to others, a focus on an ethical standard remains, Weber argues. While an unequivocally positive connotation is bestowed upon "holding your own" in the United States, persons from cultures uninfluenced by a tradition of this-worldly asceticism may well view this degree of individualism with skepticism—namely, as dangerously close to egocentrism.

6. Those who conducted themselves in an exemplary fashion according to the expectations of peer sect members received from them a clear message: You are honorable and accepted. This unequivocal and unmediated bestowal of social esteem must have served to elevate the devout psychologically and to counterbalance any fatalism residuals from the doctrine of Predestination. The religious context here determined that approval from one's fellows implied a symbolic dimension: "You are saved." However, cohesive groups in the secularized 20th century could bestow only the *caput mortuum*, or routinized, form of approval: "You are well liked." This tension between the person in search of approval (and hence conforming to group norms) and the person holding his own in the group by upholding ethical standards endures in American society to the present (See Kalberg, 2014b).

7. In this regard Weber notes Puritanism's condemnation of idolatry, or the orientation to personal wants and desires (*Kreaturvergoetterung*). Their satisfaction competes with the believer's loyalty to God. Hence, this prohibition denies legitimacy to a focus on the person and all privatized concerns (see 2009, p. 493, n. 39).

8. Weber has here in mind both Catholicism and Lutheranism. Members of these churches are absolved of an urgent necessity to hold their own. He is critical of this mode of group formation, which he found to be widespread in the Germany of his times (see Mommsen, 1974, pp. 80–81).

9. The famous *Gemeinschaft—Gesellschaft* dichotomy formulated by Ferdinand Toennies (1855–1936) was well-known to Weber. He is here, in noting

Gesellschaft features of the 17th-century Protestant sect, demarcating an antagonistic position (see Weber, 2005, pp. 284–286).

10. This point, unmentioned in Weber's texts, has been inferred.

11. This aspect of membership in a sect—the moral legitimation of members— did not obstruct geographical mobility if only because entry into a new community could be gained easily; namely, by a letter from the pastor of one's home church. Such a "letter of introduction" immediately overcame the normal suspicion of newcomers and, moreover, established their honesty, respectability, and creditworthiness (see Weber, 1968, p. 1206). (Weber would argue that consideration of such *religious* legacies must not be excluded from attempts today to explain why rates of geographical and occupational mobility in the United States were high until recently.)

12. "Business ethics" in the United States finds here its point of origin. This phrase today is viewed widely in Europe as an oxymoron.

3

Weber's Methodology

S ome interpreters view Weber as a "theorist of ideas," yet others see him as a "theorist of interests." While the former focus on *The Protestant Ethic and the Spirit of Capitalism* and emphasize the strong role in his sociology of values, religion, and culture, the latter take his analytic opus *Economy and Society* (*E&S*) as their main source. They assert that Weber offers a non-Marxist conflict theory rooted in domination, power, inequality, struggle, and individual interests. Still others understand him, as noted in the Introduction, mainly as a gifted taxonomist engaged in the creation of a vast armament of finely tuned concepts—"ideal types" (see below and Chapter 4)—intended to establish sociology on a secure conceptual foundation.

In fact, each of these interpretations legitimately flows from his complex agenda (see Kalberg, 1998, pp. 208–214; 2012, pp. 97–140). However, these commentaries all run astray by casting their focus too narrowly. The broader themes that overcome the seeming fragmentation of Weber's sociology are too often neglected: The ways in which he links—and opposes—values and interests, his concern to define the uniqueness of "Western rationalism" and "modern Western rationalism" and to provide causal explanations of their origins; his search to understand which constellations of groups give rise to widespread notions of compassion, ethical action, and individual autonomy; his attempt to analyze how action becomes substantively oriented to values to such an extent that boundaries are placed around utilitarian, practical-rational action; and his focus on the manner in which persons in different social settings create meaning for their lives.

This discussion of Weber's methodology explores these pivotal themes while calling attention to the forceful ways in which values, culture, and religion come to the fore in his sociology; domination, power, conflict, and individual interests remain central; and "clear concepts" serve as indispensable points of orientation. We first address several background ideas and presuppositions and then specific components of Weber's methodology. Both discussions will prove indispensable for comprehension of the subsequent chapters on *E&S*, the Economic Ethics of the World Religions volumes (EEWR), Weber's sociology of civilizations, and his charting of the American political culture's uniqueness. Many of the pivotal axioms of his methodology remain central to sociology today.

Background Ideas and Presuppositions

The Rejection of the Search for True Values, General Laws, and Objective Facts

Weber rejected the notion that values rooted in religions and quasi-supernatural ideas could form the basis a new social science. This position led him to oppose unequivocally the many attempts in Germany at the end of the 19th century to define the aim of the social sciences as the creation of new constellations of values appropriate to the industrial society.

His distinguished colleagues Rickert, Dilthey, Schmoller, Roscher, and Knies had all agreed that investigations of social life must be carried out *in order to* substantiate ideals and norms—indeed, even in the name of science. They feared that urban, secular, and capitalist societies would be devoid of values and argued that this abhorrent vacuum must be filled by values discovered by science. Their nightmare vision would otherwise soon become reality: Persons would become mere drifting "atoms" devoid of a reflective and introspective capacity, a sense of compassion and deep ethical obligation to others, and a sense of true community. As religion declined, a new source for desperately needed values must be found. Science offered new hope.

The notion that science should be viewed as the legitimate source of personal values was more than Weber could bear. He saw in such proposals yet another clandestine intrusion of quasi-religious legacies—now into a domain appropriately defined, he believed, as exclusively grounded in empirical investigation. Moreover, he denied the possibility that the social sciences could serve as the source of values, for an "objective science" *cannot* exist (see below, pp.). Even the hope for such a science is a deception, one rooted ultimately in a bygone world of unified and symbiotic values. It has now become clear, Weber asserts, that *each* epoch—perhaps even every generation or decade—calls forth its *own* "culturally significant value-ideas." Invariably, our observations of empirical reality take place *in reference to these*, he insists. The empirical ground on which the social sciences are based "changes" continuously (see 1949, pp. 72–78).

This unavoidable "value-relevance" (*Wertbeziehung*) of our observations always renders certain events and occurrences visible to us and occludes others. Only *some* "realities" are thrown into relief by the culturally significant values of any specific age. Those today, for example, are embodied by terms such as "equality for all," freedom, human rights, and equal opportunity, and dichotomies such as capitalism and socialism and First World and Third World. The specific vantage points dominant in any era predispose our perception in such a way that we see only selected slices of the past and present.

Consequently, our search today for knowledge cannot take the same form—as a search for concealed *absolutes*—as in the 17th and 18th centuries. The ultimate precondition for such a quest no longer exists: a widespread belief in a set of unified values. For the same reason, our knowledge can no longer be anchored in the quasi-religious ideas of the 19th century. Furthermore, owing to the invariably perspectival character of our knowledge, we can hope neither to find "general laws" in history nor to write history as the prominent historian Leopold von Ranke (1795–1886) proposed: "as it actually occurred." Thus, in the famous "debate over methods" (*Methodenstreit*), Weber opposed both the "nomothetic" position held by the economist Carl Menger (1840–1921)—the formulation of general laws must be the task of the social sciences—and the "ideographic" position held by Schmoller's "historical school of economics": The goal must be to offer exact and full descriptions of specific cases.

Weber admonished vehemently and repeatedly that all attempts to create values through the social sciences must now be seen as illusions. All such deceptions must be cast aside in the new post-religion and post–quasi-religion epoch:

> The fate of a cultural epoch which has eaten of the tree of knowledge is that it must know, however completely we may investigate history, we cannot learn its *real* meaning from the results of our research. Rather, we must be able to create this meaning ourselves. Moreover, we must acknowledge that "world views" (*Weltanschauungen*) never can be the product of the advance of empirically-based knowledge. Finally, we must recognize that the highest ideals—and those which move us most deeply—become effective influences upon us only as a consequence of their struggle with other ideals. These ideals are just as sacred to others as ours are to us. (1949, p. 57; translation altered, original emphasis; see also p. 18)

We know of no ideals that can be demonstrated scientifically. Undoubtedly, the task of pulling them out of one's own breast is all the more difficult in an epoch in which culture has otherwise become so subjective. But we simply have no fool's paradise and no streets paved with gold to promise, either in this world or the next, either in thought or in action. It is the stigma of our human dignity as men that the peace of our souls can never be as great as the peace of those who dream of such a paradise. (1909, p. 420)

Weber's Rejection of Organic Holism

Weber's sociology departs from a critique of all approaches that view societies as quasi-organic, holistic units. Their separate "parts" are then perceived as components integrated into a larger "system" of objective structures. These "organic" schools of thought understand the larger collectivity within which the individual acts as a delimited structure, and social action and interaction as particularistic expressions of this "whole." German romantic and conservative thought, as well as the sociologies of Comte and Durkheim, fall within this tradition.

Organic theories generally postulate a degree of societal integration questionable to Weber. He seldom viewed civilizations as clearly formed and closed entities with delineated boundaries. Seeing a likelihood for fragmentation, tension, open conflict, and domination and the use of power, Weber rejects the notion that societies can be best conceptualized as unified.

Moreover, according to him, if organic theories are utilized *other than* as a means of facilitating preliminary conceptualization, a high risk of "reification" arises: "Society" and the "organic whole" may become viewed as the fundamental unit of analysis rather than the individual's subjective meaning (1968, pp. 14–15). This may occur to such an extent that the activity of persons is incorrectly understood as simply the "socialized product" of external forces. Weber argues, to the contrary, that persons are *capable* of *interpreting* their social realities, bestowing "subjective meaning" on certain aspects of it, and initiating independent action: "[We are] *cultural* beings endowed with the capacity and will to take a deliberate stand toward the world and to lend it *meaning (Sinn)*" (1949, p. 81; translation altered; original emphasis).

From Eurocentrism to a
Comparative Sociology of Subjective Meaning

However weakened by secularization, capitalism, and urbanization, the West's overarching set of values remained viable in the 19th century.

They formed a measuring rod against which European social scientists evaluated societies around the globe with respect to their relative "evolution" and "rationality." Had they experienced the same degree of "advancement" as the modern West? Weber's rejection of the 19th century's quasi-religious value constellations implied both a skepticism regarding the widespread belief in "progress" and an awareness of its contingency. It also laid the foundation for the radically comparative character of his sociology and its break from Eurocentric ideas.

The shift to a fully anthropocentric sociology focused on the individual's subjective meaning and empirical reality had the effect of delegitimizing all Western-centric value configurations. As the underlying justification for a social science oriented exclusively to the "ideas of the West" disappeared, firm standards for the observation and evaluation of other cultures vanished as well.

Weber's colleagues viewed this development with extreme trepidation. They correctly perceived his methodology as threatening at its core the "superiority of the West," as well as frequently the very essence of their being. Weber, however, noted an overriding advantage for research: Social scientists were now set free to investigate "the other" on its *own* terms. This liberation from a fixed point of orientation meant to him that unconstrained empirical explorations of *subjective meaning* in Eastern and Western, ancient and modern, civilizations could now be conducted.

Weber advocated such a radical swing of the pendulum not only owing to advantages he saw for a social science methodology. Rather, an even larger dynamic induced him to bestow an unqualified legitimacy upon decentered, intercivilizational research.

"Unconstrained" comparative studies were now urgently *needed* to address effectively immediate questions in his own civilization: In what precise ways can the modern West be said to be unique? What are the *parameters* of possible social change in the West? How does the orientation of activity to values and the *formation* of subjective meaning as such take place? How can comparative-historical studies focusing on the formation of subjective meaning in civilizations far and wide shed light on and assist resolution of the crisis of meaning widespread in rapidly industrializing Western societies?

These questions deeply troubled Weber's colleagues. He alone comprehended the potential achievements of a sociology that, through rigorous empirical research, would be capable of isolating the boundaries of cases and developments, defining significant causal forces, and drawing conclusions regarding the circumstances under which subjective meaning is formed, social transformation likely occurs, and action becomes oriented to values. Such a sociology would cast a sharp beam of light on the modern West's dilemmas and conundrums—and persons would then be able to make *informed* decisions and to take clear *ethical* positions (2005, pp. 333–334). The massiveness and extreme thoroughness of his comparative studies cannot be understood without cognizance of this motivating concern.

Conflict and Ethical Action

Weber's mode of research was decentered in a further manner. In breaking from all schools of thought that stressed unifying constellations of values, transcendentally anchored value hierarchies, and—through progress and evolution—humanity's common and peaceful future, his sociology banished an array of presuppositions that placed obstacles against empirical analysis. Having done so, his research could better assess the extent to which mundane conflict appears, as well as its contours and causes.

For him, the "struggle for existence" did not take place on the grand stage of "human evolution" and in response to a "survival of the fittest" law, as for Social Darwinists. Instead, it developed exclusively as a result of the hard choices that accompany everyday activity. History unfolded out of these decisions, yet not in a unilinear or directed fashion. Paradox, irony, and unforeseen consequences, Weber insists, were manifest perpetually (see 1946a, p. 117), as well as restless, undirected conflict. The various major domains of life (the family, clan, religion, economy, law, rulership, and status groups arenas,[1] rather than congealing into a synthesis to drive progress or to propel a Parsonsian "value-generalization" process, may follow—given facilitating configurations of groups—their *own* laws of development. Indeed, they may stand empirically in relations of irreconcilable conflict to one another (see 1946b; 1949, p. 18; 2005, pp. 330–338).

In formulating "an empirical science of concrete reality" and emphasizing that persons rather than God, "natural laws," or evolution endow history with meaning, Weber's sociology unavoidably confronts several pivotal questions. How will our action be oriented in patterned ways such that groups are formed? How do we act responsibly? How is ethical action grounded? The liberation from religion-based world views and their legacies led naturally to a great potential for undirected—even random—action. To Weber, just this development called forth the question of how individuals make choices in industrialized, secularized, bureaucratized, and capitalist societies.

Weber's rejection of all schools that defined the modern person's freedom as simply the "philistine freedom of private convenience" (Löwith, 1970, p. 122) rendered these queries all the more urgent, as did his opposition to

Nietzsche's answers: Weber's insistence that patterned action occurs embedded within contexts of action prevented him from placing faith in prophets and great "supermen" (2005, p. 339). Moreover, he argued that secularism, industrialism, and the Enlightenment had already empowered "the people" with rights to such an extent that Nietzsche's call for authoritarian "heroes" went too far. They would inevitably circumscribe the open space for decision-making indispensable if ethically based choices are to occur.

Weber knew well that the social science he proposed failed to offer ethical guidance. He remained acutely aware that this position disappointed in particular the younger generation of his time (see 2005, pp. 324–235, 328–329). Would the elevation of subjective meaning and "concrete empirical reality" to the forefront be beneficial in the end? And what would become of modern individuals? Now cast adrift from all directing and obligatory values and traditions, and forced to locate and then cultivate meaning by reference to their own "demons," would they become either opportunistic actors or psychologically paralyzed?

Weber rejected the loud calls for "a romantic irrational heroism which sacrifices itself amid the delirium of self-decomposition" (Salomon, 1935, p. 384). Moreover, he viewed as utopian all hopes that a politicized proletariat would usher in a more just society. Would configurations of *binding* values capable of anchoring ethical decisions remain viable? Would the type of human being oriented to and *unified* by values survive? These crucial questions hold our attention. They can best be addressed by turning first to specific components of Weber's comparative-historical methodology.

Specific Components of Weber's Methodology

The Embrace of Multicausality

The search for a single "guiding hand," whether that of a monotheistic God, Adam Smith's "laws of the market," or Karl Marx's class conflict, remained anathema to Weber. He perceived all such overarching forces as residuals of now-antiquated world views characterized by religious and quasi-religious ideas.

Indeed, Weber's adamant refusal to define the "general laws of social life" (Menger), the "stages of historical development" (Buecher, Marx), or evolution[2] as the central point of departure for his causal explanations paved the way for a focus on empirical reality and subjective meaning. As important, it also provided the underlying precondition for his embrace of radically *multicausal* modes of explanation. Having abandoned reference to all forms of "necessity" as history's moving force, innumerable values, traditions, emotions, and pragmatic interests rose to the fore in Weber's sociology as the causes that determine our action in the past and the present.

His empirical research convinced him that historical change required "carrier" groups: social strata, organizations, and classes. These carriers were, for example, at times political and rulership groups, at other times status or economic groups, and at still other times religious groups. His investigations across a vast palette of themes, epochs, and civilizations yielded in this respect a clear conclusion: Rather than a causal "resting point," Weber found only continuous movement by groups across, above all, the rulership, economy, religion, law, social honor, family, and clan arenas (see, for example, 1968, p. 341). Without powerful carriers, even Hegel's "spirit" or Ranke's Christian Humanism could not move history. Nor could religious or secular world views or the theodicy dilemma presented by unjust suffering. This element of Weber's methodology will be referred to continuously.

Interpretive Understanding and Subjective Meaning

At the core of Weber's sociology stands the attempt by sociologists to "understand interpretively" the ways in which persons view their own social action. This *subjectively meaningful* action constitutes the social scientist's concern, he contends, rather than merely "reactive" or "imitative" behavior (as occurs, for example, when persons in a crowd expect rain and simultaneously open their umbrellas). Social action, he insists, involves *both* a "meaningful orientation of behavior to that of others" *and* the individual's interpretive, or reflective, aspect (1968, pp. 22–24). Persons are social, but not only social. They are endowed with the ability to actively interpret situations, interactions, and relationships by reference to values, beliefs, interests, emotions, power, authority, law, traditions, ideas, and so on.

> Sociology . . . is a science that offers an interpretive understanding of social action and, in doing so, provides a causal explanation of its course and effects. We shall speak of "action" insofar as the acting individual attaches a subjective *meaning* to his behavior—be it overt or covert, omission or acquiescence. Action is "social" insofar as its subjective meaning takes account of the behavior *of others* and is thereby oriented in its course. (1968, p. 4; translation altered, original emphasis)[3]

The central position of meaningful action in Weber's sociology separates it fundamentally from all behaviorist, structuralist, and positivist schools.

Sociologists can understand the meaningfulness of others' actions in one of two ways. First, "rational understanding" involves an intellectual grasp of the meaning actors attribute to their actions. Second, "intuitive" (or "empathic") understanding refers to the comprehension of "the emotional context in which the action [takes] place" (1968, p. 5).

Thus, for example, the motivation behind the orientation of civil servants to a state bureaucracy's impersonal statutes and prescriptions can be understood by the sociologist, as can the motivation behind the orientation of good friends to one another. To the extent that this occurs, a *causal* explanation of action, Weber argues, is provided.

Because it attends alone to external activity, stimulus and response behaviorism neglects the issues foremost to Weber: the *diverse* possible motives behind observable activity, the manner in which the subjective meaningfulness of action varies accordingly, and the significant differences that follow in respect to action. This capacity of the human species to lend multiple meanings to conduct implies, Weber asserts emphatically, that the social sciences should never adopt natural science methodologies.

The Four Types of Social
Action and Subjective Meaning

To him, social action can be best conceptualized as involving one of four "types of meaningful action": means-end rational, value-rational, affectual, or traditional action. Each type refers to the ideal-typical (see below) motivational orientations of actors.

Weber defines action as *means-end* rational (*zweckrational*):

> when the end, the means, and the secondary results are all rationally taken into account and weighed. This involves a serious consideration of alternative means to the end, of the relations of the end to the secondary consequences, and finally of the relative importance of different possible ends. (1968, p. 26; translation altered)

Similarly, persons possess the capacity to act *value-rationally*. This occurs when social action is:

> . . . determined by a conscious belief in the value for its own sake of some ethical, aesthetic, religious, or other form of behavior, independently of its prospects of success. . . . Value-rational action always involves "commands" or "demands" which, in the actor's opinion, are binding (*verbindlich*) on him. (1968, p. 26)

In addition, "determined by the actor's specific affects and feeling states," *affectual* action, which involves an emotional attachment, must be distinguished clearly from value-rational and means-end rational action. Finally, *traditional* action, "determined by ingrained habituation" and age-old customs, often approaches merely a routine reaction to common stimuli. It lacks a highly self-conscious aspect and stands on the borderline of subjectively meaningful action (see 1968, pp. 24–26).[4]

Each type of meaningful action can be found in all epochs and all civilizations. The social action of even "primitive" peoples may be means-end rational (see, for example, 1968, pp. 400, 422–426) and modern man is not endowed with a greater inherent capacity for a certain type of action than his ancestors. However, as a result of identifiable social configurations, some epochs may tend predominantly to call forth a particular type of action.

Weber is convinced that, by utilizing the types of social action typology as a heuristic tool, sociologists can understand—and hence explain causally—even the ways in which the social action of persons living in radically different cultures is subjectively meaningful to them. Assuming that, as a result of intensive study, researchers have succeeded in becoming thoroughly familiar with a particular social context and hence capable of imagining themselves "into" it, an assessment can be made of the extent to which actions approximate one of the types of social action. The subjective meaningfulness of the motives for these actions—whether traditions, means-end rational calculations, orientations to emotions, or orientations to values—then become *understandable*.[5] In this manner, Weber's "interpretive" sociology enables the sociologist to comprehend the actor's *own* intentions (see 1968, pp. 5–6).

This foundational emphasis on a pluralism of motives distinguishes Weber's sociology unequivocally from all schools of behaviorism, all approaches that place social structures at the forefront (for example, those rooted in Durkheim's "social facts" or Marx's classes), and all approaches that endow norms, roles, and rules with a determining power over persons. Even when social action seems tightly bonded to a social structure, a heterogeneity of motives must be recognized, he insists.

Weber argues that a great array of motives within a single "external form" is both analytically and empirically possible—*and* sociologically significant. The subjective meaningfulness of action varies even within the firm organizational structure of the political or religious sect. Hindu and Puritan sects, for example, shared a similar external form, yet the devout in each case endowed radically different action with meaning (1946c, p. 292).

However, just this reasoning leads Weber to a conundrum: How do persons orient their social action *in common* such that demarcated groups are formed? This question assumes a great urgency, for he is convinced that the absence of such orientations—toward, for example, the state, bureaucratic organizations, traditions, and values—causes "structures" to cease to exist. The state, for example, in the end is constituted from *nothing more than* the patterned action-orientations of its politicians, judges, civil servants, and citizens (see 1968, p. 13).

Far from formal methodological postulates only, these foundational distinctions directly anchor Weber's empirical studies, as will become apparent. The investigation of the subjective meaning of action stood at the very center of his "Protestant ethic thesis." Yet Weber engaged in a massive empirical effort to understand the subjective meaning of "the other" throughout his comparative-historical sociology. He aimed to do just this when he studied, for example, the Confucian scholar, the Buddhist monk, the Hindu Brahmin, the prophets of the Old Testament, the feudal ruler, the monarch, and functionaries in bureaucracies.

For what subjective reasons do people render obedience to authority? How is status defined and attributed? Weber wished to articulate a methodology that would assist researchers to understand the diverse ways in which persons subjectively "make sense" of their activities. He argues that sociologists should impartially attempt to do so even when a subjective "meaning-complex" seems to them strange or odd.

Value-Freedom and Value-Relevance

Hence, Weber's sociology does not seek to discover "an objectively 'correct' meaning or one which is 'true' in some metaphysical sense" (1968, p.4).[6] Moreover, neither empathy toward nor hostility against the actors under investigation is central here. Researchers are obligated, with respect to the research process, to set aside—as much as humanly possible—their ideological preferences, personal values, likes, and dislikes (of Puritans, for example, or the bureaucracy's functionaries, and make every effort to remain fair and impartial. Clear standards of inquiry, as well as unbiased observation, measurement, comparison, and evaluation of the sources, must be the prescriptive ideal of social scientists. Researchers must strive to uphold this ideal even if the habits, values, and practices of groups under investigation are discovered to be repulsive.

Weber knew that to uphold such an "objective" and "value-free" (*Wertfreiheit*) posture with respect to the gathering and evaluation of data is not an easy task. We are all "cultural beings," and hence values remain inextricably intertwined with our thinking and action. A thin line separates "facts" from "values," and values intrude even into our modes of observation. Indeed, modern Western science itself *arose* as a consequence of a series of specific economic, political, stratification, and cultural developments.

Nonetheless, *the social scientist* must make a concerted effort to distinguish empirically-based arguments and conclusions from normative—or value-based—arguments and conclusions. The latter should be excluded.

However, with regard to a foundational aspect of the research process, values remain appropriately central, Weber insists: the *selection* of topics. Far from "objective" in some metaphysical or predetermined sense, our choice—unavoidably so, for him—is directly related to our values (*Wertbezogenheit*) and our interests. If a sociologist strongly believes, for example, that persons of different ethnic groups should be treated equally, he may be drawn—as a result of this *value*—to study how civil rights movements have assisted heretofore excluded groups to acquire basic rights.

Nonetheless, as noted, with respect to investigative and analysis procedures, Weber maintains that researchers must strive to exclude all personal values: namely, value-judgments that pronounce, in the name of science, a particular activity or way of life as noble or base, ultimately rational or irrational, provincial or cosmopolitan. The social sciences cannot—and should not—assist us to decide with certainty which values are superior or inferior. Those of the Sermon on the Mount cannot be proven scientifically to be "better" than those of the Rig Vedas.

Nor can social scientists argue that specific values *should* guide the lives of people in a specific situation. Science provides "the tools and the training for thought" as well as insight, knowledge, and an awareness of "inconsistent facts." It also offers clarity in respect to the various primary and secondary consequences of utilizing a certain means to reach a specified goal—and hence confronts us with choices. However, it must never be allowed to take responsibility for our decisions (2005, pp. 331–336; see 2012, pp. 100–138).

Weber pronounced such an ethos of "value neutrality" as indispensable to the definition of sociology—if it wished to be a social science rather than a political endeavor:

> Science today is a "vocation" organized in *special disciplines* in the service of self-clarification and knowledge of interrelated facts. It is not the gift of grace of seers and prophets dispensing sacred values and revelations, nor does it partake of the contemplation of sages and philosophers about the *meaning* of the world. (2005, pp. 334–335)

How does the sociologist best proceed to ascertain subjective meaning in the groups under investigation? How is this task accomplished in an unbiased fashion? Answers to these questions require a brief discussion of Weber's mode of analysis grounded in *ideal types*.

Ideal Types

Although Weber takes the meaningful action of individuals as his basic unit of analysis, his interpretive sociology never views social life as an "endless drift" of solitary and unconnected action orientations. The diverse ways in which persons act *in concert in groups* capture his attention rather than the social action of the isolated individual. Indeed, he defines the sociological enterprise as oriented to the investigation of the subjective meaning of persons in delimited groups and the identification of *regularities of action*:

> There can be observed, within the realm of social action, actual empirical regularities; that is, courses of action that are repeated by the actor or (possibly also: simultaneously) occur among numerous actors because the subjective *meaning* is typically *meant* to be the same. Sociological investigation is concerned with these *typical* modes of action. (1968, p. 29; translation altered, original emphasis)

This patterned action can result, he argues, not only from an orientation to values, but also to affectual, traditional, and even means-end rational action. A fundamental theme in his sociology explores the various ways in which, as a consequence of configurations of empirical causes, merely imitative and reactive behavior is *uprooted* from its random flow and transformed into *meaning*-based regularities anchored in one of the four types of social action.

Weber's major heuristic concept—the ideal type—"documents" these regularities of meaningful action as they occur in groups. These *research tools* chart the patterned action of individuals in groups—and nothing more. His ideal type "the Puritan," for example, identifies the regular action of these believers (for example, an orientation toward methodical work and an ascetic style of life). Hence, Weber's sociology steers away from a focus upon isolated action, detailed historical narrative, and diffuse concepts (such as "society," "social differentiation," and "the question of social order"). Instead, it seeks, through the formation of ideal types, to capture patterned social action. This level of analysis prevails throughout his texts.

How are ideal types formed? Neither a summarization nor classification of social action is involved. Rather, and although construction of the ideal type is rooted thoroughly in empirical reality, it is formulated, first, through a conscious exaggeration of the *essential* features of the patterns of action of interest to the sociologist and, second, through a synthesis of these characteristic patterns of action into an internally unified and logically rigorous concept:

> An ideal type is formed by the one-sided *accentuation of one or more* points of view and by the synthesis of a great many diffuse, discrete, more or less present

and occasionally absent *concrete individual* phenomena, which are arranged according to those one-sidedly emphasized viewpoints into a unified *analytical* construct. In its conceptual purity, this construct cannot be found empirically anywhere in reality. (1949, p. 90; emphasis in original)

While inductive procedures from empirical observations are first followed, deductive procedures then guide the logical ordering of the identified patterns of action into a unified and precise construct. Nonetheless, the anchoring of ideal types empirically precludes their comprehension as "abstract" or "reified" concepts (see 1949, pp. 92–107).

Above all, according to Weber, ideal types serve *to assist* empirical, cause-oriented inquiry rather than to "replicate" the external world (an impossible task, he stresses, owing to the unending flow of events as well as the infinite diversity and complexity of even a particular social phenomena) or to articulate an ideal or hoped-for development. Thus, the "Puritan" portrays accurately the subjective meaning of neither a particular Puritan nor all Puritans (1968, pp. 19–22). The same holds for ideal types of, for example, bureaucracies, prophets, intellectuals, or charismatic leaders. As Weber notes: "Concepts are primarily analytical instruments for the intellectual mastery of the empirically given and can be only that" (1949, p. 106; translation altered).

Once formed as clear concepts that capture the regular actions of persons in groups, ideal types ground Weber's causal sociology in a fundamental fashion: They enable the precise definition of empirical patterned action. As a logical construct that documents regular social action, the ideal type establishes clear points of reference—or guidelines—against which patterns of subjective meaning in *a particular case* can be compared and identified precisely. Hence, the uniqueness of cases can be defined clearly through an assessment of approximation to, or deviation from, the theoretically constructed type:

> Ideal types . . . are of great value for research and of high systematic value for expository purposes when they are used as conceptual instruments for *comparison* and the *measurement* of reality. They are indispensable for this purpose. (1949, p. 97; emphasis in original; see also pp. 43, 90–93; 1946b, p. 323–324)[7]

The Goal of Weber's Sociology

Commentaries on Weber's works have frequently failed to note that he orients his research to discrete problems and the causal analysis of specific cases and developments. He proposes that the causal explanation of this "historical individual" should serve as sociology's primary aim:

We wish to understand the reality that surrounds our lives, in which we are placed, *in its characteristic uniqueness*. We wish to understand on the one hand its context (*Zusammenhang*) and the cultural *significance* of its particular manifestations in their contemporary form, and on the other the causes of it becoming historically so and not otherwise. (1949, p.72; translation altered, original emphasis; see also p. 69; 1968, p.10)

Hence, Weber opposed strongly the numerous positivist schools of thought in his day that sought, following the method offered by the natural sciences, to define a set of general laws of history and then to explain all specific developments by deduction. He rejected forcefully the position that the social sciences should aim "to construct a closed system of concepts which can encompass and classify reality in some definitive manner and from which it can be deduced again" (1949, p. 84).

Similarly, his opposition to the view that laws themselves comprise causal explanations was clear. Because concrete realities, individual cases and developments, and subjective meaning cannot be deduced from laws, they are incapable of providing the knowledge of reality that would offer causal explanations, Weber maintains. Particular cases and developments can be explained causally only by "other equally individual configurations" (1949, pp. 75–76; see Kalberg, 1994b, pp. 81–84). To him: "The existence of a connection between two historical occurrences cannot be captured abstractly, but only by presenting an internally consistent view of the way in which it was concretely formed" (1891, p. 2).

These pivotal components of Weber's methodology will be better understood after consideration of EEWR and *E&S*. We are now prepared to understand these demanding works and Weber's motives for writing them. *E&S*, his systematic treatise, first draws our attention.

This treatise lays out the conceptual tools and research procedures for his wide-ranging sociology of civilizations. It also provides the theoretical framework for his EEWR studies on China, India, and ancient Israel. Weber renounced in these works any search for a single, encompassing causal equation: "This sort of construction is better left to that type of dilettante who believes in the 'unity' of the 'social psyche' and its reducibility to *one* formula" (2009, p. 550, n. 142; original emphasis).

Study Questions and Thoughts to Ponder

1. The foundational methodological model in Weber's sociology—the ideal type—explicitly leaves open the question of whether "tradition to modernity" or "capitalism to modern capitalism" transformations occurred empirically. Why is this the case? Please explain.

2. Discuss the goal of Weber's sociology. Offer some comparisons on this score to Durkheim and Marx.

3. Summarize Weber's definition of "objectivity." Is it plausible?

4. Does a macrosociology based in (multiple) ideal types and the acknowledgment of extreme pluralisms of subjective meaning necessarily lead to a multi-causal methodology?

Notes

1. Domains, arenas, life-spheres, and realms are used synonymously (*Lebenssphäre, Lebensbereiche, Lebensordnungen*).

2. The frequent translation of Weber's term *Entwicklung* (development) as "evolution" has caused a great deal of confusion.

3. Following Weber, I am using the terms "meaningful action" and "social action" synonymously (see 1968, pp. 21–22).

4. Weber points out that his classification does not seek to exhaust all possibilities, "but only to formulate in conceptually pure form certain sociologically important types to which actual action is more or less closely approximated" (1968, p. 26). He does not expect to discover *empirical* cases in which social action is oriented *only* to one of these types of action. See the section below on ideal types.

5. Motives for Weber are causes of action and must be understood by reference to subjective meaning: "A motive is a complex of subjective meaning which seems to the actor himself or to the observer an adequate ground for the conduct in question" (1968, p. 11).

6. This distinguishes the "empirical sciences of action," according to Weber, from jurisprudence, logic, ethics, and esthetics, all of which aim to ascertain "true" and "valid" meanings (1968, p. 4; 1949).

7. Weber makes this general point further in the chapter on rulership in Part I of *E&S*: "Hence, the kind of terminology and classification set forth . . . has in no sense the aim—indeed, it could not have it—to be exhaustive or to confine the whole of historical reality in a rigid scheme. Its usefulness is derived from the fact that in a given case it is possible to distinguish what aspects of a given organized group can legitimately be identified as falling under or approximating one or another of these categories" (1968, pp. 263–264).

4

Economy and Society[1]

Incomplete and published posthumously in 1922, *Economy and Society* (*E&S*) addresses the ways in which the West must be understood as unique. This three-volume opus also explores the causal origins of the West's singular developmental pathway. Finally, and unlike EEWR and *PE*, *E&S* seeks to provide a systematic grounding for the discipline of sociology as distinguished from the fields of history and economics.

Written over a period of nine years (1909–1918), this labyrinthine study ranges across an astonishing comparative palette. Weber examines, for example, status groups, the nation, classes, ethnic groups, the family, the clan, and political groups on the one hand, and a vast array of economies, cities, salvation religions, and rulership and legal groups on the other hand. Rather than by reference to the 20th century or a single society alone, he does so in sweeping comparative-historical and civilizational perspective. At times broad, his strokes scrutinize patterns of action in a variety of civilizations and compare developmental trends over centuries and even millennia. Throughout, it is apparent that thorough research underpins Weber's discussions.

Herein lies the claim of *E&S* to be one of the 20th century's most remarkable contributions to the social sciences. Weber is engaged in a breathtaking project: a *systematization* of his detailed empirical knowledge of the ancient, medieval, and modern epochs in China, India, and the West, as well as of the ancient Middle Eastern civilizations. By doing so, he seeks to create an *analytic* treatise that will provide guiding ideal types and research procedures to social scientists for the practice of a comparative-historical *and* interpretive sociology of civilizations.

When combined with the perpetual formation of analytic generalizations, Weber's attention to historical detail renders *E&S* a difficult, even tortuous work. Numerous models heuristically useful to researchers are created in every chapter. While some are more limited in scope and pertain to a specific historical period, others range broadly; some are more static, others are more dynamic and include sets of hypotheses; still others are "developmental forms" (*Entwicklungsformen*) comprised of many stages. All serve as conceptual yardsticks designed to assist identification of predominant patterns of action in empirical cases. While the shorter Part I (pp. 3–310), which was written later, emphasizes model building, and indeed often appears as a compendium of concepts, the longer Part II (pp. 311–1374) stresses both historical cases and model building. It also often provides brief—and usually incomplete—causal analyses of particular developments.

The patience of even the most enamored reader is repeatedly tested by the sheer dryness of the ideal types in Part I and the disjointed, back and forth movement between the historical evidence and the construction of ideal types in Part II. Unfortunately, Weber never provides an adequate summary statement of his aims, themes, or procedures.[2] Perhaps not surprisingly, interpreters of *E&S* have generally discussed only those chapters that have become *de rigueur* reading for both theorists and sociologists engaged in specialized research: the sections on law, status groups, prophets, charisma, rulership in general, the bureaucracy, and the city.

Over many decades, these chapters have provided the point of departure for innumerable articles in the social sciences. However, and although each chapter deserves careful scrutiny, this focus fails to unlock the true originality and enduring usefulness of *E&S* as a far-reaching analytic treatise. Moreover, this narrow-focus manner of utilizing *E&S* has neglected entirely the large—even civilizational—themes at the core of this ambitious study.

An exploration of the *five axes* that dominate *E&S* will articulate its overall goals, themes, and trajectories, as well as serve to acquaint us with Weber's manner of constructing models. In the process, the major modes of analysis and research procedures of his comparative-historical and interpretive sociology of civilizations become apparent. A brief perusal of each of these axes must suffice. The building blocks provided by *E&S* are substantial.

"Locating" Social Action: Societal Domains and Ideal Types

Convinced that the crystallization of social action and its empirical appearance in multiple patterns is neither random nor to be grasped by reference to a "social system," "cultural order," "social fact," or "generalized other," Weber aims throughout *E&S* to specify *where* such regularities are *likely* to arise. To the extent that he succeeds in *analytically locating* meaningful action, the foundation for his entire agenda has been laid. Indeed, this task must be completed if his interpretive approach to the study of civilizations—the understanding by the sociologist of the subjective meaning persons across the globe in diverse groups attribute to their action—is to constitute more than an empty, formalistic enterprise of little utility to researchers.

Based on massive comparative-historical research, *E&S* contends that social action—largely though not exclusively—congeals frequently in a number of "societal domains" (*gesellschaftliche Ordnungen*): the economy, rulership, religion, law, status groups, family, and clan arenas.[3] To him, persons are "placed into various societal life-spheres, each of which is governed by different laws" (1946a, p. 123).

E&S undertakes the huge task of delimiting analytically these major realms. It does so by identifying, themes, dilemmas, and sets of questions indigenous to each. For example, explanations for suffering, misfortune, and misery distinguish the arena of religion, while the life-sphere of rulership is concerned with the possible motives for rendering obedience and the reasons why persons attribute legitimacy to commands. The status group realm involves various notions of social honor and corresponding styles of life. In this manner, analytic boundaries for each domain become established (see Kalberg, 1994, pp. 104–105, 149).

Action by persons "located" in these arenas may become uprooted from its random, reactive flow and become social action, Weber argues. Given facilitating contextual dynamics, this action may become patterned action, and most *E&S* chapters discuss the particular features of domain-specific regular action. For example, with respect to economic activity, action becomes social action "if it takes account of the behavior of someone else . . . [and] in so far as the actor assumes that others will respect his actual control over economic goods" (1968, p. 22; see also p. 341). And action oriented to status becomes social action wherever a specific mode of organizing life is acknowledged and restrictions on social intercourse become effective (1968, p. 932).

Here we find, with societal realms, a major heuristic tool for the interpretive sociologist's research. In Weber's terminology, each domain implies a potential domain of subjective meaning (*Sinnbereich*) within which patterned social action and cohesive groups may arise.

Nonetheless, and however conceptually pivotal to his entire interpretive agenda, Weber concludes that arenas are too diffuse to ground his empirically based sociology. With respect to this *E&S* task—*locating* social action—they constitute a beginning step only. Patterned orientations of subjectively meaningful action can be far more rigorously conceptualized and "located," he holds, by reference to *ideal types*. These *models* capture regular social action with great precision. As an analytic treatise, *E&S* takes the formation of ideal types as one of its main tasks.

When Weber forms an ideal type construct of, for example, the prophet, the functionary in a bureaucracy, the Puritan, the market or natural economy, the feudal aristocrat, the peasant, and the intellectual, he is in each case conceptualizing patterned orientations of social action. Thus, the "bureaucratic functionary" concept implies regular orientations by a group of people toward punctuality, reliability, specialized tasks, a hierarchical chain of command, certificates of competence, and the disciplined organization of work; the "charismatic leader" model implies the orientation of a group of people (disciples, followers) toward persons viewed as extraordinary and a willingness to follow them even if a violation of convention and custom is necessary.

Each ideal type signifies an uprooting of action from its amorphous flow and a demarcation of constellations of social action. It also implies the possibility that action similar to that described by this construct will appear empirically—perhaps even in the form of patterned orientations of social action endowed with a degree of endurance, firmness, and continuity. Hence, the social action delineated by ideal types indicates the possibility that an indigenous *causal thrust* may exist empirically: To Weber, each such model—the regular action-orientations it implies—retains the potential, depending on the push and pull of the arrays of regular action within which it is embedded, to assert an autonomous (*eigengesetzliche*) influence.

In this manner, each of the multiple ideal types in *E&S* locates patterned social action in a far more specific manner than do its societal domains. This capacity of this far-ranging analytic matrix to locate meaningful empirical action by reference to ideal types and societal domains fulfills an important task: The attempts by sociologists to identify empirical regularities of social action are assisted.

However, the *E&S* analytic comprised of multiple spheres and sphere-specific ideal types performs a further crucial service in Weber's sociology: It helps researchers *understand* how a vast variety of action on an expansive, comparative-historical spectrum *can become* subjectively meaningful to persons. In other words, the sheer expanse of its multiple domains and ideal types facilitates the sociologist's comprehension of social action *contextually*—that is, on its own terms or "from within." In doing so, this opus accomplishes for Weber's interpretive understanding project another pivotal task: It opposes any proclivity for sociologists engaged in interpretive comparative research to explore social action solely from the vantage point of *their own* accustomed (and perhaps unexamined) presuppositions. Whenever this occurs, a greater likelihood exists that social scientists will, Weber is convinced, define "unusual action" as odd, "irrational," and incomprehensible rather than as subjectively meaningful.

In sum, in locating empirical subjective meaning with the assistance of numerous ideal types and societal domains, *E&S* facilitates comprehension by researchers of how values, interests, emotions, and traditions in diverse settings may provide meaning to action, call forth patterned social action, and hence formulate the bases for social groups (see Kalberg, 1994, pp. 30–46). By enabling an understanding of putatively "irrational" actions as indeed meaningful, this analytic opus *expands* the imaginations of sociologists.

For example, the ideal type "missionary prophet" assists "we moderns" to comprehend the ways in which this charismatic figure, who views the cosmos as internally unified by God's Commandments and intentions (1968, pp. 450–451), attributes meaning to his actions—however "irrational" they may appear from the point of view of today's widely held scientific and secularized presuppositions. Moreover, wherever patterned action in one group congeals with patterned action in another group, some action-orientations may "line up" in a concerted fashion and form the foundation for internally consistent—and even methodically organized—lives. Several of Weber's ideal types (the mystic, the ascetic, and the prophet, for example) chart just such systematically directed action. As we will see, he attributes to such figures the possibility of possessing great historical importance.

Ideal Types as "Yardsticks"

As noted, as conceptual tools the ideal types of *E&S* "document" patterned social action and demarcate its location vis-à-vis a series of domains. In addition, when utilized as yardsticks, or standards, against which the empirical patterns of action under investigation can be compared and defined, they assist the clear delineation of this empirical action. A vast diversity of ideal types of varying scope are formulated in *E&S* (for example, feudalism, patriarchalism, priests, the Oriental city, natural law, canon law, asceticism, and warriors).

Several ideal types formulated by Weber have been highly influential in sociology for at least 60 years: his "types of rulership"[4] and "status groups." The definition here of these familiar models further illustrate Weber's comparative-historical mode of procedure. And a discussion of their capacity to serve the researcher as yardsticks illustrates their usefulness for empirical investigations (see also Kalberg, 1994, pp. 87–91).

Legitimate Rulership

Rulers have been obeyed for millennia. Of course, rulership has often been overthrown—only to be established again under new rulers. A great deal of "glue" exists in those civilizations where authority and domination are firm; however, they often become corrupt and lose their legitimacy. To Weber, an important query must be answered: *What reasons* do people give to themselves for obeying authority?

Rather than a "social fact," an expression of natural laws, or an inevitable culmination of evolutionary forces, *rulership* implies for Weber nothing more than the probability that a definable group of persons (as a result of various motives) will empirically orient social action to giving commands, that another definable group of persons will direct social action to obedience (as a result of various motives), and that commands are in fact, to a sociologically relevant degree, carried out.[5] In his famous formulation, rulership refers "to the probability that a command with a given specific content will be obeyed by a given group of persons" (1968, p. 53). It may be ascribed to diverse persons, such as feudal princes, judges, civil servants, monarchs, bankers, craftsmen, and tribal chiefs. All exercise rulership wherever obedience is claimed and in fact called forth (1968, pp. 941, 948).

Weber's major concern focuses on *legitimate* rulership, or the situation in which a degree of legitimacy is *attributed* to the rulership relationship. Obedience here importantly acquires a voluntary element. Whether rooted in unreflective habit or custom, an emotional attachment to the ruler or fear of him, values or ideals, or purely material interests and a calculation of advantage, a necessary minimum of compliance, unlike sheer *power* (see below), always exists in the case of legitimate rulership (1968, p. 212).

To Weber, the establishment of a rulership relationship's legitimacy exclusively through material interests is likely to be relatively unstable. On the other hand, purely value-rational and affectual motives can be decisive only in "extraordinary" circumstances, he holds. A mixture of custom and a means-end rational calculation of material interests generally provides the "motive for compliance" in everyday situations (1968, pp. 213–214, 943).

Nonetheless, in Weber's analysis, these motives alone never form a reliable and enduring foundation for rulership. A further element—at least a minimum belief on the part of the ruled in the legitimacy of the rulership—is crucial: "In general, it should be kept clearly in mind that the basis of every rulership, and correspondingly of *every* kind of willingness to obey, is a *belief,* a belief by virtue of which persons exercising rulership are lent prestige" (1968, p. 263; see also p. 213). In essence, Weber maintains that wherever persons *believe* that a particular rulership is justified a willingness to obey arises that secures rulership more effectively than does force or power alone.

The character of the typical belief, or claim to legitimacy, provides Weber with the criteria he utilizes to classify, *as ideal-typical models*, the major *types* of legitimate rulership (see 1968, p. 953). Again, why do people obey authority? From the vantage point of his extensive comparative and historical studies, Weber argues that all ruling powers, "profane or religious, political as well as unpolitical," can be understood as appealing to *rational-legal, traditional,* or *charismatic* principles of legitimate rulership. What typical beliefs establish the "validity" of these "pure types" of legitimate rulership? Weber notes three:

1. Rational grounds—resting on a belief in the legality of enacted rules and the right of those elevated to rulership under such rules to issue commands (legal rulership; 1968, p. 215).

2. Traditional grounds—resting on an established belief in the sanctity of immemorial traditions and the legitimacy of those exercising rulership under them (traditional rulership; 1968, p. 215).

3. Charismatic grounds—resting on devotion to the exceptional sanctity, heroism, or exemplary character of an individual person, and of the orders revealed or ordained by him (charismatic rulership) (1968, p. 215). Under the motto, "it is written—but I say unto you," this mission opposes all existing values, customs, laws, rules, and traditions (1968, pp. 1115–1117; see also pp. 262–263, 953–954, 947).

These issues define the "rulership" domain and distinguish action oriented to it from action oriented to the other life-spheres. How does, for example, "rational-legal" rulership in Weber's sociology constitute a model that sets standards for the guidance of research?

This widely discussed type of rulership is manifest in the bureaucratic organization. It becomes all-pervasive in industrial societies, Weber argues. Its legitimacy rests on a belief held by people that it has been properly enacted through rules and impartial procedures rather than on a belief in persons or in the legitimacy of traditions established in the past. Thus, bureaucratic administration stands in radical opposition to both charismatic rulership and all types of traditional rulership (patriarchalism, patrimonialism, feudalism). Diverse social action is now patterned in reference to stable prescriptions, regulations, rules, and specialized tasks—indeed, the ordering of action in this manner accounts for the *comparative* technical superiority in regard to the completion of tasks of bureaucratic rulership vis-à-vis traditional and charismatic rulership. Moreover, rights and duties are defined in this organization that enable the issuing of commands and the expectation of obedience:

> Orders are given in the name of an impersonal norm rather than in the name of a personal authority; and even the giving of a command constitutes obedience toward a norm rather than an arbitrary freedom, favor, or privilege. (1946c, pp. 294–295; see also 1968, pp. 229, 945, 1012)

Furthermore, Weber's ideal type emphasizes that bureaucracies orient labor toward general rules and regulations in a systematic fashion. Work occurs in offices, on a full-time basis, and involves the formulation of written records and their preservation; employees are appointed and rewarded with a regular salary as well as the prospect for advancement. And labor procedures maximize calculation: Through an assessment of single cases in reference to a set of abstract rules or a weighing of means and ends, decisions can be rendered in a predictable and expedient manner.

Compared to the traditional forms of rulership, such decisions occur with less equivocation. Arenas of jurisdiction, task specialization, competence, and responsibility for each employee are delimited on the one hand by administrative regulations and on the other by technical training. According to this model, this technical training can be most effectively utilized when realms of competence are defined and an unquestioned hierarchy of command reigns in which "each lower office is under the control and supervision of a higher one" (1968, p. 218). Rulership, including a superior's access to coercive means, is distributed in a stable manner and articulated by regulations (see 1968, pp. 217–226, 973–975).

Weber's construct stresses that "formal rationality" reigns in bureaucracies. Problems are solved and decisions made by the systematic and continuous means-end orientation of action to abstract rules, each of which has been enacted through discursively analyzable procedures. Because decision-making and the giving of commands takes place in direct reference to these rules, bureaucracies typically imply—compared to the traditional and charismatic types of rulership—a reduction of affectual and traditional action. Weber repeatedly calls attention to the extremely impersonal character of bureaucratic rulership. For example:

> Bureaucracy develops the more perfectly the more it is "dehumanized," the more completely it succeeds in eliminating from official business love, hatred, and all purely personal, irrational, and emotional elements which escape calculation. (1968, p. 975).

This complex ideal type, Weber argues, can be utilized as a standard against which the particular empirical case under investigation—the American, English, Turkish, Chinese, or German bureaucracy, for example, or a state bureaucracy vis-à-vis a bureaucracy in private industry—can be compared. Through an assessment of deviation from this heuristic tool, the main features of the particular case will then become defined. Its distinctiveness will then become apparent.[6]

Weber's model "status group" further illustrates the manner in which ideal types "document" a particular cluster of patterned action. Empirical cases can then be "measured" against this construct and thereby defined clearly.

Status Groups

He contends that *status groups* constitute an independent foundation for social inequality. How is this ideal type defined and how does it serve as a conceptual yardstick that assists research?

"Status situation" implies "every typical component of the life of men that is determined by a specific, positive or negative, social estimation of honor" (1968, p. 932). Thus, social esteem—claims to it and acknowledgment of it—orients social action in this domain. The "way of leading a life" (*Lebensführung*) comes here to the fore. It varies in particular according to socialization processes, family prestige, and occupational prestige (1968, pp. 305–306; see also 1946c, p. 300).

In this model, a status group (*Stand*) appears when persons share a style of life—that is, consumption patterns, common conventions, specific notions of honor, and, conceivably, economic and particular status monopolies. For Weber, status situations, due to an implied evaluation of one's own situation relative to that of others as well as a subjective awareness of common conventions, values, and styles of life, may often lead to the formation of groups. These groups vary across a spectrum, at times remaining amorphous and at other times cultivating firm boundaries that throw status differences into relief. Here social interaction is absent or restricted. Stratification by status always implies the "monopolization of ideal and material goods or opportunities," as well as social distance and exclusiveness (1946c, p. 300; 1968, pp. 927, 935). Opposing Marx, Weber sees status concerns as demarcating an axis of inequality independent from classes.

He emphasizes again subjective meaning. A subjective sense of social honor and esteem must be acknowledged; it may have a significant impact. To him, "stratification by status" stands in opposition to, and may restrict, *even* action oriented to classes, material interests, the development of the free market, class conflicts, and hard bargaining. Again, Weber's illustrations typically move across centuries and civilizations. He discovers examples of exclusion and inclusion according to status considerations universally.

Guilds in the Middle Ages, for example, now and then struggled more fervently over questions of precedence in festival processions than over economic issues. Distinguished families throughout the world permit courtship of their daughters only by status peers, and members of "old families" have frequently cultivated a variety of techniques of exclusiveness, as have the descendants of the Pilgrim fathers, Pocahontas, and the First Families of Virginia (1958, pp. 34, 125; 1968, pp. 933, 937).

Likewise, court nobles and humanist literati imprinted significantly the character of education in the 17th century, and various "carrier strata" have prominently influenced the formation of religious doctrines and ethical teachings (see below). This has occurred to such an extent that belief systems undergo profound alterations whenever they acquired a new carrier stratum (see 1946c, pp. 279–285; 1968, pp. 490–492, 1180–1181; 2009, pp. 238–241). A single status group might occasionally set its stamp on the long-range development of a civilization, as did intellectuals (the "literati") in China, the samurai warriors in Japan, and the Brahmin priests in India.

As ideal type models, each status group can be employed as a standard against which the particular empirical case under investigation can be "measured." Its uniqueness can be defined in this manner. Without these constructs to assist conceptualization, it is not possible, Weber argues, to conduct the comparative "mental experiments" (*Gedankenbild*) central for the rigorous isolation of significant *causal* patterns of action.

These yardstick ideal types—status groups and types of rulership—from *E&S* (as well as many others that could be addressed) place Weber in direct opposition to Marx: ownership of property does not constitute the single axis of inequality. Weber's sociology repeatedly contends that a variety of causal forces are effective in history and that social change across various civilizations occurs in a nonlinear, complex fashion (see below).

Ideal Types as Hypothesis-Forming Models

E&S's ideal types facilitate the clear conceptualization of specific empirical cases and developments. They also chart hypotheses that can be tested against specific cases and developments. Ideal types are employed in *E&S* as hypothesis-forming constructs in four major ways.

Their *dynamic* character is the focus of Weber's first type of model. Rather than being static, ideal types are constituted from arrays of regular action. Relationships—delimited, empirically testable hypotheses—among these patterns of action are implied. Second, *contextual* models that articulate hypotheses regarding the impact of specific social contexts on regular action are constructed in *E&S*. Third, when examined in reference to one another, ideal types articulate *logical interactions* of patterned, meaningful action. Hypotheses regarding "elective affinity" and "antagonism" relationships across ideal types abound in *E&S*. Fourth, Weber utilizes ideal types to chart analytic *developments*. Each construct hypotheses a *course* of regular action, or a "developmental path."

By erecting a demarcated analytical framework, every model facilitates a conceptual grasp on otherwise diffuse realities and formulates causal hypotheses regarding empirical patterned action. In doing so, each construct assists attainment of the overall goal of Weber's sociology: the causal explanation of cases and developments (see above, pp. 44–45). Hence, a strongly theoretical dimension is injected by each model into the very core of Weber's comparative-historical sociology. Only a few of his elective affinity, antagonism, and developmental constructs can be noted here.[7]

Weber informs us explicitly that he is concerned in *E&S* with the ideal-typical relationships between the economy and "society"—that is, the interactions between the economy and "the general structural *forms* (*Strukturformen*) of human groups" (1968, p. 356)[8] in the major societal domains. In great detail and on a vast scale, he charts out, through constellations of ideal types, the diverse ways in which the various stages in the development of the economy (the agricultural and industrial organization of work; the natural, money, planned, market, and capitalist types of economies; see Kalberg, 1983) relate to—and influence—the various major stages in the other arenas: for example, the traditional, natural, and logical-formal types of law; the paths to salvation in the religion domain (through a savior, an institution, ritual, good works, mysticism's withdrawal from the world, and asceticism's activity; see Kalberg, 1990); the charismatic, patriarchal, feudal, patrimonial, and bureaucratic types of rulership; the family and clan universal organizations; and an array of major status groups (such as intellectuals, civil servants, and feudal nobles).

Nonetheless, this attention to the interactions between the economy and the other domains never implies its elevation to a position of causal dominance. On the contrary, in distinguishing a *series* of realms, Weber wishes to argue that questions of causality cannot be addressed by exclusive reference to economic forces and material interests—or *any single* arena. As he notes: "The connections between the economy and the societal spheres are dealt with more fully than is usually the case. This is done deliberately so that the autonomy (*Eigengesetzlichkeit*) of these domains vis-à-vis the economy is made manifest" (1914, p. vii). Hence, each domain, as manifest through its ideal types, implies the possibility of empirically significant patterns of action, Weber contends. This opus cannot accurately be depicted as addressing only the manner in which diverse groups influence—and are influenced by—the economy. The elevation of a particular arena to a position of general causal priority, Weber insists, must not occur.

Moreover, *E&S* charts much more than the analytic relationships between the various groups in the economy arena and the various groups in the other realms. Weber examines also the ideal-typical relationships, for example, between clans and religious groups, legal and rulership groups, groups in the spheres of religion and law, the family and rulership groups, and religious and rulership groups. More specifically, he scrutinizes the relation of logical-formal law to bureaucratic rulership, the family to various salvation paths, and the "ethics" of various status groups to the major salvation paths on the one hand and the types of law and rulership on the other hand. How, then, do the various domains relate analytically to one another? *E&S* proclaims that they do so in two patterned ways.

Elective Affinity and Relations of Antagonism Models

Two concepts in *E&S* capture cross-arena relationships: relations of "elective affinity" and relations of "antagonism." While elective affinity models imply hypotheses regarding a compatible intermingling—a nondeterministic though typical and reciprocal interaction of regular social action—of two or more ideal types that share internal features, antagonism models indicate hypotheses of "inadequacy" and a clash, a hindering, even an excluding of patterned action from other arenas.

These "logical interactions" of domains-based regular action constitute, to Weber, hypothesis-forming models. For example, the intensely personal character of relationships in the family and clan are viewed as *antagonistic* to the impersonal relationships characteristic of the marketplace (an orientation of social action to the "laws of the market" over orientations to persons) and bureaucratic rulership (an orientation to statutes, regulations, and laws over persons). Similarly, the relationships of compassion and brotherhood typically cultivated by the great salvation religions are seen as opposing the formal rationality that appears in the later developmental stages of the economy (capitalism), rulership (bureaucracy), and law (logical-formal) domains. And charismatic rulership stands in a relationship of antagonism to all routine economic action: "From the point of view of rational economic activity, charismatic want satisfaction is a typical anti-economic force" (1968, p. 245; see Kalberg, 1994, pp. 102–117).

On the other hand, innumerable cross-sphere *affinity* relationships abound as well in *E&S*. For example, and despite wide diversity, Weber detected a series of elective affinities between the status ethic of intellectuals and certain salvation paths. Due to their *typical tendency* to ponder the world passively, to search for a comprehensive meaning to life, and to deplore the meaninglessness of empirical reality rather than to undertake "tasks" and act regularly *in* the world as "doers," intellectuals are generally predisposed to formulate notions of salvation "more remote from life, more theoretical and more systematic than salvation from external need, the quest for which is characteristic of non-privileged strata" (1968, p. 506; translation altered).

Weber also sees logical interactions of elective affinity as typically occurring between the universal organizations and both ritual-based and salvation-based religions. Ritual religions simply appropriated the general virtues practiced in the family, kin group, and traditional neighborhood (such as fraternity, truthfulness, loyalty to the sibling, respect for older generations, and reciprocal assistance), and salvation religions typically bestowed distinctly positive premiums on an ethic of brotherhood and compassion. In all cases, personal relations and person-oriented values predominated. Similarly, Weber discovered elective affinity relations between traditional types of law and patriarchal rulership, as well as bureaucratic rulership and logical-formal law (see Kalberg, 1994, pp. 108–116)

In this manner, *E&S* articulates a wide array of cross-domain analytic relationships, all of which are formulated as hypotheses.[9] Indeed, this opus constructs a *broad-ranging analytic*—one that can be utilized as a theoretical framework to facilitate the clear conceptualization of empirical relationships, as well as their analytical location.[10] One further type of hypothesis-forming construct central in *E&S* must be examined: the developmental model.

Developmental Models

Weber's *E&S developmental models* hypothesize *courses* of patterned action in the economy, rulership, religion, and law spheres. In doing so, they (a) set a standard that facilitates the clear conceptualization of the particular development under investigation and (b) postulate delimited, empirically-testable developmental pathways of regular action. In effect, as "technical aids" constructed with a "rational consistency . . . rarely found in reality" (1946c, p. 323), each model charts paths that will be taken if certain "irrational" empirical disturbances do not intervene (1949, pp. 101–103). "Even developments," according to Weber, "can be constructed as ideal types, and these constructs may have quite considerable heuristic value" (1949, p. 101). Only one example can be offered here: the "routinization of charisma" model.

Charismatic rulership is exercised by a person over followers who believe that this figure possesses extraordinary powers. These leaders, who arise in "emergency situations," may be prophets, war heroes, politicians, leaders of the hunt, demagogues, oracle-givers, or magicians. In all cases, the attributed "right to rule" derives from recognition of highly unusual qualities, ones not possessed by the average person.

Once genuineness is acknowledged, followers feel duty-bound to devote themselves completely to charismatic leaders. They obey commands as a result of an immense affection and the conviction that a genuinely personal relationship exists. Indeed, Weber sees an "emotional conviction" as central to the belief of followers in the charismatic leader's authority, one that "internally" revolutionizes their entire personalities: "Charisma . . . manifests its revolutionary power from within, from a central *metanoia* [change] of its followers attitudes" (1968, p. 1117; see pp. 241–244, 1112–1117).

The highly personal character of charismatic rule, as well as its lack of concern for everyday routine, leads it to reject all "external order." The "objective" law received by possessors of charisma as a "gift from God" bestows upon them a unique and new mission. For this reason, Weber sees charisma as standing in fundamental opposition to all means-end rational action, as well as to all existing and stable forces of daily life (see 1968, pp. 291, 1112–1120).

However, he also stresses the fragility of charismatic rulership. As a consequence of its location strictly in the "supernatural qualities" of great leaders and the necessity for the "superhuman" personality repeatedly to demonstrate unusual powers and a "right to rule," "charismatic authority is naturally unstable" (1968, pp. 1112–1114). Even great personal devotion cannot guarantee the perpetuation of the charismatic figure's teachings in their pure form. Instead, Weber's "routinization" model proclaims, charisma follows a developmental path characterized by its weakening: it becomes repeatedly absorbed into the permanent institutions of everyday life. Indeed, followers have always sought such a transformation in the hope that, in the process, a *permanent* protection against sickness, disease, and natural catastrophe will be acquired (see, for example 1968, pp. 1131–1133, 1146–1149, 1156).

The material and power interests of the charismatic community of followers constitute, in Weber's routinization construct, an important driving force in institutionalizing the "transitory gift of grace . . . into a permanent possession of everyday life" (1968, p. 1121). Preserved in depersonalized (*versachlichte*) form, a weakened charisma becomes attached to the community of followers. It plays an indispensable role in attracting new believers, this model hypotheses, as well as in establishing the legitimacy of new status groups, forms of rulership, and religious doctrines.

Now as a part of "everyday life" and capable, often through ceremonies involving elaborate ritual, of being transmitted to family members, or institutions, "hereditary," "institutionalized," and "office" charisma serve to legitimize "acquired rights." Altered into these impersonal and routinized forms, charisma is often upheld, according to this developmental construct, at all these stages not only by the values of followers, but also by persons in possession of economic and political interests in doing so. It is further supported by all those in possession of power and property who view their positions of advantage as legitimated by routinized charisma's authority—for example, court officials, priests, monarchs, high dignitaries, and party leaders (1968, pp. 251, 1122, 1139–1141, 1146–1148; 1946c, p. 297).[11]

In formulating developmental models, Weber repeatedly notes their basically "unhistorical" character. As ideal-typical constructions, as discussed, each captures the *essence* of an empirical development, presenting it in a manner more internally consistent and systematically unified than ever actually occurred.

Hence, because the stages of his developmental models should never be viewed either as accurate renderings of an historical pathway or as themselves constituting "effective forces," *E&S* diverges distinctly from all evolutionary schools of thought that search either for society's "scientific laws" or history's "invariable stages." Weber's developmental constructs serve a more modest task: they aim on the one hand to provide the researcher with clear and practical "means of orientation" to diffuse empirical landscapes and on the other hand to offer an array of hypotheses regarding a pathway of development. Whether the analytic course laid out by a particular model is followed always remains an issue for detailed investigation by specialists, Weber insists (1949, p. 103). His developmental constructs testify further to the centrality of model building and hypothesis formation in his sociology.

Weber's yardstick, affinity, antagonism, and developmental constructs appear throughout *E&S*. They contribute decisively to the rigor, analytic power, and uniqueness of his comparative-historical sociology. As "constructed schemes," all models "serve the purpose of offering an ideal-typical means of *orientation*" (1946b, p. 323; original emphasis). With respect to antagonisms across domains, for example, "the theoretically constructed types of conflicting 'societal domains' are merely intended to show that at certain points such and such internal conflicts are *possible* and 'adequate'" (1946b, p. 323; original emphasis). By performing this modest task, each model provides a purchase on amorphous and ceaselessly flowing realities, thereby facilitating clear conceptualization of the empirical patterned action of interest to the researcher. Each hypothesis regarding conflict can then be tested through an in-depth investigation.

Weber expects his "logical constructs," because designed alone as conceptual tools that assist causal analysis, to be "dislocated" once the empirical case or development has been rigorously examined. Complex circumstances and contexts will invariably "strengthen" or "weaken" particular hypothesized relationships. Nonetheless, unlike history, sociology *must* include a rigorous analytical framing—through models—of the problem under investigation, he stresses. Indeed, just the immersion of sociologists deeply in empirical realities *requires* such models if significant causal patterns of action are to be identified, he insists. This remains all the more the case because, according to Weber, the fundamental character of empirical reality—an unending cascade of diffuse events and happenings—presents a continuous danger: namely, that causal inquiry will too easily become mired in an endless, description-based regression.

By constructing arrays of empirically anchored models in *E&S* that conceptualize patterned meaningful action, Weber aims to draw sociology *away* from a focus on demarcated social problems on the one hand and flat historical narrative on the other hand. Nonetheless, his research procedures steadfastly avoid the other side of the spectrum: his grounded models never move to the level of broad, diffuse, epoch-transcending, and evolutionary generalizations. Rather, the *E&S* constructs offer delimited hypotheses designed to be tested against specific cases and developments.

To Weber, unique to the sociological enterprise is always a back and forth movement between conceptualization—the formation of ideal-type models and domain-based theoretical frameworks—and the detailed investigation of empirical cases and developments. If the goal of offering causal explanations for the rise and expansion of the specific case or development is to be realized, the researcher's attention to *both* the empirically particular and conceptual generalization is indispensable.

Driving Forces: The Multicausality of *E&S*, Social Carriers, Power, and Ideas

Although *E&S* gives priority to the task of model building over causal analysis, Weber's unequivocal embrace of multicausal modes of procedure is apparent. Throughout this treatise, as noted, he focuses on patterned social action within the status groups, universal organizations, religion, law, rulership, and economy domains. An array of ideal types in *E&S* is connected analytically to each arena, and each indicates the empirical possibility, given conducive contexts of further patterned action, of *regular* social action endowed with a degree of endurance.

In other words, each ideal type implies the possibility of an empirical causal thrust and staying power or, to Weber, an *autonomous* push. Nonetheless, and even though the meaningful action of persons anchors his sociology, the question "within what *carrier* group action occurs" remains fundamental to his sociology. Social action becomes sociologically significant action *only* in demarcated groups.

In every society, only *certain* traditional, affectual, value-rational, and means-end rational patterns of social action acquire strong exponents and become important parts of the social fabric. For Weber, status groups, classes, and organizations serve as the most prominent bearers of action. Each "carries" a configuration of delimited action patterns. He calls attention, for example, to the ideal-typical "status ethic" of functionaries in bureaucracies (duty, punctuality, the orderly performance of tasks, disciplined work habits, etc.; see 1968, pp. 956–1003) and the class ethos of the bourgeoisie (opposition to privileges based on birth and status, a favoring of formal legal equality; see 1968, pp. 477–480).

Attention to such *carriers* is central to Weber's sociology. He connects this focus closely to an emphasis on the potential of demarcated groups to set into motion an autonomous causal thrust. As he notes, "Unless the concept 'autonomy' is to lack all precision, its definition presupposes the existence of a bounded group of persons which, though membership may fluctuate, is determinable" (1968, p. 699; translation altered). These three themes—autonomy, multicausality, and carrier groups—surface throughout *E&S* in a number of crucial passages.

In introducing his chapters on traditional and charismatic rulership in *E&S*, for example, Weber summarizes his aims as involving not only an evaluation of the extent to which the "developmental chances" of the major "structural principles" of each rulership type can be said to be subject to "economic, political or any other external determinants"(1968, p. 1002). In addition, he seeks to assess the degree to which the developmental chances of the types of rulership follow "an 'autonomous' logic inherent in their technical structure" (1968, p. 1002; see also p. 341).

Weber insists that this "logic" must be *conceptualized as capable* even of exerting an independent effect on groups oriented to economic interests (1968, pp. 578, 1002, 654-5). Moreover, he discusses, whenever a "bounded group" crystallizes as its social carrier, many empirical cases when this does occur. He is especially aware of the extent to which the attribution of *legitimacy* to rulership contributes to the formation of an independent driving force.

Hence, even while remaining cognizant of the frequent impact of economic and political interests, Weber's research procedures emphasize the necessity for a broadly multicausal approach (see 1968, pp. 341, 935). In arguing on behalf of the autonomous *potential* of social action in the economy, law, rulership, religion, status groups, and universal organizations domains, Weber aims in *E&S* to conceptualize action oriented to the economy within a broadened analytic framework and to emphasize the multidimensionality of all causal analysis (see Kalberg, 1994, pp. 50–78).

The "level of analysis" in *E&S*—the subjective meaning of persons in groups located in an array of societal arenas, constellations of domain-specific ideal types, and social carriers—itself further demonstrates his far-ranging multicausality. It is evident as well from Weber's frequent reference in *E&S*, EEWR, and *General Economic History* (1927) to the importance of a further variety of causal forces: historical events, technological innovations, and geographical forces. Moreover, conflict and competition, as well as interests generally and economic interests in particular, constitute to him effective causal forces—as does, not least, power. In his classical formulation, Weber defines power thusly: "Within a social relationship, power means any chance (no matter whereon this chance is based) to carry through one's (individual *or* collective) own will (*even* against resistance)" (1968, p. 53).[12]

New patterns of action frequently fade or become victims of suppression by opposing patterns of action if power is lacking and alliances across groups fail to take place. Rulers are particularly adept, Weber insists repeatedly, at forming coalitions of carrier groups with the sole purpose of maintaining and aggrandizing power. They seek to balance classes, status groups, and organizations against one another as a matter of course. Power plays a central role in his multicausal analyses of how new patterns of social action arise, spread, and set historical developments into motion. His investigations of how regular action becomes circumscribed and rendered less influential also attend to power.

Finally, *E&S* also endows *ideas* with causal efficacy. *Religious* ideas, especially those that address the conundrum of frequent and seemingly random human suffering despite the presence of an all-powerful God (the problem of theodicy), might cast their imprint across centuries and even millennia, Weber argues. Just the attempts to explain misery and injustice played a particularly significant role in the development of religions from ones anchored in magic to ones rooted in notions of salvation, ethical action, and an "other-world." Ideas regarding the stubborn persistence of misfortune, as articulated by prophets, priests, monks, and theologians, pushed this development rather than economic and political interests alone.

Repeatedly, ideas were formulated that clarified the relationship of believers to the transcendent realm—and these ideas implied new meaningful action "pleasing to the gods." Eventually, doctrines were formulated that offered broad-ranging views of the universe, explained suffering in a comprehensive sense, and defined action that promised to bring an end to suffering (see 1968, pp. 349–350, 399–439, 577–579; 1946a, pp. 122–123; 1946c, pp. 269–276, 280–285; Kalberg, 1990).

In sum, attention to a diversity of causal patterned action characterizes *E&S*, as does Weber's unwillingness to elevate particular groups to positions of general causal priority.[13]

The Interweaving of Past and Present

Weber's attempts to define and explain the uniqueness of a particular configuration of groups always acknowledge the many ways in which the past perpetually interweaves causally with the present. This remains the case despite the heroic capacity he sees in charismatic leaders: to sever, given constellations of facilitating conditions, abruptly past and present. Yet even drastic transformations, he holds, and the abrupt advent of "the new" never fully ruptures ties to the past (1968, pp. 29, 577). To him, "that which has been handed down from the past becomes everywhere the immediate precursor of that taken in the present as valid" (1968, p. 29; translation altered). Even the monumental structural alterations called forth by industrialization failed to sweep away the past. Viable legacies live on, he argues repeatedly.

Weber's orientation in *E&S* to societal domains and ideal types stands at the foundation not only of this treatise's multicausality, but also of its capacity to analyze the multiple and subtle ways in which the past interlocks with the present. As discussed, to him, the various societal spheres are endowed with a potentially independent, or "autonomous," capacity rooted in their indigenous questions and problems. They develop at times in a nonparallel manner and at their own pace. And each ideal type, in "documenting" patterns of meaningful action, implies the possibility of an autonomous sustaining element. Moreover, as also noted, Weber endows further forces—historical events, geographical constellations, power, social carriers, conflict, competition, and technology—with an unequivocal causal capacity. The patterned social action of persons in groups is conceptualized as having many and diverse sources.

Weber's sociology offers a "view of society" as constituted from an array of moving—even dynamically interacting—"parts." All "general axiom" schools that depart from encompassing dichotomies (*Gemeinschaft/ Gesellschaft*, tradition/modernity, particularism/universalism), broad themes (the question of social order), or assumptions that support the "organic unity" and "lawfulness" of societies stand radically in opposition to Weber's "open" theoretical framework rooted in arrays of moving ideal types and societal domains.

E&S's fundamental features enable civilizations to be conceptualized as ranging across a wide spectrum of empirical cases characterized on the one hand more by flux, competition, conflict, tension, and disintegration and on the other hand more by internal unity and harmony. The influence of the past on the present varies accordingly. And the dichotomy frequently viewed by commentators as capturing Weber's "view of history"—a contrast of the stable and routine character of tradition to the revolutionary character of charisma (see Mommsen, 1970)—fails to render the complex relationship in his sociology between past and present.

The vast variety of patterned action located in groups, their "open" interaction, and their variable degree of closure allows Weber forcefully to demonstrate the many ways in which the past and present interweave. Regularities of social action in some groups can be recognized as becoming firm and acquiring powerful carriers, even to the extent of developing in reference to their own indigenous problematics and penetrating deeply into subsequent epochs; other groups fail to do so and prove fleeting; still others cast their imprint vigorously and then fade quickly. The "view of society" that flows out of *E&S*—as constructed from numerous causally effective, competing, and reciprocally interacting patterns of social action located in ideal types and societal domains—easily takes cognizance of the "survival" of some regularities of action from the past and their significant influence, as viable legacies (*Ueberbleibsel, Vermaechtnisse, Reste*), on patterns of action in the present.

Weber often charts legacies. He is especially cognizant of those in the religion domain. In the United States, for example, central values in Protestant asceticism remain integral in American life today: disciplined and routine work in a profession, the perpetual formation by persons of goals, the orientation to the future and the attempt to "master" the world's challenges (*Weltbeherrschung*), and an optimism regarding the capacity to shape personal destinies. Moreover, a strong intolerance of "evil" also endures today despite the fact that most who strongly oppose evil have no awareness of this viewpoint as linked intimately to now-elapsed religious ideas and values from American Puritanism (1968, p. 1187; see also 1927, pp. 368–369; 2009, pp. 84, 157–159, 547, n. 122; Kalberg, 2014).

Furthermore, the "direct democratic administration" by the religious congregation, as it took place in the Protestant sects in the United States, left a legacy crucial for the establishment of democratic forms of government, as did the unwillingness of sect members to bestow a halo of reverence on secular authority. The Quakers in particular, in advocating freedom of conscience for others as well as for themselves, paved the way for political tolerance (see 1968, pp. 1204–1210; Kalberg, 1997).

Examples that interweave past and present run perpetually throughout *E&S*. This pivotal feature of Weber's sociology stands in strict opposition to all present-oriented, functionalist modes of analysis. To him, the past always penetrates into the present, at times deeply and in ways that mold its core contours. He is especially convinced that an identification of the modern West's uniqueness and its possible course of further development *require* investigations of its historical development.[14]

Although never discussed by Weber in an organized manner in *E&S*, the five axes investigated in this chapter remain central throughout this analytic treatise. We have now identified and discussed the major concepts, research strategies, and modes of analysis at the foundation of his comparative-historical and interpretive sociology, sociology of civilizations, and sociology in general. Weber's methodology was introduced in Chapter 3 and Chapter 2 examined the "Protestant ethic thesis." Chapter 1 summarized major streams in the intellectual debates of his era, many of which set the stage for the development of his sociology of civilizations.

Before turning to this complex project, the major parameters of the *social and political* contexts within which Weber lived must be briefly charted. Taken together, they formulate a further viable background to his sociology of civilizations. The monumental shifts in these contexts are familiar to us today—namely, the transformations from rural to urban, sacred to secular, feudalism to capitalism, and monarchy to democracy. A further alteration also confronted this epoch: the European aristocracy experienced, amid a general expansion of social egalitarianism, a distinct loss of status and wealth.

Intense anxiety across Europe arose from this upheaval. It highly influenced Weber's scholarship. Indeed, the works of all sociologists can be best comprehended when situated within the social and political contexts specific to their historical eras. The exploration in the following chapter of these contexts assists greatly our understanding of the purposes, procedures, and boundaries of his sociology of civilizations. It serves to further introduce Chapters 6, 7, 8, and 9.

Study Questions and Thoughts to Ponder

1. How is the ideal type formed?

2. Weber contends that ideal types "document" patterned action. What exactly does he mean?

3. *E&S*'s "societal domains" (the economy, law, religion, rulership, status groups, and universal organizations [the clan and the family] domains) assist the capacity of researchers to "locate" patterned action. Please explain.

4. To debate: Weber's notion of status honor constitutes an independent axis of inequality. It must be seen as a strong improvement over the explanation of inequality by reference alone to ownership of property, or lack thereof, held by Karl Marx.

5. How does Weber define "status groups"? Is this concept itself a legacy of the hierarchical (feudal) societies of the past? Should "social honor" and varying "styles of life" be seen today as without relevance in 21st century egalitarian and high mobility societies?

6. Explain how Weber's developmental models assist identification of empirical developments.

7. Discuss the analytic framework offered by *E&S*. What domains does it include? How have they been chosen?

8. Examine the role of "carrier groups" in Weber's sociology.

9. How does Weber's methodology rooted in ideal types differ from the methodology of organic holism schools?

Notes

1. The German editors of the complete works edition (*MWG*) have concluded that *Wirtschaft und Gesellschaft* (*E&S*), which was originally edited posthumously by Weber's wife, was never intended by Weber as a single work. Hence, the *MWG* edition breaks "*Wirtschaft und Gesellschaft*" into several separate volumes. Because *E&S* is now well-established in the English-speaking world and no plan exists to publish its chapters as separate volumes, I will cite *E&S* throughout this volume. Moreover, in terms of themes, procedures, and presuppositions, the *E&S* chapters exhibit a high degree of unity (see Kalberg, 1994; 2012, pp. 13–42, 94–139, 285–290).

2. The introductory chapter—"Basic Sociological Terms"—is quite incomplete.

3. For this reason, *E&S* is organized around these domains. The unfortunate title of this treatise, which stems from Weber's wife, leaves the impression that his sociology is organized around a notion of "society." The title Weber gave to *E&S*'s

Part II—"The Economy and the Societal Domains [*gesellschaftliche Ordnungen*] and Powers"—points to the centrality of societal domains.

4. *Herrschaft* is normally translated as either "authority" or "domination." Neither of these terms captures *Herrschaft*'s *combination* of both authority and domination. I am using Benjamin Nelson's translation: "rulership."

5. Weber emphasizes explicitly the character of rulership as nothing more than meaningful action-orientations:

> Rulership does not mean that a superior elementary force asserts itself in one way or another; it refers to a meaningful interrelationship between those giving orders and those obeying, to the effect that the expectations toward which action is oriented on both sides can be reckoned upon. (1968, p. 1378)

6. Charismatic rulership is examined below. With regard to traditional rulership, Weber emphasizes: "The validity of a social order by virtue of the sacredness of tradition is the oldest and most universal type of legitimacy" (1968, p. 37). On traditional rulership generally, see 1946c, p. 296; 1968, pp. 216, 226–227, 958, 1006–1007, 1041.

7. On Weber's dynamic and contextual models, see Kalberg, 1994, pp. 95–98, 39–46, 98–102.

8. As opposed to "culture" (literature, art, science, etc.).

9. For further examples, see Kalberg, 1994, pp. 108–116. These pages also include a discussion of *intra*-domain relationships of antagonism (for example, the antagonism of charismatic rulership to traditional and bureaucratic rulership).

10. *E&S* also constructs numerous models of antagonism *within* domains. For a discussion of these models (see Kalberg, 1994, pp. 106–108).

11. Weber's attention in this model to the role played by pragmatic interests reveals the "sober realism" side of his sociology. Further developmental models outline the rise of formal rationality in regard to the free market and the state, and a "theoretical" rationalization process in the domain of religion (see Kalberg, 1994, pp. 128–140).

12. This is the excellent translation given by Walliman, Rosenbaum, Tatsis, and Zito (1980).

13. For a further discussion of Weber's multicausality, as well as of his contextual and "conjunctural" mode of establishing causality (see Kalberg, 1994, pp. 32–35, 50–77, 143–192).

14. On the exceedingly complex relationship between past and present in Weber's sociology, see further Kalberg, 1994, pp. 158–167; 1996, pp. 57–64.

5

The Social and
Political Context

Very rapid industrialization was occurring in Max Weber's Germany. Moreover, compared to England and Holland, industrialization began late and, hence, was accompanied by a sense of urgency. However, German elites were convinced that, if the powers of the state were harnessed comprehensively, their nation would soon surpass its competitors.

This "industrialization from above" placed in motion a number of forces that inhibited the unfolding of a democratic political culture on German soil. It implied above all that business elites would be more closely aligned with the state than took place in most other industrializing nations. Moreover, a strong and independent class capable of standing against state power—as a countervailing force seeking to open a public arena of participation and the free exchange of divergent views—failed to arise. Economic development occurred more under the hegemony of a caste of government functionaries than occurred elsewhere.

Three further features of German society proved central. Although largely a secularized nation by 1850, Weber saw that powerful legacies of Luther's political ideas had endured, albeit now manifest as accepted conventions and values rather than as religious belief. They assumed the form of a deep respect for authority in general and for the state in particular (especially in Prussia), even to such a degree that a halo of trust and legitimacy was bestowed in many regions upon the state, its laws, and its civil service functionaries.

In addition, the particular character of feudalism in many of the old German principalities—innumerable small kingdoms—had rendered the authoritarian rulership of the feudal master direct and immediate. Hence, notions of self-rule, individual rights, and representative government never found fertile ground.

Finally, and as a result of all these developments, the German working class remained politically weak. Unlike the French, the Germans failed in their attempt to introduce modern forms of egalitarianism and democratic self-governance. Prussian troops crushed the Revolution of 1848.

These features of its political culture erected significant obstacles to the monumental tasks Germany confronted at the turn-of-the-century. Whereas a stable democracy existed in the United States *before* industrialization, Germany faced the burdensome task of cultivating and extending region-based democratic traditions *in the midst* of industrialization. In many important ways, these two political cultures were located at opposite ends of the authoritarianism–democracy spectrum (see Kalberg, 2012, pp. 227–248).

Although Chancellor Bismarck (1815–1898) had molded a variety of small kingdoms into a unified nation in 1871, a "modernizing ideology"—an embrace of democracy, political rights, and a legal system that institutionalized a division of powers—never accompanied his nation building on a wide scale. Furthermore, Bismarck's authoritarian rulership precluded an assertive and independent role for the German parliament and for the leaders of political parties (see Weber 1968, pp. 1381–1463).

An active, participatory citizenry could scarcely arise amid this overwhelming centralization of power and its possession in the hands of small elites. Politics was dominated by the Chancellor, his functionaries, and an antiquated class of agrarian aristocrats unwilling to place the development of the nation above narrow class interests (see 1988, pp. 470–507). While successful at calling forth rapid industrialization, as well as a notion of social trust grounded thoroughly among elites in a respect for the state and its laws on the one hand and enduring hierarchical, quasi-feudal social conventions on the other, the German political culture opposed all developments in the direction of a democratic political culture.

Civic sphere values and ideals that could be nourished failed to appear on a widespread basis. By the turn into the 20th century, the non-political elites had either turned to introspective endeavors (scholarship, education, art, music, philosophy) or simply withdrawn into private sphere relationships (see 2005, pp. 339–340). Others condemned unequivocally the modern, "impersonal and harsh society" (*Gesellschaft*) and sought a return to the putatively stable and compassionate community (*Gemeinschaft*) of the preindustrial epoch. Varieties of Romantic movements oriented to the past arose. Still others found refuge in fulfilling the old Lutheran notion of vocation: the reliable and dutiful performance of one's workday obligations provided dignity and self-worth. Industrialization rapidly occurred, rooted in part in just this diligent Lutheran work ethic and obedience to authority. However, it took place devoid of the energy borne out of an optimistic view of the industrial society as offering upward mobility dreams and democratic self-governance.

Despite traditions of parliamentary government and citizen activism in a number of regions, a severely restricted civic sphere and feudalism's hierarchical legacies prevented the widespread development in Germany of social egalitarianism and representative democracy. Not surprisingly, "cultural pessimism" became widespread among the educated classes in the 1890s. Indeed, despair, doubt, and a sense of crisis extended throughout much of German society (see Mosse, 1964; Ringer, 1969).

Amid this situation, many asked repeatedly: what public sphere *standards* and values can guide persons in the industrial society? How do we live in this new era? *Who* will live in the modern world? How can ethical and compassionate action survive amid capitalism's unavoidable "cosmos" of instrumental action patterns in reference to the market? "Where are to be found," the philosopher Wilhelm Dilthey (1833–1911) queried, the instruments for surmounting the spiritual chaos which threatens to engulf us" (see Kalberg, 2012, pp. 227–248; Salomon, 1934, p. 164)?

These burning questions were also Weber's burning questions. However, unlike many intellectuals of the time, he refused to withdraw from political activism; nor did he become a resigned cultural pessimist.

An omnipresent actor and life-long player on the stage of German politics, Weber proved an indefatigable critic, marshalling his piercing ammunition in innumerable speeches and newspaper articles, directing it alike against nearly all major classes and groups. He condemned Bismarck for crushing all independent leadership; the German monarchy for blatant incompetence and dilettantism; the bourgeoisie for its weak class consciousness and unwillingness to struggle for political power against the state bureaucracy; the agrarian aristocrats in Prussia for their militarism, authoritarianism, attempts to deny citizenship rights to the working class, and inability to place the nation's interests above their own concerns for material gain; and the German civil servants for their slavish conformity, obsessive adherence to rules and regulations, meekness, and general unwillingness to take responsibility for their decisions. Weber seemed to admire only the German workers; nonetheless, he criticized them as well: while appreciating their competence and craftsmanship skills, he lamented their general passivity in the face of authority (especially compared to their counterparts in France).

Major components of Weber's commentary on modernity can only be understood as a complex, even convoluted, attempt to address glaring internal weaknesses in the German political culture and to offer realistic mechanisms to overcome them. He wished to retain high standards of living and efficient modes of organizing work and producing goods—and capitalism, he was convinced, offered the best opportunity for realization of these aims. However, the many dehumanizing components of this economic system were apparent to him. Weber's thoroughly sociological analysis of his epoch must be explained briefly.

Weber's Analysis

Formal rationality appeared in a nearly omnipresent manner, Weber argued, in the multiple public and private bureaucracies of the industrial society. Here it is expected that decision-making occurs "without regard to persons" and by reference to sets of universally applied rules, laws, statutes, and regulations. As well, favoritism is precluded in respect to hiring, promotion, and certification. An adherence to the dictates of abstract procedures holds sway over all concern for distinctions in respect to social status or personality.

The "logical-formal" law of our day, for example, is implemented by trained jurists who insure that "only unambiguous general characteristics of the case are taken into account in terms of purely processual and legal factors" (1968, pp. 656–657). In the economy arena formal rationality increases to the degree that all technically possible calculations within the "laws of the market" are carried out. Those who would seek to acquire a mortgage are treated by a bank's specialists in reference to impersonal criteria: credit reports, savings, monthly income, and so on (see 2005, pp. 251–254).[1]

Weber sees a different type of rationality as dominant in *daily life* (*Alltag*) in the industrial epoch: *practical* rationality. The individual's egoistic interests and merely adaptive capacities are here apparent, and pragmatic, calculating strategies are typically employed in order to deal with the common obstacles of everyday life in the most expedient manner. As a consequence of their normal activities, all business-oriented strata in particular exhibit a strong tendency to order their ways of life in a practical-rational manner (1946c, pp. 279, 284; 2009, p. 241).

Weber understands modern societies as pervaded also by *theoretical* rationality; in fact, their new "world view"—science—cultivates this type of rationality. An abstract confrontation with reality is prevalent here, and rigorous experiments, precise concepts, and logical deduction and induction become the tools to address and master reality. Whereas theologians and priests in an earlier age adjusted and refined inconsistencies in religious doctrines through theoretical rationalization processes, the same systematic, cognitive search for explanations takes place today—yet now alone in reference to an *empirical* reality.

In both cases, reality is mastered through systematic thought and conceptual schemes. Because requiring a step beyond that which can be observed— "a leap of faith"—religion becomes defined as "irrational" to the same degree that a scientific world view ascends to a dominant position (2005, pp. 337–341; see Kalberg, 2012, pp. 13–42). However, Weber insists in his classic "Science as a Vocation" essay (2005, pp. 321–335, 337–340) that science cannot produce a comparable world view endowed with binding values (see below, pp. 193–199). And the scientist of today is engaged in an enterprise that stresses, as the locus of "truth," empirical observation, description, and abstract synthesizing. Knowledge, insight, clarity, and the "tools and the training for thought" result from satisfactory scientific work rather than from values (see 2005, pp. 333–336).

Formal, practical, and theoretical rationality invariably play central roles in industrial societies, Weber argues. They push aside clusters of values, as well as traditions, from the past. However, all these types of rationality remain incapable of calling forth and giving sustenance to new sets of *noble values*, he contends. Modern-day functionaries in Weber's bureaucracy model orient their action predominantly to duty, caution, security, conformity, order, reliability, and punctuality. Laws and regulations must be implemented according to procedures of formal correctness and legal precedent rather than by reference to higher substantive issues—justice, freedom, and equality—or the character of the accused. Calculations of interests and advantage dominate daily life's practical rationality.

What domains of *modern* secular life, Weber queries frequently, carry and cultivate a *substantive rationality*—namely, a configuration of values that includes compassion, a brotherhood ethic, and charity? He searches, but finds none. On the contrary, now unconstrained by constellations of noble values such as those found in the doctrines of the great salvation religions, formal, practical, and theoretical rationality develop more and more freely and unhindered.

And how does Weber view modern capitalism? He sees that, characterized by the hegemony of formal, practical, and theoretical rationality, a high utilization of scientific innovations, and a bureaucratization of the labor force, modern capitalism has expanded into the far corners of many societies. He appreciates its economic achievements: a large share of the population experiences a standard of living heretofore unknown. He queries, however, whether capitalism today will allow values, and especially *public sphere ethical* values, to orient action in a viable manner. Will they survive exclusively as dead legacies (*caput mortuum*) of restricted influence—namely, as a religious heritage now lacking a binding, obligatory element and powerful social carriers?

To Weber, impersonal and nonbinding relationships unceasingly rise to the forefront in this modern "cosmos." While once firmly anchored and given direction by a "devotion to a cause"—a "calling"—rooted ultimately in coherent configurations of values, social relationships are now largely adrift. At times they approximate purely utilitarian interactions that follow momentary interests, strategic calculations, cognitive processes, power and rulership orientations, and interpretations of statutes and laws (see 2011, pp. 177–179).

The life methodically *directed* toward a set of ideals becomes less and less possible, according to Weber, and an uninterrupted flow of practical-rational activity more and more holds sway. Whereas the motivation to join an ascetic Protestant church or sect could once be explained by reference to sincere belief, the external benefits of membership—acquisition of an entire community's trust and hence its business—often now become central (see 2005, pp. 277–290). A cynical posture, Weber fears, will expand. He asks: "What type of human being will live in this cosmos" (1949, p. 27).

In this historically unique epoch in which "material goods [have] acquired an increasing and, in the end, inescapable power over people as never before in history" (2011, p. 177), the "interests of daily life" are becoming empowered to such an extent that they consistently manipulate and exploit values. A clear *disjunction* is lessening between firm values and ideals held dear on the one hand and the raw, utilitarian flow of life on the other hand, Weber holds. Without such standards and principles, the "pragmatic approach to life" more and more pushes aside ethical ideals, notions of responsibility, and the autonomous and integrated—or "unified"—personality "directed from within" by beliefs and values (1949, p. 18; 1946b, pp. 327–340). Individual autonomy will disappear and massive conformity will result.

Weber wished to see a constellation of noble values and ideals in place that would effectively orient social action and offer dignity to individuals. These were the values of individual autonomy, responsibility, the personality unified by values, ethical action, brotherhood, compassion, charity, and a sense of honor. However, his studies had convinced him that values die out whenever denied their means of sustenance: strong social carriers *and* vigorous competition with other values.

Values become viable when chosen and then defended against other values. They guide meaningful action and enable the formation of dignity and honor; they also provide a firm grounding for initiative-taking and leadership, Weber maintains. Nonetheless, only certain groups cultivate values to the point where they become obligatory despite opposing material interests: namely, groups in *dynamic* competition. Only this "open" situation nourishes sustained struggles across a pluralism of values (*Wertkampf*). In this milieu, persons become "responsible" in reference to a set of values and capable of consistently upholding ethical conduct.

Owing to wide-ranging bureaucratization in industrial societies and the powerful influence of formal, practical, and theoretical types of rationality, Weber feared that the contending arenas indispensable for both a realm of values-based freedom and a flourishing of competing values were losing their distinct boundaries and collapsing. As this occurs, societies will become closed and leaders—defending values—will fade from the social landscape, Weber argues. Societal ossification, driven by a managerial orientation to technical efficiency and not unlike the extreme stagnation that had long ago afflicted Egypt and China, more and more appeared to be on the horizon (see 2005, pp. 251–254).

Indeed, Weber saw an ominous "passion for bureaucratization" that would lead only to "a parcelling out of the soul" (1956, pp. 127–128) and a societal-wide passivity in which people are "led like sheep" (1978, p. 282). How would it be possible "to save *any remnants* of 'individual' freedom of movement" (1968, p. 1403; original emphasis)? "We 'individualists' and partisans of 'democratic' institutions," he proclaimed, "are swimming 'against the tide' of materialist forces" (1978, p. 282; translation altered), and "everywhere the *house of bondage* is already in place" (1978, p. 281, translation altered, original emphasis; see also pp. 281–282; 1968, pp. 1402–1403).

Ideals, ethical action, and noble values must not become, Weber insists, simply dead legacies from the past, for in the end utilitarian calculations will neither offer *dignity* to persons as unique individuals nor prevent the rule of force. *Who* will live in this "steel-hard casing" (*eisener Gehaeuse*) of "mechanized ossification"? Will only "narrow specialists without minds" and "pleasure-seekers without heart" inhabit the new cosmos (2011, p. 178)? Ethical action, he fears, will be pushed out of the realms of work and politics and recede into the private sphere (2005, pp. 338–339). As Albert Salomon, in his classic interpretation of Weber, asks: "Can man— ... conceived as molded by the passions and tensions of a lofty human soul—still find a place for himself in the modern world" (1934, p. 153)?

Despite this bleak view of the future, Weber refused to idealize the past, as did many of his colleagues. Albeit intensely worried, he responded vigorously in two ways. First, he sees a number of possibilities for diminishing harmful trends now in motion. He formulated a cluster of proposals that sought to counter German society's ills and to ameliorate the dangers confronted by Western Civilization. Second, he broadened out his scholarship agenda after 1910 to include in-depth studies of non-Western civilizations. By turning primarily to the long histories of China, India, and ancient Israel (see 1951, 1952, 1958), these investigations sought to isolate through precise comparisons the singularity of the West and its specific trajectory of development.

Does the West, he ponders, retain maneuvering room that will allow significant change? Rigorous comparisons will cast new beams of light, Weber believes. Perhaps they will assist understanding of the quandaries faced by Germany and the West. And perhaps they will offer the insight and clarity that will lead to viable new efforts and reforms. Given the title "The Economic Ethics of the World Religions," these works played a pivotal role in the formation of his empirical sociology of comparative civilizations.

We turn first to a discussion of Weber's proposals to address the central dilemmas of his age. He queries: what modes of practical action remain available to confront fundamental dangers and dilemmas? His sociology of civilizations is our focus in the three chapters that follow.

Weber's Response

In what ways did Weber offer a realistic response to the "crisis of Western civilization"? What measures could address these fundamental ills? His proposals point to a series of complex strategies for action. Only an outline can be offered here.[2]

The Support for Strong Parliaments

Weber maintained vehemently that modern societies need institutions capable of cultivating leadership qualities on a regular basis. This could occur in parliaments; here the aggressive articulation of political positions and the hard competition of political parties is institutionalized and viewed as the normal course of affairs. In the process of open debate and conflicts over values and interests, yet also negotiation and compromise, leaders in possession of the "three pre-eminent qualities" for politicians would emerge: passion, responsibility, and a sense of proportion. Perhaps even leaders endowed with "inner charismatic qualities" would appear, though also leaders with the sense of detachment that allows judgment (see 1946a, pp. 113, 115–116).

Thus, parliaments cultivate leaders in possession of an "ethic of responsibility" and a "passionate devotion to a cause," Weber contends. In addition, they prepare leaders to undertake an indispensable task: on the basis of their values and policies, they are empowered to stand against the formal rationality of functionaries, managers, and technocrats. In doing so, parliaments contribute to the expansion of a civic sphere within which citizens can debate, make responsible decisions, exercise political rights, and defend values.

However, if to serve as a viable "training ground" for leaders, parliaments must stand strong against other branches of government. Weak parliaments, dominated on the one hand by the state's civil servants and on the other hand by authoritarian politicians, such as Bismarck, will not attract persons capable of becoming leaders, Weber holds (1946a, p. 113; see 2005, pp. 255–272).

The Support for Democracy

Far more than other forms of governance, parliamentary democracies are capable of giving birth to and sustaining the societal dynamism indispensable for the creation of a viable civic sphere, Weber believed. And *here* decisions can be rendered in reference to values. Moreover, like strong parliaments, strong democracies will assist the development of strong leaders, as will democracy's ideals: freedom of speech, individual rights, the rule of law, and the right of assembly. "It is a gross self-deception," Weber argued, "to believe that without the achievements of [the Enlightenment] age of the Rights of Man any one of us, including the most conservative, can go on living" (1968, p. 1403). The contesting of power and rulership monopolies of all sorts, he is convinced, occurs more effectively in democracies (2005, pp. 253–272, 277–290).[3]

The Support for Capitalism

Ambivalence characterizes Weber's attitude toward capitalism. On the one hand he laments repeatedly the ways in which the impersonal "laws of the open market" introduce a merciless struggle, formal rationality, and functional relationships that cannot realistically be influenced by a brotherhood ethic or ideals of compassion and charity. The merging of such humanitarian concerns with economic relationships taking place in competitive markets almost always leads to economic inefficiencies and bankruptcies—"and this would not be helpful in any way" (see 2009, pp. 426–430).

On the other hand, capitalism's open competition and private enterprise call forth vigorous entrepreneurs and risk takers. These energetic actors, as well as the sheer irregularity and unpredictability of market forces, introduce societal dynamism (1968, pp. 1403–1404). Socialism not only fails to do so, but also implies a further large step in the direction of a closed and stagnating society: to manage the economy, it introduces yet another "caste" of functionaries and administrators (2005, pp. 130–134).

The Necessary Constriction of Science

If defined as an endeavor empowered to prescribe values, science poses a threat to the individual's autonomy and, ultimately, to ethical action, Weber believes. Wherever understood as offering "objectively valid" conclusions and wherever a "caste of experts" are perceived—in the name of science—as legitimately constructing norms for conduct, science becomes capable of elevating decision making out of its rightful domain: the individual's conscience, values, and "demons." Science cannot—and *must* not—inform us how we *should* live, Weber insists (1949, p. 54; 2005, pp. 328–336). Notions of ethical responsibility, honor, dignity, and devotion to a cause can develop only when persons are starkly aware of their own values, Weber argues—and this takes place only if persons are repeatedly confronted with the necessity of making decisions *for themselves*. Moreover, if a science—understood as prescribed norms—becomes broadly institutionalized, decision making by "specialists" poses a threat to a society's dynamism and capacity for pluralistic conflict.

Hence, firm boundaries must circumscribe the domain of science. Its tasks must remain limited to "methods of thinking, the tools and the training for thought," and clarity regarding assessment of the suitability of means to reach a given end (including an ethical ideal) and assessment of the unintended consequences of action (2005, pp. 332–336). By fulfilling even these delimited tasks, science can promote self-awareness and enhance a sense of responsibility vis-à-vis a set of values:

> If you take such and such a stand, then, according to scientific experience, you have to use such and such a *means* in order to carry out your conviction practically. . . . Does the end "justify" the means? . . . Figuratively speaking, you serve this god and you *offend the other* god when you decide to adhere to [a particular] position. . . . Thus, if we [as social scientists] are competent in our pursuit, . . . we can force the individual, or at least we can help him, to give himself an *account of the ultimate meaning of his own conduct*. . . . I am tempted to say of a teacher who succeeds in this: he stands in the service of "moral" forces; he fulfills the duty of bringing about self-clarification and a sense of responsibility. (2005, pp. 333–334; original emphasis)

Accordingly, Weber insists that professors in university classrooms must not offer value judgments, personal views, and political opinions. "So long as [they wish] to remain teacher[s] and not to become demagogue[s]," they must refrain from discussing the conclusions of their research as "truth."[4] Owing to their high prestige vis-à-vis students, doing so presents a great danger: a constriction of their autonomous decision-making powers might occur. In turn, students should not expect leadership and guidance from their professors, Weber maintains. Unlike politics, science excludes the activity— the clash of values and the defense of values—on the basis of which leaders arise (see 2005, pp. 332–336; see below, pp. 192–199).

The Support for a Strong National State

Weber is well-known as a proponent of a strong German nation. Some interpreters view him as an unreconstructed nationalist who favored the power of the German state for its own sake. This interpretation evidences little understanding of Weber's sociology, his appreciation of the underlying dilemmas confronted by industrial societies, and his own ultimate ideals and values.[5]

As noted, he perceives arrays of Western values as threatened by a specter of societal stagnation and ossification. However, neither the smaller states of Europe nor England or the United States are capable of defending them, he is convinced. He sees a crass materialism and an exploitative commercialism in these nations as having weakened Western values—and hence the arena within which autonomous individuals *can* arise. These nations, he argues, remain incapable of mobilizing internally to resist threatening forces effectively.

In addition, Weber sees the West as contested by the East. However, Russian authoritarianism, civil servant rulership, and economic underdevelopment had failed to give rise to the values of the Enlightenment—reason and rationality—as well as to the "Rights of Man" (see 1978, pp. 281–283).

In this crisis situation, together with the majority of his colleagues, Weber perceived the German state as a bulwark against the encroachment on the West's noble values. A *strong* state would be best equipped to make a stand in defense of action on behalf of these values: individual autonomy, self-responsibility, the unified personality, ethical action, brotherhood, compassion, charity, and a sense of honor. Furthermore, according to him, the German state would not, if it acts alone on behalf of German nationalism, fulfill its "responsibility before history." Rather, Germany now must undertake a far more monumental task: to defend Western values for *all* Western countries.

Weber hopes that strong parliaments, a dynamic democracy, a vigorous capitalism, a modern science lacking legitimacy to pronounce "correct" values, and a strong German state will curtail the advance of bureaucratization on the one hand and formal, practical, and theoretical types of rationality on the other. To the extent that this occurs, societal ossification and the trajectory toward "steel-hard" societies devoid of ethical action will be opposed. A dynamic *civic* arena can then unfold. As this takes place, the fundamental precondition for the nourishing of values will appear, Weber argues: a societal openness and dynamism that allows—even fosters— perpetual value conflicts of moderate intensity.

All those aspects of the West Weber holds dear will be defended, he is convinced, where noble values become empowered to orient action. The random push and pull of daily life interests and mundane concerns, and the mere "sterile excitation" they give rise to, will be counterbalanced. Life will become *directed* on behalf of ethical ideals and a passion for "causes" will be awakened: "For nothing is worthy of man as man unless he can pursue it with passionate devotion" (2005, p. 140).

Individuals will then become accountable for their own actions and prac- tice an "ethic of responsibility." Of great significance to Weber, ethical ideals will be empowered to place a thrust toward community into motion: "The ethical norm and its 'universal validity' create a community, or at least in so far as an individual might reject the act of another on moral grounds and yet still face it and participate in the common life" (1946b, p. 342).

As noted, Weber's worries regarding Germany and the future of the West took him also in another direction: he expanded massively his scholarship agenda and became a sociologist of civilizations. This new pursuit consti- tutes an additional attempt to address the dilemmas and dangers he per- ceived. He is now convinced that only comparative investigations will assist his quest to define clearly how Western economies, laws, rulership forms, and religions are unique, to comprehend precisely the *direction* of their development, to assess in detail realistic possibilities regarding social change in the West, and to understand better the ways in which certain constellations of groups succeed in anchoring social action in values and ethical ideals. Do civilizations, he queries, regularly fulfill noble values? Weber's gaze encompassed China and India above all. His new explorations began. The next three chapters directly investigate his formidable sociology of civilizations.

Study Questions and Thoughts to Ponder

1. What are, according to Weber, "noble values?" Why are they called "noble"?

2. Why was Weber disillusioned with the West?

3. Explain the phrase "industrialization from above."

4. Think through the contours of Germany's political culture in Weber's time and offer comparisons to the American political culture. (For hints, see Chapter 10.)

5. Weber fears "societal ossification" and praises societal dynamism. Note the disadvantages of the former and the advantages of the latter.

6. Note the variety of ways in which, for Weber, "open" societies cultivate democracy.

7. Explain the capitalist economy's "formal rationality."

8. Explain why modern science cannot—and should not—become, according to Weber, a new world view that offers "correct" values to all.

9. Explain, according to Weber, how modern capitalism weakens the orientation of patterned action to values.

10. Weber's "five proposals" aim "to address the central dilemmas of his age." Are they successful?

11. It would seem that Weber's support for strong parliaments and the "necessary constriction of science" go a long way toward confronting the dangers of our epoch. Do you agree or disagree with this statement? Provide reasons.

12. Weber's agenda now seems clear: modern societies need to create *ethical* individuals endowed with compassion. Do you agree that this agenda is an urgent one? Or does Weber exaggerate the ills modern societies confront?

Notes

1.   Weber is here formulating ideal types. He is well aware of the many ways in which rule-bound efficiency can be diminished by both red tape and favoritism.

2.   Weber's response was elaborate and complex. The focus here is on his sociological thinking rather than, as is often the case, his political activity. He was, in this regard, a vigorous defender of individual rights (see Beetham, 1974; Coser, 1971, pp. 242–243, 254–256; Honigsheim, 1968).

3.   Several commentators have argued that Weber's commitment to democracy was not one in principle, but was rooted in his view that modern industrial societies confronted a great danger of societal ossification. It is apparent that Weber distrusted the citizenship skills of the Germans. Owing in part to the authoritarian rule of Bismarck, which left the nation far behind its Western European neighbors in respect to the development of these skills (see below, pp. 199–205), a long period of tutelage in the practices of democracy would be necessary, he believed (see Beetham, 1974; Loewenstein, 1966).

4. Weber continues: "Whether, under such conditions, science is a worthwhile 'vocation' for somebody, and whether science itself has an objectively valuable 'vocation' are again value judgments about which nothing can be said in the lecture-room" (2005, p. 334).

5. The extreme cosmopolitanism of his own family (see Roth, 1993, 1997, 2001) also speaks against the interpretation that sees Weber as a nationalist (see also Beetham, 1974, pp. 119–150; Loewenstein, 1966, p. 101).

6

"Rationalism" East and West: The Economic Ethics of the World Religions and the Turn Toward a Sociology of Civilizations

This chapter proceeds step by step through the foundational themes, concepts, and methodological procedures of Weber's sociology of civilizations. It focuses at the outset on his volumes on Confucianism and Daoism (1951), Hinduism and Buddhism (1958), and ancient Judaism (1952) in the Economic Ethics of the World Religion series. Each study enhances greatly the comparative component in Weber's sociology.

This chapter also discusses, again relying largely on EEWR, how Weber defines civilizations and one of his pivotal concepts: a civilization's "rationalism." The subsequent three chapters utilize this construct. They address the large-scale cases central to his sociology of civilizations: the rationalisms of the West, the modern West, China, and India. Hence, this chapter moves to the core of the theme at the center of his latter decades. In important ways, *PE*, many of the methodology writings, and *E&S* can be viewed as constructing large preliminary steps toward Weber's comparative-historical and interpretive sociology of civilizations. A brief overview of EEWR's themes and causal framework proves indispensable as a means of setting the stage.

The EEWR: The Major
Themes and Causal Framework

Weber's exploration of the "world religions" in EEWR broadens the range of his research far beyond *PE*'s themes. Whereas this classic study investigates the religious sources of the spirit of capitalism in the West, EEWR examines whether the religions of China, India, and ancient Israel possess economic ethics. If so, Weber queries, are they capable of giving birth to a spirit of capitalism?

In addition, through a series of rigorous and cross-civilizational comparisons that address, for example, the development of forms of law, types of rulership, and forms of cities, the EEWR volumes explore Weber's enduring interest in the presence—or absence—of capitalism and modern capitalism outside the West. He asks whether certain forms of law, types of rulership, and forms of cities proved conducive to the rise of capitalism and modern capitalism. What underlying long-term patterns of action, he questions, congealed in various settings in support of—or in opposition to—the development of capitalism and modern capitalism?

The EEWR studies offer a distinct causal framework. In tracing the origins of a spirit of capitalism in the West back to ascetic Protestantism, *PE* examines only "one side of the causal equation" (see 2009, p. 159). Conversely, the EEWR volumes rest on expansive multicausal procedures. Weber now scrutinizes not only a push toward change emanating from certain devout believers in congregations, but also the impact of groups of people "located" in the economy, rulership, law, universal organizations, and status groups life-spheres. Was their influence significant? What was, he queries, its direction?

Thus, Weber expanded his causal analyses after *PE* to include patterns of action in a *variety* of life-spheres and in *multitudes* of groups interacting in arrays of constellations. He insists in EEWR, as in *E&S*, that rigorous, macro-causal studies require a comparative and multicausal methodology. In a central passage in the EEWR introduction, Weber notes the complex ways in which "both sides" are intertwined:

> Every . . . attempt at explanation, recognizing the fundamental significance of economic factors, must above all take account of these factors. However, the opposite line of causation should not be neglected if only because the origin of economic rationalism [modern capitalism] depends not only on an advanced development of technology and law but also on the capacity and disposition of persons to organize their lives in a practical-rational manner. Wherever magical and religious forces have inhibited the unfolding of this organized

life, the development of an organized life oriented systematically toward *economic* activity has confronted broad-ranging internal resistance. Magical and religious powers, and the belief in them anchored in ethical notions of duty, have been in the past among the most important influences upon the way life has been organized. (2009, p. 216; original emphasis; see also 1968, p. 341)

In this pivotal statement, Weber rejects several lines of causality frequently believed to be behind modern capitalism's origin. And elsewhere he emphatically opposes, for example, greed and a material interest in becoming wealthy: both have been universal, yet modern capitalism developed only in a few regions and during a particular historical epoch. Because Weber insists on focusing on empirical factors, the putative "general evolutionary sweep of history" is also omitted as a viable cause.

And what of economic interests? Although acknowledging their importance, he rejects all explanations that view economic ethics as exclusively the "superstructure" of economic interests. Similarly, the class of formally trained jurists that congealed in the West, he maintains, should not be understood as arising universally from the interest in economic stability of a dominant business class—for then a salient question appears: why did these interests not lead to the same development in China or India (2009, p. 215)? Furthermore, Weber contends that organizations—and even tightly knit sects—do not, as social structures, uniformly call forth the same values or activities: "Structurally identical religious sects . . . existed in Hinduism as well as in Christianity, yet their sacred values pointed [the social action of believers] in radically different directions" (1946c, p. 292).

In opposition to many of his colleagues, he is convinced that research rooted mainly in interest-based calculations, the domination of a particular class, and the flow of power omits too much. The *various* ways in which persons orient their action to values, social honor, the supernatural realm, the family, laws, and rulership must not be neglected, he holds. And the age-old influence of customs and conventions must be also acknowledged. Moreover, Weber's foundational methodological tool—the ideal type—explicitly leaves open, for empirically based investigation, whether "tradition to modernity" or "capitalism to modern capitalism" transformations actually occur. Thus, he also rejects, as insufficiently empirically grounded, all societal differentiation models and cyclical views of history (1976, p. 366).

Weber's insistence on complex, multicausal procedures leads him away from the conclusion that modern capitalism's failure to develop earliest in Asia resulted from an absence of this-worldly asceticism, as many of his sympathetic interpreters have argued. *One* focus, when examining Confucianism, Hinduism, Buddhism, and ancient Judaism in the EEWR series, concerns the question of whether devoutness bestowed "psychological premiums" upon methodical economic activity. However, Weber holds that single factors never determine history's pathways. Always central to him are *constellations* of patterned action by persons in groups and the dynamic interactions of groups.[1]

By "applying" his domains-based, *multicausal* framework from *E&S* (see above, pp 48–51.) to his EEWR investigations, Weber identifies the divergent arrays of regular action in every civilization that permeate groups in the rulership, religion, economy, status groups, family, clan, and law domains. The many clusters of groups that carried patterns of action conducive to the unfolding of modern capitalism in China and India, Weber discovers, were in the end outweighed by a series of opposing groups.

For example, he identifies a variety of nonreligion obstacles to economic development in China, such as extremely strong sibling ties and an absence of "a formally guaranteed law and a rational administration and judiciary" (1951, p. 85; see also pp. 91, 99–100). He sees a series of barriers also in India, such as constraints by the caste system placed on migration, the recruitment of labor, and credit (1958, pp. 111–117, 52–53, 102–106). However, in both cases he discovers as well an entire host of facilitating patterns of action that nonetheless failed to introduce widespread capitalism *or* modern capitalism—such as, in China, freedom of trade, an increase in precious metals and population growth in the 17th century, occupational mobility, and the presence of a money economy (1951, pp. 12, 54–55, 99–100, 243).

Moreover, Weber is quite convinced that modern capitalism can be *adopted* by—and would flourish in—a number of Eastern civilizations, including China. Yet adoption involved different processes than his concern, he insists: the *origin* in a specific region of a *new* economic ethos and a *new* type of economy. Weber contends repeatedly that a broadly multicausal and conjunctural methodology—one capable of assessing the dynamic interactions of groups—is indispensable for his comparative research.

His cross-civilizational causal analyses in EEWR are largely anchored in *E&S*'s array of domains: the economy, rulership, law, religion, family, clan, and status honor life-spheres. Their cross-group coalitions and tensions offer a bounty of hypotheses to guide Weber's empirical research. To him, these arenas constitute an *open-ended conceptual grid*. Resting on its pluralistic foundation, multicausal analysis designed to identify the sources of those groups unique to a civilization can commence, he maintains.

In sum, in conjunction with the *E&S* domains, the EEWR volumes in Weber's macro sociology fulfil a crucial task: they assist, in a rigorous manner, the identification of a civilization's uniqueness. Indeed, an attempt to define the particular singularity of *each civilization* guides Weber's EEWR research. Pivotal throughout his analyses are an orientation to multiple groups in important spheres of life and answers to major queries: do central groups lend support to the development of capitalism? Do they prove conducive even to the appearance of modern capitalism? Do they stand in a relationship of antagonism to capitalism's birth and unfolding? Rather than studies of "entire civilizations," which Weber regards as impossible owing to his value-relevance maxim (see above, pp. 41–42), his sociology of civilizations retains throughout this particular focus on the multiple predecessors for the birth of capitalism and modern capitalism.

It must be stressed that these big picture themes and complex causal procedures coalesce regarding a project only rarely attempted in the entire history of the social sciences: Weber is here engaged in the construction of a rigorous, comparative-historical, and empirical sociology of civilizations rooted in the subjective meaning of persons as located mainly in arrays of life-spheres and their subsidiary groups. Many commentators, casting their focus on *PE* and on specific chapters in *E&S*, have failed to note the centrality in Weber's sociology of this ambitious endeavor. Large groups of scholars concerned with economic modernization, as he was, have neglected to this day the *civilizational* component Weber saw at the very foundation of long-term economic transformations.

His sociology stands nearly alone on this score. As is discussed later, it emphasizes, for example, that any examination of the West's particular historical trajectory must *also* acknowledge the unique extent of its "structural heterogeneity" (see below, pp. 109–112). Yet this crucial component, he argues, becomes visible to sociologists *only* if wide comparisons are undertaken. *Compared to* China, India, the Middle East, and the ancient West, a higher degree of pluralistic tension across quasi-independent and independent life-spheres distinguished the Western pathway, Weber contends. The resulting conflicts called forth a comparative openness—and hence a societal flexibility and resilience that facilitated further cross-sphere conflict and competition. Competing spheres in the West introduced a degree of civilizational dynamism that Weber sees as both specific to Western rationalism and conducive to modern capitalism's unfolding (see 1968, pp. 1192–1193).

Throughout EEWR, he seeks, first, to offer comparisons and contrasts of Chinese rationalism, Indian rationalism, and the rationalism of ancient Judaism to "Western rationalism" and "modern Western rationalism." Having isolated each civilization's unique rationalism and route of development, he then provides multicausal explanations for each civilizational rationalism and for its singular rationalization of action pathway.

Major questions remain to be scrutinized: How should a civilization's rationalism be comprehended? How can qualitatively different rationalisms be understood? How can the distinctiveness of their origins and pathways be explained? These queries stand at the center of Weber's sociology of civilizations; he pondered them throughout the last decade of his life. They are addressed. A major question can no longer be postponed: What are civilizations?

Civilizations and a Civilization's "Rationalism": The Turn Toward a Sociology of Civilizations

Civilizations are comprised of innumerable clusters of groups, Weber maintains. New groups crystallize regularly, often in reaction to cross-group conflict. Captured by ideal types, each group is constituted from persons who share subjective meanings; indeed, common meanings may *pull* people into groups, he argues. They may be characterized by relatively firm boundaries and, wherever supporting arrays of carrier groups congeal into configurations of groups, they may endure over longer periods. At this point alliances may form on a large scale and social *contexts* may crystallize capable of laying down parameters, ones that may facilitate the birth and development of compatible groups.

For example, in the EEWR volumes clusters of groups in various epochs oriented to "religion" groups became aligned with "world" groups oriented variously to rulership, status honor, laws, families, and clans. Conversely, arrays of world groups repeatedly coalesced with constellations of religion groups. And groups in coalitions often created more configurations of groups, Weber contends—that is, further contexts comprised of amenable groups. And, if the patterns of action they carry are compatible to some degree, further groups in the process of formation may be strengthened. Yet further groups-based contexts are then formed. To the extent that this dynamic occurs, some groups become defined to the same degree as incompatible. They are firmly opposed. However, these groups, may form alliances and attract strong carrier groups.

In these ways, Weber's sociology of civilizations rests on a groups-based foundation. It is oriented toward multiple groups, groups in constellations, and the dynamic interaction of groups. Whether firm alliances are formed remains crucial—yet always dependent upon empirical developments. If coalitions are formed, the influence of groups in clusters of groups expands across further groups, in the process repeatedly forming firm social contexts. Far from static, groups are perceived by Weber as either in the process of forming boundaries or as constituted with viable boundaries that require defending. That is, groups are comprehended as perpetually in relationships with other groups, whether ones that lead to mergers or ones that call forth power struggles and conflict.

Throughout EEWR, as well as E&S, he traces the formation of social contexts in this way and how they, as the yield of configurations of compatible groups, perpetually interweave with—or reject—other constellations of groups. And, as a consequence of this orientation to multitudes of groups developing in their own directions and at their own speeds, Weber sees questions of power, domination, and conflict as perpetually arising. They stand at the very core of his sociology of civilizations. Groups, on the basis of predisposing features held in common, may peacefully merge and form coalitions; conversely, owing to incompatible patterns of action, they may fall into "relations of antagonism." Weber's groups-based level of analysis acknowledges that empirical landscapes vary across a wide spectrum.

According to him, when multitudes of groups substantively coalesce with further multitudes of groups, *contexts* for regular action are then formed. At this point, a civilization's unique features—its rationalism—become visible. And as further groups crystallize in reference to—in alliance with or in opposition to—these contexts, a civilization's rationalism becomes more clearly demarcated. Even a specific developmental pathway, or "track," becomes delineated in this manner. To a significant albeit variable extent, patterned action and groups may congeal even in reference to this "world view."

In sum, to Weber, a civilization's rationalism is constituted from configurations of groups that form multiple social contexts. These groups evidence varying developmental directions, directional momentum, and degrees of internal coherence and internal conflict.[2] As will be apparent in the following chapters, his empirical cases fall across a spectrum that ranges from the high internal unity that characterized Chinese rationalism to Western rationalism's structural heterogeneity. However, in all cases a civilization's rationalism implies a significant degree of acknowledged commonality across multiple arrays of groups and across centuries.

Weber defines the unique rationalisms of several civilizations in EEWR. Nonetheless, and although massive, his discussions of "Chinese rationalism," "Indian rationalism," and "the rationalism of ancient Israel" comprise only "one half" of his sociology of civilizations. He also importantly offers, first (and mainly in E&S), comparisons and contrasts across all the civilizations he examines (for example Chinese rationalism and Indian rationalism). Albeit in passages lacking strong organization, he then charts comparisons and contrasts between the rationalisms of China and India and the rationalisms of the West and the modern West. Only in this way can the uniqueness of *each* civilizational rationalism become demarcated.

The question of the extent to which a civilization's rationalism indicates groups-based dynamics and demarcated social contexts that facilitate the development of capitalism—and even modern capitalism—constitutes the major focus of Weber's sociology of civilizations. Also pivotal to him are the ways in which the rationalisms of some civilizations create barriers against capitalism and modern capitalism. Finally, by reference to clearly defined comparative cases, his sociology of civilizations forms in-depth, multicausal explanations—for both the uniqueness of a civilization's rationalism and its particular route of development. Significantly, Weber sought throughout his studies to comprehend the range of indigenous subjective meanings specific to the major groups comprising each civilizational rationalism.

His general introduction to EEWR, perhaps the last essay from his pen (2011, pp. 233–250), succinctly conveys this *civilizational* level of analysis. Weber seeks here to identify those multiple groups in the modern West that can be said to be unique to this civilization (see chapter 7). His focus on a variety of life-spheres (for example, the religion, rulership, economy, and law arenas), the groups that constitute them, and their innumerable interactions is apparent.

Nonetheless, Weber also discovers "autonomous" developments in certain domains and in certain epochs. What complex causes, he queries, led to the economy sphere's relative autonomy—or "take off"—in the 18th century in the West? Why did a parallel development in this domain not occur in China and India in this century or earlier? And how can the significant autonomy of the law sphere in the West's 18th century be causally explained? Only a cross-civilizational, comparative, and multicausal methodology is equipped to answer these questions, Weber contends.

At this point, causal analysis to him must take cognizance of group configurations and the manner in which—and extent to which—they merge and form social contexts that endow a life-sphere with some degree of autonomy. Also indispensable is the precise isolation of lines of causality through rigorous comparative experiments across civilizations. The degree of internal cohesion among arrays of aligned groups, the power of carrier groups, and their capacity vis-à-vis new groups must be investigated in each empirical case, he holds. Weber frequently charts in both *E&S* and EEWR how this occurred, although often in an unorganized manner.

As noted in Chapters 3 and 4, arrays of ideal types, affinity and antagonism constructs, and developmental models are formulated in abundance in *E&S*. All these concepts erect useful analytic schemes—at times of such a scale as to enable identification of the substance, contours, and parameters of civilizations in regard to the question of the development of capitalism and modern capitalism. Indeed, the capacity of these constructs to assist the researcher's conceptualization of a civilization's rationalism in these ways, as well as of long-term macro processes, and to uphold multicausal explanations, bestows upon these research tools a central place in Weber's approach to the study of civilizations. The formation in *E&S* of a multi-sphere orientational matrix advances the methodology of his sociology of civilizations far beyond the usual linear—or "yardstick"—applications of ideal types.

Weber's definitions of civilizations and a civilization's rationalism must be examined in more precise terms—namely, by reference to his major civilizational theme: how did the various arrays of social contexts specific to Western rationalism and modern Western rationalism *prove conducive* to the rise and expansion of modern Western capitalism. His widely dispersed and fragmented analysis must be assembled. This is the task of the next chapter.

Parallel reconstructions are offered in the subsequent two chapters—namely, of the constellations of groups that, according to Weber, comprised Chinese rationalism and the rationalism of India. In what specific ways did each of these rationalisms differ from Western rationalism and modern Western rationalism? What accounts for their unique substance, parameters, and developmental directions? In what ways do many of their major social contexts *oppose* the birth and development of modern capitalism? To what extent? Rigorous comparisons are indispensable on behalf of these questions, Weber maintains. Only such queries and procedures will enable clear definitions of Western rationalism, modern Western rationalism, Chinese rationalism, and the rationalism of India. Large-scale reconstructions prove necessary in the following three chapters.

Weber's ideal types move now to center stage owing to their capacity to capture each civilization's major constellations of patterned action and their location in clusters of groups. Multiple configurations of groups regularly establish the social contexts in each civilization in reference to which patterned action occurs and new types of groups congeal. Weber's notion of a civilization's "world view" and developmental track is also emphasized. It will become evident that, according to him, constellations of groups indigenous to modern Western rationalism facilitated the rise and expansion of modern capitalism. The quite different rationalisms established in China and India erected powerful barriers against modern capitalism.

At the forefront of the following three chapters stand three summary questions from Weber: How did the rationalisms of some civilizations call clusters of diverse groups into contexts that proved conducive to capitalism's sustained rise? How did further amenable contexts in some civilizations drive its metamorphosis into modern capitalism? How did the rationalisms of other civilizations place—and sustain—obstacles against the birth and expansion of capitalism and modern capitalism?

Study Questions and Thoughts to Ponder

1. What are civilizations?

2. Does Weber make his case that the study of civilizations requires a multicausal methodology?

3. What role does *E&S* play in the EEWR investigations?

4. Does a macrosociology based in (multiple) ideal types and the acknowledgment of extreme pluralisms of subjective meaning necessarily lead to a multicausal methodology?

5. Weber distinguishes strongly between civilizations that originally call forth modern capitalism as opposed to civilizations that adopt, once in motion, modern capitalism. Is this distinction moot in our age of "globalization"?

6. The uniqueness of a civilization can be clearly defined, according to Weber, only after rigorous cross-civilizational comparisons. Do you agree with Weber?

7. Weber's contention that each civilization calls forth unique patterns of subjective meaning can be seen as a red thread running throughout this chapter. Debate the importance of this presupposition.

8. Summarize major features of Weber's groups-based methodology.

9. Summarize EEWR's major themes.

Notes

1. Even great charismatic figures, such as prophets, are not viewed by Weber a-contextually. Their influence requires a preexisting "certain minimum of intellectual discourse" (see 1968, pp. 486–487).

2. Nonetheless, Weber insists that civilizations must not be conceptualized as juggernauts or as organic and structurally unified. Of course empirically, during certain epochs and as a consequence of identifiable causes, some civilizations may become rigid and "ossified." In this regard, he notes postclassical China and ancient Egypt.

7

The Sociology of Civilizations I: Western Rationalism and Modern Western Rationalism

C entral passages throughout *E&S* and EEWR turn to the "specifically formed 'rationalism' of Western civilization" and "within this particular type of rationalism, the characteristic features of modern Western rationalism." "Our concern," Weber continues, "is to identify this uniqueness and to explain its origin" (2011, pp. 245–246).

Its major aspects include, for example, a legal system characterized by procedures formulated in reference to abstract, universally applicable prescriptions and executed, as well as interpreted, by specially trained jurists (see 1927, p. 313; 1968, p. 883). Typical of large-scale organizations in the West was bureaucratic rulership, as carried out by trained officials and managers administering their delineated tasks in an organized fashion and in a professional manner (1968, p. 998). Parliaments, which involve regularly elected representatives, also possess exclusively Western roots, Weber contends (2011, p. 236).

Similarly, in the West traditional forms of rulership (patriarchalism, feudalism, patrimonialism) have been replaced, as the major "political organizations," by a constitutional state anchored in a "rationally enacted 'constitution' and rationally enacted laws" (2011, p. 236). Administration is carried out by civil servants "possessing *specialized arenas of competence* and oriented to rules and 'laws'" (2011, p. 236). And modern science, characterized by the dominance of highly trained and specialized personnel, called forth systematic procedures based on the rigorous application of the experimental method (see 2011, pp. 233–234). Since the 17th century, "modern capitalism," grounded in a systematic organization of free labor, businesses with fixed capital, certainty of calculation, and a unique "economic rationalism" rooted in a methodical economic ethic, came to dominate the West "as part of the rationalization of life in the public sphere which has become familiar in this part of the world" (1946c, p. 293; see also 1968, p. 505; 2011, pp. 236–237).[1]

"Again and again [we] discover in the West, and *only* in the West, specific *types* of rationalism" (2011, p. 250; see 1927, pp. 311–312). Weber queries in general: "How did it happen that scientific, artistic, and economic development, as well as state-building, were not directed in China and India into those tracks of *rationalization* specific to the West" (2011, p. 245; emphasis in original)? Although he remained convinced that modern capitalism, for example, could be *adopted* by, and would flourish in, a number of Eastern civilizations, he insisted that adoption involved processes different than his concern: the *origin* in a specific region and in a particular historical epoch of a *new* economic ethos and a *new* type of economy.

However, Weber seeks not only to define the West's "particularity," but, as mentioned, he aims also to offer explanations of its origins (2011, p. 246). One of his latest methodological writings expresses succinctly the importance to him of the causal question: "European and American social and economic life is 'rationalized' in a specific way and in a specific sense. To explain this rationalization, and to construct concepts appropriate to it, is one of the chief tasks of our discipline" (1949, p. 34).

This quest—to define and explain the modern West's "specific rationalism" and its origins—endured as Weber's overarching concern at least since 1910. As noted in the last chapter, he insists that comprehension of the ways in which modern capitalism uniquely crystallized and expanded in the West is possible only on the basis of a comparative and context-oriented mode of analysis. This procedure must acknowledge multiple causes, the congealing of configurations of groups, and the significance of continuously forming cross-group coalitions and tensions. He rejects firmly all linear and mono-causal research designs that fail to situate groups contextually and to acknowledge the influence of group contexts on newly formed groups.

Indeed, on the basis of the conceptual innovations apparent in *E&S* and EEWR, his comparative query can be formulated more precisely: How did it occur that particular alignments of groups *in the West* called forth, cultivated, and sustained modern capitalism? Weber's position is clear: This type of capitalism appeared in the 18th and 19th centuries as a consequence of singular mixtures at this time of multiple groups oriented to the law, rulership, and economy domains ("the world") and other groups oriented to certain salvation paths. These mixtures of groups constitute to Weber configurations of groups he calls "Western rationalism" and "modern Western rationalism."

He offers highly detailed investigations on the capacities of Western rationalism to give birth to configurations of groups conducive to the rise and expansion of modern capitalism. Weber's emphasis on both deep contexts and long-range developments will be apparent throughout this chapter, and his contrasts between Western rationalism and the rationalisms of China and India will be discussed frequently. Doing so will assist isolation of the West's uniqueness, its historical trajectory, and the specific causes behind its development.

Comprehension of Weber's analysis of the rise and expansion of Western rationalism and modern Western rationalism also requires attention to a further Weberian theme alluded to above: the degree to which the separate life-spheres becomes "autonomous." To what extent do deep ties to families, clans, traditional forms of rulership and types of law, the natural economy, and magic and ritual remain uncontested? Or, as a consequence of multiple antagonistic groups, are these bonds weakened and even shattered? As will becomes evident, *formal* rationality comes to the fore with a greater likelihood to the extent that the law, economy, and rulership domains begin to "follow their own laws."[2] Weber's analysis commences with the West's distant past.[3]

Although he locates certain roots in Antiquity, Western rationalism's major sources congealed largely in the Middle Ages (476–1050CE), he contends. Certain salient and powerful groups in particular life-spheres became allied. Furthermore, they became manifest in various constellations of groups. In combination, all these powerful groups carried capitalism's expansion in this era, Weber holds.

After an intermediate period of slower economic growth in the 17th and 18th centuries, additional groups concatenated in a manner that supported modern capitalism's development. An unusual juxtaposition of groups gave birth to modern Western rationalism in the 19th century. This civilizational rationalism, in Weber's analysis, established the configurations of groups prerequisite to industrial capitalism's expansive growth.

Western Rationalism's Track I: Independent Cities, Christianity, Law, and Citizens in the Western Middle Ages

Weber insists that the West's historical route cannot be comprehended as a progressive, linear, and unhindered advance from the Middle Ages to the present. Nonetheless, Western rationalism's long-range unfolding proceeded in reference to a particular *track*, he maintains, one that juxtaposed ancient Judaic and Christian monotheism, ancient and medieval Roman law, and distinct ancient and medieval urban areas. If Christianity's merger with a unique type of city in the Middle Ages had not occurred, this world religion would have developed in a different manner, Weber argues—with fateful consequences for Western history (see 1952, pp. 3–5; 1968, p. 472). Innumerable comparisons to China, India, and the Middle East led him to this conclusion.

Emanating from early Christianity, the medieval city and its guilds, and Roman law, Western rationalism's powerful universalistic thrusts weakened the authority of the clan, the tribe, and ethnic groups. Anchored in this city's cultivation of citizenship, these impulses confronted, challenged, and significantly ameliorated the severe insider—outsider and friend—enemy dualisms typical in these groups. They also contested magic and traditional forms of rulership.

How did Western rationalism acquire clear contours in the cities of the Middle Ages? Weber offers a fine-grained analysis; only its major features can be noted here. Contrasts to China and India throw into relief the uniqueness of these cities and, in the process, serve to delineate the boundaries of Western rationalism.

Unlike the urban areas of Antiquity, which developed on the foundation of political and military groups, the cities of the Middle Ages were grounded in the economy and its growth, Weber holds. However, he distinguishes sharply between southern and northern European municipalities. While sea-trading commerce dominated by a stratum of wealthy patrician nobles developed in the southern urban areas (Venice, Genoa), the northern cities (Cologne) were based more thoroughly on profits acquired through the production of goods and retail trade. This "inland industrial"—or "producer" city—"is . . . one of the crucial factors inseparably linked with [modern capitalism's] . . . rise" (1968, p. 1323).

The shaping of this urban area's economy by capitalism became manifest in a variety of ways, Weber argues. As specialized products and new forms of production were introduced, trade volume came to greatly outstrip that of the ancient West, especially across nonlocal and international markets. Consumer demand increased dramatically, and slave labor, which had hindered the efficient utilization of capital in the ancient era, was no longer used. Rooted in competition, capitalist free enterprise grew slowly but steadily. The urban workplace, characterized by a differentiated division of labor and systematic production processes, largely replaced the rural *oikos* (1976, p. 394). However, Western rationalism must not be viewed only in reference to this high level of wealth, Weber contends. Rather, a deep context of interacting multiple groups, only a few of which were directly oriented to the economy, must be acknowledged.

The *political* consequences of this wealth were significant. As their economic strength grew, residents of the northern inland industrial cities eventually sought to sever all ties with powerful rural nobles and to establish politically autonomous—even democratic—urban areas. Importantly, as warfare between patrician cities continued, the noble clans found it necessary, unlike in China and India, to arm the lower classes—ultimately thereby transferring political power to them. Moreover, the capacity of urban artisans to produce goods, particularly for military endeavors, led to yet greater wealth for this class.

This class soon proved capable of protecting its interests against the urban patrician clans and of forming autonomous corporate groups, or *guilds*. In possession of social, political, and economic power, free craftsmen and artisans became organized on a large scale and oriented the medieval city "immeasurably much more than [occurred in] any city of Antiquity . . . towards acquisition through rational economic activity" (1968, p. 1362). To Weber, "modern capitalism emerged on the basis prepared by the medieval organization of commerce and industry, using its material and legal forms" (1976, p. 354; see 1927, pp. 327–330; 1968, p. 1347; 2009, pp. 370–374).

He emphasizes that the guilds acquired legal rights and great social importance. Their capacity to call forth *confraternization* was also central. As "functional associations," membership "transcended existing class contrasts" (2009, p. 370). Rather than from particular groups, whether classes, status groups, clans, or tribes, members were recruited on the basis of competence. Once formed, these organizations founded a new and autonomous "separate community"—one which possessed wealth and, as a consequence of its military independence from both feudal lords in the countryside and patrician nobles in the cities, acquired political power. Thus, a subordinate social position could not be accepted. "The urban citizenry . . . usurped the right," Weber maintains, "to dissolve the bonds of seigneurial [feudal] rulership; this was the great—in fact, the *revolutionary*—innovation which differentiated the Western cities from all other cities" (1968, p. 1239; see 1927, pp. 324–326; 1976, pp. 370–374).

The guilds' political independence, economic means, and fundamentally democratic character transformed the inland industrial city. Administrative districts and juridical organs were formed; a legal status separate from the rulership of the great rural and urban clans was acquired. Endowed with political rights and an economic policy-making role, this city *commune* "became an institutionalized association, autonomous and autocephalous, an active 'territorial corporation'; . . . [and] urban officials . . . became officials of this institution" (*Anstalt*) (1968, p. 1249; see p. 1323). Significantly to Weber, although found also in the ancient Western city, these features existed nowhere else (see 2009, pp. 371–372, 375–376). He holds that a central cornerstone of Western rationalism had been laid with this "urban revolution" (1951, p. 14; see 1968, pp. 1249–1250).

China, India, and the Middle East

His comparative research demarcated these features of Western rationalism and their uniqueness. Although Weber noted the great financial strength of the guilds in India and China, a "decisive difference" remained—namely, the crucial capacity to oppose rulers militarily. The Chinese geopolitical configuration—the necessity of river regulation and irrigation projects gave birth to royal bureaucracies—opposed the transformation of a stratum of armed men into a commune of citizens (1951, pp. 14–15, 17–20, 76). Collectivities of urban citizens never effectively challenged the dominance of clan associations in China (1951, p. 14) and castes in India. Hence, they never introduced confraternization among city inhabitants and corporate bodies capable of executing legally binding contracts (1968, pp. 1228–1229).

Cities of the Middle East under Islamic rule in the medieval period reached a stage of development comparable only to the Western ancient city, Weber contends. In both, urban patrician clans, in possession of military training and power grounded in wealth from trade, ownership of land, enslaved debtors, and purchased slaves, retained a "rather unstable autonomy" over patrimonial rulers and their administrative officials. Nonetheless, despite their strength, they never became consolidated into a "city patriciate"—namely, into an association of kinship groups capable of uniting an urban area into an independent commune (see 1968, pp. 1228–1229).

Moreover, although merchant and artisan guild associations occasionally undertook organized action, urban citizens as a "collective" never did so. Such an incorporated, and politically autonomous, association that included a municipal financial administration and independent military power was lacking. Hence, an "association of burghers based on religious and secular equality before the law, connubium, commensality, and solidarity against non-members" could not arise (1968, p. 1241). Such a city was unknown: "The city commune in the full meaning of the word appeared as a mass phenomenon only in the West" (1968, p. 1226; see also pp. 1227–1248; see 1951, pp. 15, 20, 93; 2009, pp. 374–375).

Why was this the case? Trade associations, because discovered universally, possessed an "essentially indirect" effect, Weber argues (1968, p. 1258; see 1951, pp. 14–15, 16–19). Instead:

> For the development of the medieval city into a citizenship association two circumstances were of central significance: on the one hand, the fact that at a time when the economic interests of residents urged them toward an institutionalized association (*anstaltsmässige Vergesellschaftung*), this movement was not frustrated by the existence of magical or religious barriers, and on the other hand the absence of a rational administration enforcing the interests of a larger political association. (2009, p. 376)

Weber addresses the latter theme in a succinct manner: Rural nobles never possessed the administrative capacity—"a trained apparatus of officials able to meet the need for an urban administration" (1968, p. 1351)—to exercise political rulership over the cities. The sheer capacity of magic or religious barriers to obstruct change must be examined in more detail. The weakening of sorcery in the West will prove foundational to Western rationalism.

Christianity I: The Decline of Magic

As a consequence of Christianity's requirement that believers focus their lives around ethical teachings, all orientations to magic and ritual became weakened. This development in the religion sphere ultimately assisted the expansion of cities during the West's Middle Ages, Weber saw.

Unlike the religions of Asia, both ancient Judaism and early Christianity turned seekers of salvation *toward* the world. Their monotheistic and omniscient God required nothing less: His commandments must be upheld *amid* daily activity. Moreover, this injunction held for the charismatically endowed—prophets and immediate disciples—*and* the lay faithful. And the unity of God's decrees, once combined with an unquestioned recognition of His omnipotence, diminished and degraded magic and ritual—for their incapacity to influence the supernatural realm now became apparent. As articulated forcefully by charismatic figures, His commandments must be practiced. For salvation, prophets demanded *ethical* action amid mundane activities.

Weber charted out the further implications of the "turn toward the world" by believers: Confronted by the *meaningfulness* of religion-oriented action, the devout experienced the random ebb and flow of routine life as lacking. In addition to challenging magic and ritual, religion now also contested directly all patterning of activity around practical concerns and utilitarian calculations—that is, all practical rationality. Hence, heretofore untouched by religion, daily life was more and more penetrated by it, and the importance of *the world*—and ethical activity *in* the world—became intensified for lay and virtuosi devout alike. All *flight from* the world became stigmatized as meaningless and irrelevant to the salvation quest (1946b, pp. 326–328).

Weber stresses the central significance for Western rationalism of Christianity's emphasis on ethical action and the consequent weakening of magic and ritual: Insider-outsider dualisms, so common and unbending among clans, tribes, and ethnic groups, and regularly "stereotyped" by magic and ritual, could now be directly contested. In some cases they could be abolished.

This confraternization breakthrough struck a firm blow against all ritual-based exclusiveness, which "had already begun to wane in the ancient city, . . . [and] was never strong [in medieval Europe]. . . . Sibs soon lost all importance as constituencies of the city" (1968, p. 1243). To Weber, a direct contrast to China is evident: "In consequence of [the persistence of reliance upon magic], the power of the clans could not be broken, as happened in the West through the development of the cities and of Christianity" (1927, p. 339).

In addition, in keeping with St. Peter's pronouncements at Antioch, the ideals and values of this salvation religion were *universalistic*: "We are *all* God's children." Loyalties to clans, tribes, and ethnic groups, as well as invidious distinctions of all sorts, must be laid aside—because *all* were connected to the Christian God through the soul. Allegiance to Him was expected even over duties to the family (see 2009, pp. 246–247). These developments established central components in Western rationalism and distinguished it from the rationalisms of China, India, and the Middle East.

Christianity II: The City, the Formation of the Congregation, and the Further Weakening of Clan Ties

A further development in the religion life-sphere contributed greatly to Western rationalism and, eventually, to the rise of modern capitalism, Weber contends: medieval Catholicism's formation of congregations (see 1968, pp. 452–467). Christianity's declaration that clan, tribal, and ethnic ties were devoid of meaning for the believer's relationship to the supernatural not only weakened the magical and ritual practices specific to these groupings, but Christianity's universalism also contested *all* invidious dualisms and united "unknown others" *as believers* into a single organization. The congregation, within which this new *confraternization of faith* took place, played a central part in this urban religion of salvation. An "equality of believers" reigned, and a universal compassion, brotherhood, and love for one's neighbor now became an obligation for all Christians (1951, pp. 37–38; 1968, pp. 1243, 1247).

The congregation served in this manner to mediate between, and connect persons of, diverse clan, tribal, and ethnic backgrounds. Believers who "joined the [city's] citizenry as individuals," rather than as members of ritually sanctioned groups, could now associate with one another freely— indeed, even on the basis of economic and political interests. Activity oriented to work and profit, and the formation of organizations designed to pursue economic endeavors, could occur simply as goal-oriented activity. Whether in guilds of artisans or trade organizations, economic interests in "free associations" could be pursued, as well as coalitions across heretofore separate groups. "In dissolving clan ties," Weber argues, "[the Christian religion] importantly shaped the medieval city" (2009, p. 375). These features of Christianity also, for example, contributed central preconditions for the birth of *individual* households and *individual* heads of households (1968, pp. 1243–1249).

Unlike under Chinese rationalism, where kinship bonds reinforced by magic-anchored ancestor worship prevailed, capitalist activity in the West could now expand more in reference to the laws of the market. Indeed, the enduring authority of the clan in China and a centralized patrimonial officialdom, which "stood directly over the artisan and small peasant," opposed the rise of an urban, entrepreneurial middle class (1951, p. 83). The caste system in India also constricted severely the arena of market freedom. And Islam in the Middle East, characterized in its early period as a "religion of a conquering army of tribes and clans, . . . never really overcame the divisiveness of Arab tribal and clan ties." Cities in the Middle East remained "typical clan towns all through the Middle Ages and almost up to the present" (2009, p. 375; see also 1968, pp. 1231–1232).

In sum, to a far greater degree than occurred in China, India, and the Middle East, configurations of groups uprooted magic and ritual in the West and weakened insider-outsider dichotomies rooted in clans, tribes, and ethnic groups, Weber argues. Orientations to monotheism and the quest for ethical salvation by believers in congregations played influential parts, especially when interwoven with politically independent cities. Here craft guilds developed and independently carried confraternization, further surmounting invidious dualisms.

To Weber, the multiple groups that constituted Western rationalism and the deep context they were forming for economic activity were now becoming demarcated—namely, a distinct configuration of groups conducive to the birth of a coherent class of urban artisans organized in guilds and oriented to the marketplace. Absent these background developments, economic growth would not have been sustained, Weber is convinced. Economic interests in China, India, and the Middle East proved incapable of doing so as a consequence of the quite different constellations of groups and deep context shaped by Chinese rationalism, the rationalism of India, and the rationalism of the Middle East (see 2009, p. 215). Crucial in the West, Weber saw, was a unique juxtaposition between "world" and "religion." Although Christianity's capacity to confront and weaken clan, tribal, and ethnic ties provided a foundational precondition for urban artisans to join together in *associative* relationships in the city commune, a reciprocity in fact reigned, he contends:

> It is highly unlikely that Christianity . . . could have developed as it did apart from an "urban" community life, . . . [which] greatly facilitated the renewed reception of [the destruction of all taboo barriers between kin grps], the concept of office, and the concept of the community as a compulsory organization (*Anstalt*) and as an impersonal and incorporated structure that serves goals. (1968, p. 472; translation altered)

Further features of the Middle Ages and High Middle Ages (*ca.* 1050–1450CE) proved distinct and also contributed to Western rationalism. Their appearance during Western antiquity and in China, India, and the Middle East was blocked. Roman law and Canon law provided key additional components to Western rationalism. In the end, they also formulated contexts that enhanced economic growth.

Roman Law and Canon Law

Roman law arose during the Middle Ages in the Italian city-states. It broke clearly from all "primitive law" anchored in magic and ritual, Weber holds. It also contrasts in a striking manner to "all law produced by the East and by Hellenic culture" (1968, p. 978).

Roman law's "legal formalism" and foundation in statutes marked a dramatic shift away from all modes of *ad hoc* folk justice rooted in the extraordinary qualities of charismatic figures. Moreover, owing to a reliance on reason, Roman law stood opposed to all "lawfinding" oriented to unknowable supernatural forces.

Rules of evidence now came to dominate over magically effective formulae; law acquired a strongly analytical nature and became viewed as enacted by persons in groups. Systematic categories were utilized and Roman legal thinking followed the rules of logic. Formal procedures and coherent legal doctrines developed; deductive arguments were derived from ultimate legal principles. The formal training of jurists commenced and a division of power between political administrators and judges arose (see 1927, pp. 339–340; 1968, pp. 795–798, 853–854, 1313; 2009, pp. 404–405). With Roman law, the "Western world had at its disposal a formally organized legal system.... Officials trained in this law were superior to all others as technical administrators" (2009, p. 404; see 1968, p. 797).

Weber's domains-based orientational matrix from *E&S* identified here a crucial interweaving of the law and rulership life-spheres. Patrimonial emperors, ruling over large territories in the central and northern territories of Europe in the High Middle Ages, were the social carriers of this systematization of law: It served their attempts to establish legal uniformity, unity, and cohesion across their regions. Moreover, an "immanent need of patrimonial monarchical administration" was apparent—namely, the necessity for monarchs to "eliminate ... the supremacy of [feudal] privileges" (1968, p. 846). Indeed, "the stronger and more stable the monarch's power," the more the law became unified and systematized. Hence, further social carriers—"officials"—revived and rendered available the more formalized aspects of Roman law. The practice of law as a profession expanded (see 1968, p. 853).

Ultimately, legal justice in the medieval West came to be characterized by a "juristically formal character" and a high degree of codification, Weber maintains, rather than by a "patriarchal administration of justice in accordance with standards of substantive welfare and equity," as occurred under patrimonial empires elsewhere (see 1968, pp. 241, 853). Roman law, "with the exception of England, northern France, and Scandinavia, ... conquered all of Europe from Spain to Scotland and Russia." It cast its shadow forcefully down through the centuries to the "logical-formal" law of the present (1968, p. 855).

Nonetheless, and although Roman law established one of Western rationalism's crucial cornerstones, Weber argues that the law arena never pursued a linear advance. Rather, for centuries Roman law was contested. Popular assemblies and folk justice remained widespread. And feudal law, rooted in personal rights and status-based privileges and devoid of a universalistic thrust, opposed Roman law in the countryside.

Moreover, patrimonial rulership in the West also promoted a notion of substantive justice—a social welfare ideal—that clashed with Roman law's emphasis on formal procedures and universalism. The monarch's mission vis-á-vis his subjects—the "good king" must serve as the guardian of his people and protect their general welfare, especially against privileges claimed by feudal nobles—stood opposed to a sharp separation of ethics, law, and administration. Decisions under patrimonial law were often rendered on a case-by-case basis and by reference to an ethical ideal rather than, as in Roman law, to codes, statutes, and formal standards. An unlikely source offered support for Roman law: the Catholic Church's *Canon Law*.

Several centuries after its founding, the Catholic Church attained a level of development and influence that precluded a continued separation from secular authorities. "Compelled to seek relations" with them, it sought to strengthen its position by drawing on "a rational body of ideas" compatible with the value-based position of the Church in respect to ethical action and social justice—namely, the notion of natural law found in Stoic philosophy. For the same reasons, the "most formal components" of Germanic law were appropriated. And the rational aspects of Roman law continued to influence the administration of the Church (1968, pp. 828–830). Indeed, the "sober practical rationalism" of ancient Roman law, which directly opposed all orgiastic and ecstatic modes of interacting with the supernatural realm, was "the most important legacy of [ancient Rome] to Christianity" (2009, p. 255).

The relationship between the Church and the universities thrust the development of Canon law in the same direction. Uniquely, "the structure of the Western medieval university separated the teaching of both theology and secular law from that of Canon law and thus prevented the growth of such theocratic hybrid structures as developed elsewhere" (1968, p. 828). A "clear dualism" between sacred and secular law became strengthened, and this division itself allowed each type of law to develop formally rational procedures further.

Weber sees that Canon law's manner of organizing relations to the supernatural influenced doctrinal controversies regarding the problem of unjust suffering. The Church's increasing subordination to a "monocratic," or single, authority proved also significant. A firm obstacle was now placed against severe doctrinal polarization and fragmentation: Unlike in both the Eastern Christian and Russian Orthodox churches, an infallible, single authority *did* exist and *did* arbitrate disputes. Consequently, and despite great vigor and a continuous expansion of church dogma, pivotal debates concerning unjust suffering and the problem of theodicy generally remained within the Church's jurisdiction. "A considerable degree of hierocratic development, especially the existence of an autonomous office hierarchy and education [within the Church]," proved central, Weber holds, to "the development of all systematic theology" (1968, p. 1175).

He notes the long-range impact of the Catholic Church *as an organization* just in this regard. Influenced by the Roman concept of office, characteristic of this Church was a "rigorously rational hierarchical organization" and "rationally defined bureaucratic offices" that implied responsibility at each level. More than in any other religious community, legislation was rationally enacted—not least because, Weber contends, administrators in this "first institution" were not merely narrowly trained, secular specialists in the law. Rather, because they labored in an institution directly connected to God, their mission transcended both narrow legal issues and self-interests—and *must* be executed rationally. Moreover, a religious aura surrounded, and legitimated, each office. This "office charisma" separated the organization from the particular office incumbent and endowed each position in the hierarchy with an inviolable dignity and trust. These central features of the Catholic Church's internal structure, Weber maintains, established clear precedents on the road toward modern capitalism's characteristic organization: the bureaucracy (2009, p. 398; see 1952, p. 5; 1968, pp. 828–829, 1192–1193).

Also these components of Western rationalism are rendered more precise through comparisons. And their uniqueness becomes more vivid.

The Law: Comparisons to China, India, and the Middle East

As a consequence of all these developments, a far more rationalized version of law distinguished Western rationalism than could be found elsewhere. A "rational judicial system," trial procedures designed to acquire evidence systematically, and "continuous lawmaking on the basis of rational jurisprudence," Weber insists, could not be found outside the West (2009, p. 398).

Furthermore, as theocratic elements in legal thinking in the East lost their hegemony, the practice of law never became incorporated into a secular, oath-bound legal entity (such as occurred in the city of the Western Middle Ages) or carried by a stratum of professionally trained jurists. Rather, it remained "essentially patriarchal" (1968, p. 845). And absent in the East was the development of law by priests and theologians in an ecclesiastical institution characterized by "organs of rational lawmaking": the Councils, the bureaucracies of the dioceses, the Curia, and the Papacy (1968, p. 792). Instead, legal development was generally carried by priests attached to the royal courts of rulers—thereby uniting secular and sacred realms of justice. The formation of an independent status group of secular specialists in the law was excluded.

Under Islam, for example, jurists were theologians. On the basis of their intimate knowledge of the *hadiths*, which describe the exemplary living of the prophet Mohammed and his disciples, these lawmakers responded to concrete inquiries. Although also an "officially licensed legal consultant," as the jurist in the West standing in the Roman law tradition, the *mufti* (lawmaker) acquired his knowledge of the law from a school explicitly oriented to the teachings of Islam. Teaching, which remained "predominantly theological," became a "routinized recitation of fixed sentiments" in universities (1968, p. 821).

Weber discovered from his comparative studies that Islamic law located its legitimation in the infallibility of the founder Mohammed and in agreements among the founding prophets. Sacred texts—the Koran and Sunna—compiled law. The arbitrariness and unpredictability of patrimonial rulership in the Middle East invigorated a subjugation to sacred law, Weber argues. In turn, "the theoretical rigidity and immutability of . . . shariah [law] was 'corrected' by judges through subjective and often quite unpredictable interpretation" (1968, p. 1096). Decisions were frequently rendered according to local custom, yet the perpetual intervention of religious decrees prevented a systematization of secular guidelines. Hence, justice was often administered in a dualistic—religious and secular—manner, yet neither body of law favored juridical unification, consistency, and rationalization. Interpretations became fixed ("stereotyped") over time.

Moreover, Islam's application of law to the Muslim alone rather than also to non-Muslims strengthened legal particularism. A universal law of the land (*lex terrae*) and formal rationality rooted in secular postulates and statutes could not develop amid the "vagueness and precariousness of sacred law" and the varying interpretations of theologian-jurists. Nor could either the domain of law as such, or legal development, acquire independence, as occurred under Western rationalism. Thus, a theocratic *kadi*-justice, which operated on a case-by-case basis and in reference to nonlegal axioms, prevailed over a unified, calculable, and predictable law: "In Islam . . . the validity of . . . commercial norms did not derive from enactment [through legal processes] or from stable principles of a rational legal system" (1968, p. 822).

Hence, despite the strong influence on Islam of ancient philosophy and its pronounced emphasis on logic, there prevailed a sacred law rooted in "traditional observance" and procedurally less rational than Canon law. In the Islamic world "all beginnings of rational juristic thinking" were contained and tamed by theological thought (1946b, p. 93; 1968, pp. 799–800, 810–811, 821–822).

The extent of formal rationality found in Western rationalism's Roman and Canon law proved unique, Weber holds. This "two-fold rationalization of action procedure from the profane and spiritual sides" pushed the West forward, on a winding pathway, to the logical-formal procedures of modern Continental law (1927, p. 340; 1968, pp. 790–791, 799). However, also distinct to the West was a strong differentiation—a "clear dualism" of spheres of jurisdiction—between the spiritual and the secular. A public space became demarcated within which secular monarchs and parliaments could legitimately form law, impose law, and systematize its procedural elements to ever higher degrees of formal rationality—unlike in India, China, and the Middle East.

The severe tension indigenous to Western rationalism between the secular and spiritual realms, and the ensuing competition, in part *itself* drove legal development in the Middle Ages and High Middle Ages, Weber contends. This antagonism laid a cornerstone that strongly contributed, particularly in later centuries, to the dynamic tension and competition—or "structural heterogeneity"—across major domains typical of Western rationalism and largely absent from the rationalisms of China, India, and the Middle East. Weber charts a series of crucial differences in a vivid passage on China:

> No estate of jurists existed because there was no advocateship in the Western sense. It was absent because the patrimonialism of the Chinese welfare state, with its weak office authority, could not comprehend the *formal* development of secular law. . . . The tension between sacred and secular law was completely absent. . . . Chinese patrimonialism, after the unification of the empire, had neither to reckon with powerful and indomitable capitalist interests nor with an autonomous estate of jurists [as in the West]. But it had to take account of the sanctity of tradition, which alone guaranteed the legitimacy of patrimonialism, and of the limited intensity of its administrative organization. Therefore, not only did formal jurisprudence fail to develop, but a systematic, substantive, and thorough rationalization of law was never attempted. In general, the administration of law retained the nature which usually characterizes *theocratic* welfare justice. (1951, pp. 148–150; translation altered; see 1968, p. 845)

Origins of the Modern State

A variety of groups that contributed to the formation of Western rationalism in the Middle Ages indirectly called forth, Weber insists, a large-scale modern organization: the state. As manifest in "formal juristic thinking" and the organization of law in general, Roman modes of thought served as an early precursor. In addition, the city of the Middle Ages was "inseparably linked" with the rise of the state. Owing both to its independent and self-governing status and its capacity, especially once a symbiotic relationship with

Christianity had developed, to weaken the clan, this city constituted a "crucial" antecedent, Weber argues (1927, p. 339; 1968, pp. 259, 714–715, 1323).

The power of the clan, as well as of clan charisma, to penetrate into and dominate a variety of social groups was limited owing to this interlocking in the West of Christianity and independent cities. Weber is convinced that this interweaving also helped sustain an expansion of individualism and egalitarianism—both of which then eventually assisted the development of the bourgeoisie. Because its economic interests both supported the extension of a demarcated *political* community and carried the pacification indispensable for trade, this class would become a pivotal social carrier of the modern state and formal legal equality (see 1968, pp. 908–909; 2009, pp. 403–404).

Simultaneously, the binding contract, as formulated under feudalism in the countryside, introduced an important precedent for the modern state. At the foundation of this form of rulership stood the notion that the holder of a fief would be, in return for services rendered (including in the lord's army if necessary), guaranteed a social position. Hence, this "bilateral contract" implied more than a granting of privileges by the lord and an economic exchange; pivotal issues of social status were involved. Weber saw that this encompassing of the lord-vassal relationship by a "separation of powers" contract restrained the ruler's arbitrariness and discretion, holding them within predictable boundaries. Political power was regulated in this manner to such an extent that, he contends, feudalism "turned . . . into an approximation of the *Rechtsstaat* [constitutional state]": "As the basis of the distribution of political power," the feudal contract anticipated constitutionalism (1968, p. 1082).

A brief summary of the Western rationalism of the High Middle Age must now be offered. Its marked tensions—or "structural heterogeneity"—is scrutinized. This discussion then turns to the Reformation. Once again, contrasts to the rationalisms of China, India, and the Middle East serve to illuminate the uniqueness of Western rationalism—namely, its formation of configurations of multiple groups that shaped a social context conducive to the rise of modern capitalism.

Western Rationalism's Tracks II: The West's Structural Heterogeneity and the Reformation

Theologians and priests systematized the message of Christianity's founder in the Western Middle Ages and High Middle Ages and rendered it comprehensible to larger populations. As persons oriented to this religion's values founded and sustained the Roman Catholic Church, an organization quite distinct from the ancient charismatic community arose.

The earlier epoch's salvation paths—through faith and through a savior—were now placed alongside two further redemption routes: through the institution of the Church and through good works. Performance of prescribed sacraments and rituals, regular Confession, and occasional good works offered an affirmative answer to the believer's central query: "Am I among the saved?" Importantly, magic became now permanently subordinate to the question of salvation and the ideal of ethical action. And the Church, having established its own law and hierarchies of authority, became politically autonomous. Furthermore, although "apart" from the world, it existed *within and oriented to* the world. Finally, as a demarcated community legitimated by its ethos of charity, compassion, universal love, and inclusion, Catholicism continued to oppose vehemently the insider-outsider dualisms practiced by clans, tribes, and ethnic groups. It also stood against all exchange relationships oriented to the market's impersonal laws: Because impersonal, they could not be regulated to the same extent by the ethical claims of the Church (2009, pp. 426–430).

The political and legal autonomy of Catholicism in the West must be understood as linked unequivocally to its *location* in incorporated cities, Weber holds. As discussed, these urban areas had, unusually, established independence from feudal and patrimonial rulers. Often organized into guilds, their *citizens* participated in forms of self-governance separate from clan, tribal, and ethnic loyalties and uninfluenced by magic and ritual. These city-based developments found support from a salvation religion opposed to magic and in favor of confraternization and a universalistic ethos of compassion: Christianity.

The effect of the juxtaposition of all these groups was manifest: Urban economic activity was influenced far more now by city-anchored legal statutes and laws, as well as by the trader's skills and business interests, than by magical practices or clan, tribal, and ethnic loyalties. Hence, here again a world-religion interaction characterized Weber's multicausal and contextual analysis of Western rationalism's origins, substance, and developmental direction. Puritanism's "world mastery" frame of mind and modern economic ethic must be understood as existing within this broader context—namely, within Western rationalism's constellation of groups (see Nielsen, 2005).

Hinduism and Buddhism, in requiring ethical action only of elites, diverged radically from Christianity. Moreover, the search for redemption by their "virtuosi" devout was directed *away* from daily life activities; a *flight from* the world was pursued. Any attempt to uphold ethical standards *in* the world was perceived as meaningless for salvation. Thus, the supernatural realm in India never directly confronted the religious practices anchored in magic and ritual widespread among the broader population. Furthermore, an ethos that, on the basis of universal claims, contested clan, tribal, and ethnic insider-outsider dualisms remained absent. And the caste system, once entrenched, foreclosed all patterning of daily life by reference to universalistic ideals. A religious halo never sanctified utilitarian activity "in the world." Weber renders these crucial differences succinctly:

> The unrestricted lust for gain of the Asiatics . . . was a "drive for gain." It was pursued with every cunning means and with the assistance of a universal mechanism: magic. It was lacking precisely that which was decisive for the economy of the West: the refraction and rational modulation of the *drive* character of the striving for goods and its alignment into a system—namely, a rational, this-worldly ethic of action. Protestantism's "inner-worldly asceticism" . . . in the West had managed to accomplish just this. The development of religion in Asia was lacking the presuppositions for doing so. . . . In the West the establishment of a rational, this-worldly ethic was bound up with the appearance of thinkers and prophets who developed out of a social context alien to Asiatic civilization. This context consisted of the *political* problems engendered by the *city's* status groups—without which neither Judaism nor Christianity nor the development of Hellenic thought is conceivable. The origin of the "city" in the Western sense was inhibited in Asia partly through the sustained power of clans [China] and partly through caste alienation [India]. (1958, pp. 337–338; translation altered; see 1927, pp. 312–314)

Finally, neither of India's salvation religions of "world indifference" and "world flight" helped create politically autonomous institutions that carried their own forms of law. For this reason also the utilitarian and practical rationality of daily life in India was never contested and pushed aside. And, unlike under Western rationalism, the conduct and ethos of political rulers remained largely unchallenged by religious organizations.

Far greater patterned tension reigned under Western rationalism than appeared in the ancient West or in China, India, or the Middle East, Weber maintains. Rooted in a pluralism of antagonistic life-spheres, conflicts in the Western High Middle Ages far excelled in intensity and duration those that arose in more unified civilizations anchored in the dominance of either Caesaropapism or theocratic rulership. Struggles between a relatively autonomous church—or "hierocratic power"—and secular political elites were severe (1968, p. 1174; see also pp. 1173–1181; 1946c, p. 288). Whereas a state-appointed clergy lacking an autonomous "office hierarchy" remained frequent in India and the Middle East, an unusual openness characterized the "less unified" West, Weber holds. A "Western hierocracy lived in a state of tension with the political power and constituted its major restraint" (2009, p. 398).

A "structural heterogeneity" became constituent to Western rationalism. It spurred a political and economic dynamism that contrasted starkly with the relative structural homogeneity widespread in non-Western civilizations. "In the West," Weber argues, "rulership was set against rulership, legitimacy against legitimacy, one office charisma against the other" (2009, p. 398). Indeed, the *world* (above all the economy, rulership, and law spheres)—*religion* antagonism *itself* introduced "a strongly dynamic element into the West's unfolding" (1968, pp. 578–579).

Weber sees the Protestant Reformation as constituting the last major component of Western rationalism. It will have eventually a strong impact on the development of capitalism, he is convinced. A further unique interaction of "religion" and "world" is apparent.

The Reformation: World and Religion Tensions

Weber insists that the Reformation's new religious movements arose not only from the abstract syntheses of theological postulates formulated by religion-oriented intellectuals. Distinct groups oriented to status honor, rulership, the economy, the law, the family, and the clan significantly influenced the religion domain in this era, he maintains. The Reformation "was certainly codetermined by economic factors" (1968, p. 1196) and the decisive weakening of Papal authority had "political reasons":

> [It] lost ground because of the caesaropapist inclinations and secularizing tendencies of the princes who had strengthened their power tremendously through administrative rationalization, and after the ecclesiastic tradition became discredited in the eyes of the intellectual circles and the noble and bourgeois strata. (1968, p. 1196)

Moreover, facilitating contexts comprised of particular rulership and economic groups had to be in place for Calvinism and the other ascetic Protestant groups to arise: "The ascetic varieties of Protestantism have prevailed wherever the bourgeoisie was a social power, and the least ascetic churches of the Reformation, Anglicanism and Lutheranism, wherever the nobility or the princes had the upper hand" (1968, p. 119; see also pp. 431–434, 471–472; 1927, pp. 352–369; 1958, pp. 337–338).

As the Reformation spread, lay believers increasingly communicated with ministers and theologians on a regular basis in reference to scriptural standards rather than age-old tradition, clan loyalties, or Catholicism's hierocratic authority. In turn, the Protestant clergy, as a result in part of the intense competition across varieties of churches and sects in the 16th and 17th centuries, more and more acknowledged "lay rationalism." Weber points out that Puritanism in England, arising out of a politically powerful middle class, "became saturated with [a plebeian] intellectualism." As an empowered laity demanded answers to the problem of suffering and the Predestination conundrum, ministers and theologians responded—at times even adjusting doctrine (2009, p. 411; 1968, p. 467; see above, pp. xxx).

Pastoral care expanded as this dynamic unfolded. It was pushed along by an unusual command of scripture among the lay devout, their uncertainty regarding salvation in light of the harshness of the Predestination doctrine, and the practical—even economic—concerns of church and sect elites. In contrast to China and India, where "pure religion[s] of intellectuals" maintained hegemony and "priestly labors of systematization concerned themselves more and more with the most traditional, and hence magical, forms of religious notions and practices" (1968, p. 466), a widespread lay rationalism in the West often initiated dramatic and urgent dialogues among theologians and the clergy. At stake was the salvation of anxiety-plagued believers. Whereas the lay faithful in the East remained "submerged in magic," this post-Reformation dynamic in the West uprooted the devout even more from magic and ritual and pushed religion-oriented conduct more forcefully toward ethical action *in* the world. Ascetic Protestantism's orientation to work, profit, wealth, and a vocational ethos eventually crystallized.

This examination of the West's independent medieval cities, citizenship, Christian doctrine, and Roman and Canon law, as well as the modern state's origins, the Reformation, lay rationalism, and structural heterogeneity, has sought to define the configuration of groups that together erected the unique contours of Western rationalism in the Middle Ages and High Middle Ages. Contrast cases—the rationalisms of China, India, and the Middle East—have been referred to throughout to articulate Western rationalism's substance, parameters, and trajectory precisely. An array of causes behind its development have been identified.

The West's "world and religion" configuration became empowered to facilitate a strong turn toward modern capitalism, it would appear, by the High Middle Ages. A firm alliance—the coalition of early Christianity's monotheism, universalism, and world-oriented salvation-striving with guild craftsmen in autonomous cities—had significantly weakened the grip of magic and surmounted clan, tribal, and ethnic dualisms by the Middle Ages to a qualitatively greater degree than had occurred in China, India, or the Middle East. Both Roman law and Canon law had contributed to this development; ethical action oriented *toward* daily activities arose on a widespread basis in the Western cities. Western rationalism now assumed quite distinct contours.

However, Weber rejects the view that capitalism expanded from the Middle Ages and the High Middle Ages in a linear manner to modern capitalism. History's flow never pursues a straight line, he contends; "market-irrational" groups often held firm—even despite the powerful antagonism to them by the Protestant ethic. Indeed, an array of groups became allied in opposition to capitalism's growth. And powerful barriers were erected against its transformation into modern capitalism, whether in the form of patrimonial empires struggling against politically independent and incorporated cities in the High Middle Ages, the scorn of feudalism's ethos for all systematic pursuit of wealth, Catholicism's traditional economic ethic and struggle against capitalist entrepreneurs, the "market-irrational" aspects of patrimonial rulership, or the English monarchy's opposition to industrious Puritans. Groups carrying values, traditions, and interests interact in multiple and unpredictable ways, Weber is convinced.

Although the Middle Ages and High Middle Ages gave birth to an "urban revolution" and a period of dynamic capitalism, this era constituted an anomaly of high economic growth *between* the ancient world and the patrimonial rulers of the 15th, 16th, and 17th centuries, Weber contends. As their empires became dominant to varying degrees in the different European countries, Western rationalism's parameters shift. *Modern* capitalism, carried significantly by ascetic Protestants and groups upholding the spirit of capitalism, will crystallize only with the weakening of these great empires, Weber holds. A further concatenation of many groups in supportive configurations must occur if further steps toward modern Western rationalism are to be taken.

The Patrimonial Empires: Absolutism, Mercantilism, and the Decline of the Urban Revolution

The cross-sphere conflicts and severe structural heterogeneity of the Middle Ages and High Middle Ages proved short-lived as defining features of the Western developmental pathway and Western rationalism. Patrimonial empires expanded across much of Europe. Amid this centralization of rulership, would a slow but steady societal ossification follow? Weber's research continues.

Rulers extended hegemony over large territories. Kings amassed military power and created complex administrative organizations, hence whittling away the military, judicial, and economic independence of cities. Legal prohibitions were placed on citizens of the urban areas and the independent power of most cities to tax was eliminated. This patrimonial subjugation decreased the economy's growth and weakened the guilds (1968, pp. 1328–1330, 1351). Weber identifies several specific causes for the economic and political decline of the medieval city.

The Putting Out System. The putting-out economy[4] gradually replaced production by urban craftsmen in guilds. Experienced merchants with access to markets began hiring workers in their own homes on a contract basis. Labor could now be more thoroughly organized and exploited than under the guild mode of production. The beginnings of an entrepreneurial middle class were apparent.

Although its extent and tempo varied enormously from country to country (see 1927, pp. 153–159), and even though the old and the new modes of production existed for centuries side-by-side, the domestic system gradually won out. England led the way, followed by France, which moved decidedly toward this "cottage" industry in the 14th century. It expanded widely as market-savvy merchants developed buying monopolies, delivered raw materials to workers, exercised control in respect to quality and scheduling over the production process, provided workers with the necessary tools, and established monopolies over the marketing and distribution of products. Wherever this mode of production expanded, the power of the guilds, which had anchored the medieval city's economic and political power, was disrupted. The autonomy of urban areas was accordingly weakened.

The domestic system proved unique to Western rationalism, Weber contends. Workers were elsewhere often unable freely to enter into contracts; frequently their mobility was restricted by the necessity to perform ritualistic and magical acts. In China the dominance of clan-based production methods, and the distribution of the product only to the kinship group, constituted a strong barrier to the growth of this system. Merchants were prevented in India from controlling the means of production owing to its caste-based, hereditary location. Hence, a subjugation of craftsmen could not occur (see 1927, pp. 160–166).

The Decline of Feudalism. Weber saw feudal authority as precarious owing to the unstable anchorage of the vassal's obedience. While a relationship of loyalty underpinned the following of commands, possession by vassals and subvassals of administrative authority over demarcated territories implied the constant possibility of aggrandizement and usurpation of the ruler's domination. For stability to endure, the voluntary component—the "feudal ethos" of personal allegiance—must be continuously cultivated and strengthened. Conflict remained "chronic," according to Weber (see 2009, p. 406–409; 1968, pp. 255–262, 1078–1088).

The lord's wish to place his rulership on a more secure footing led repeatedly to attempts to create a directly subordinate administrative staff. These efforts frequently were successful in Europe—and feudalism more and more became transformed into patrimonial rulership. The necessity for tighter administrative control, amid warfare across competing regions and then among patrimonial "states," furthered this development. The push by jurists interested in legal reliability and the search by an expanding bourgeoisie for cross-regional economic stability did so as well.

Feudalism gradually lost out to expanding patrimonial kingdoms. In addition, exploitation and control of the cities intensified as absolutist monarchies commenced a period of intense competition and empire building. In possession of large armies and utilizing officials trained to administer extended areas, rulers throughout Europe in the 15th, 16th, and 17th centuries succeeded in eroding the autonomy of the city communes. Western rationalism's urban revolution came to an end. Democracy and citizenship in the cities was suppressed in the process (1968, p. 1351; see also pp. 257–259, 971, 1089).

The Rise of Patrimonial Empires and Mercantilism. The advance of large-scale administrative organizations and rulership over huge territories occurred as patrimonialism bestowed economic privileges on new groups of entrepreneurs with roots in the putting-out system. In exchange for fees or profit sharing, the awarding of monopolies and private trade rights to "state commercial enterprises" and specific craft organizations became widespread practices. Moreover, patrimonial rulership's antagonism to the formal rationality of the marketplace proved less intense than that of feudalism; indeed, Weber saw an affinity between certain aspects of patrimonialism's ethos and the market economy.

Far more tolerant of upward mobility, trade, new property formation, and the search for riches than their feudal counterparts, patrimonial rulers and officials viewed feudalism's indigenous status barriers as placing limitations on acquisition and trade. To Weber: "The 'financier' is . . . feasible under almost all conditions of rulership, especially under patrimonialism." Western rationalism's "Age of Mercantilism," in which a direct relationship between the state and capital congealed, had commenced. Now patrimonialism's economic achievements enhanced its capacity to maintain hegemony over the urban areas (see 1968, pp. 1091–1094, 1097–1099; 2009, pp. 381–383, 349–351).

A larger dynamic came into play to alter Western rationalism in the 16th and 17th centuries: Princes and monarchs across Europe became engaged in ruthless competition for political power and the resources of the new world. "Ever more capital for political reasons, and because of the expanding money economy," was required (1968, p. 353). Precisely this competition, which Weber saw as unique to the West in this epoch, endowed the alliance between the state and an expanding class of merchants, financiers, and colonial adventurers with a special firmness and intensity. These emerging states promoted financial rationalization, introduced an expanded money economy, and "created the largest opportunities for modern capitalism," Weber holds (see 2009, p. 397).

Mercantilism's Opposition to Modern Capitalism. Once again, a linear unfolding to modern capitalism could be envisaged. However, according to Weber, this "political capitalism" never introduced modern capitalism. Twists and turns characterized its origins. Indeed, patrimonialism's mercantilism in the end opposed the growth of the market. Due to its person-oriented values, patrimonialism's ethos stood in a relationship of antagonism to the market's formal rationality. Moreover, owing to its claim to legitimacy, this ethos remained more oriented to the welfare and loyalty of subjects than to the revolutionary changes placed into motion by the widening powers of business-oriented groups and the growth of the marketplace (2009, pp. 408–409). Finally, frequent tensions between the ruler, his court, and local officials created a degree of instability that hindered the growth of formal rationality.

In general, the "spirit of patrimonial administration" sought to preserve the traditional economic ethic; it "is alien to and distrustful of capitalist development" (2009, p. 408). Even where great wealth was obtained, the proclivity of patrimonialism to immobilize riches through monopolies opposed a high degree of formal rationality (1968, pp. 1091, 1094–1098). How then, Weber queries again, did Western rationalism give birth to modern capitalism?

The 17th and 18th Centuries: Technology, Science and Religion, the Factory, and Commercialization

Despite the growth of great patrimonial empires, Western rationalism continued to be characterized by a certain structural heterogeneity conducive to economic activity. By the end of the 16th century, trade and economic development in general had increased to heretofore unequaled levels. Compared to the ancient world, China, India, and the Middle East, a greater dynamic of competing groups and a political situation of relative openness existed. All in all, an entrepreneurial middle class planted deep roots and gradually expanded its power during the 16th, 17th, and 18th centuries. Weber maintains that technology, science, the factory, and new commercialization mechanisms (such as the stock market) played pivotal parts in this expansion. Only a brief overview can be offered.

The Role of Technological Change

Although an entire series of technological innovations in the West contributed to the growth of modern capitalism, Weber contends that an independent causal weight cannot be attributed to them. Indeed, in the ancient world capitalism developed in the absence of technological advance—even "one could say simultaneous with the cessation of technical progress." The view that "certain *technical* 'achievements' constituted the obvious origin of capitalist development" must be seen as a "popular error" (2009, p. 447; 1976, pp. 353–354).

Weber's reluctance to endow technology with a clear causal capacity derives from his sociology's general proclivity to view single groups as located in configurations of groups. He then emphasizes the decisive role of the social context. Did the milieu—Western rationalism's salvation paths, forms of rulership and law, and cities—facilitate or constrain the impact of a specific innovation? Did "the development of . . . technology . . . acquire pivotal invigorating impulses from opportunities offered by capitalism" (2009, p. 214)? Did a specific context singularly configure a facilitating milieu, thereby enabling innovations to take hold and have an impact? While "the origin of mathematics and physics was not determined by economic interests," Weber maintained, the *technical* applications of scientific knowledge were (2009, p. 214). Even the influence of warfare on the unfolding of modern capitalism and the demand for luxury goods depended on a social context, he held, as evident from an examination of comparative cases (see 2009, pp. 389–390).

The Influence of Science: Material-Technological Interests and Religious Belief

Science began to play a part in the unfolding of modern capitalism in England when market forces became capable of offering sustained incentives to inventors, according to Weber. In the form of technological innovations, the application of science would lessen production costs, it was widely hoped. An entirely new, and more systematic, *motivation* was created among inventors and scientists quite different from Leonardo's: "Science meant the path to *true* art" (2005, p. 325; see 2009, pp. 390–399). With the expansion of markets, the question of whether an invention possessed "practical" utility now became pivotal.

However, Weber refuses to see a "feverish pursuit of invention" as driven alone by material incentives. The social context was more complex, he insists; religious belief also proved again salient (see 2009, p. 516, n. 169). He rejects at the outset a view widespread among his colleagues: Devoutness must be understood as an obstacle to the development of empirical science. Instead, the origin of modern natural science was intimately *interwoven* with religious faith, Weber maintains, particularly with Puritanism. Indeed, "most of the natural science heroes in England from the seventeenth century right up until [Michael] Faraday [1791–1867] and [James] Maxwell" [1831–1879] were sincere believers (2005, pp. 324–325; 2009, p. 447).

He is convinced that the religious dimension played a significant part in linking scientific innovation and the expansion of the economy in England's 17th and 18th centuries. Above all, Puritan scientists sought to unveil God's will through an exploration of the universe's natural laws—and this quest frequently yielded knowledge that could be placed into the service of new technologies. Hence, the natural sciences assisted economic growth in a more *practical* manner than in earlier epochs—and, given previous technological innovations, did so at a critical time for the economy's growth. Finally, the religious component in the motivational configuration of Puritan scientists inserted a *methodical*—"and not just occasional"—element into this interlocking of scientific innovation and economic growth (see 2005, pp. 325, 340; 2009, pp. 447, 516 n. 169). Western rationalism acquired a further pivotal and unique feature with this interweaving of science and religion.

The Rise of the Factory

Factories are centers of production that bring together a concentration of freely contracted workers under one roof. Nonhuman sources of power—machines—are typical, as is capital accounting. On the basis of mechanization, tasks are specialized and labor is organized, coordinated, and disciplined. An elaborate differentiation of functions, and their rational organization in reference to questions of technical efficiency, characterizes the factory's division of labor. A continuity of operations prevails.

This manner of organizing work stands in contrast to the putting-out system in two ways: The factory centralized labor and accumulated fixed capital to a far greater extent; it also appropriated land, tools, installations, and means of production to one owner. Thus, far higher degrees of efficiency accompanied the organization of labor and a more exact calculation of costs became possible. In the 18th century, the factory gradually displaced the putting-out system (see 2009, p. 384; see also 1927, pp. 163, 169–173; 1968, pp. 117, 135; 1976, p. 44).

Largely because of its requirement for a large supply of free and mobile labor, the factory rarely appeared before the 18th century and infrequently outside the West. The requisite supply of labor proved difficult to assemble in India, and the perception by castes of each other as "impure" hindered easy cooperation on the factory floor. Moreover, each caste held to its own set of rituals, rest breaks, and holidays. In China, the cohesiveness of clans in villages limited the supply of mobile labor and fostered "communal clan" workshops rather than factories. Similarly, the scarcity of unfree labor created obstacles to factory development in Antiquity and the Middle Ages in the West.

On the other hand, Western rationalism assembled arrays of groups that assisted the birth of the factory, a "mechanization of technology," a type of science oriented to practical innovations, and ascetic Protestantism's vocational ethos. A strong push in the direction of modern capitalism ensued, Weber contends (1927, p. 184; 2009, pp. 384–385).

Commercialization

The economies of England, the American colonies, and the early United States witnessed a broad-ranging commercialization in the 18th and 19th centuries. This development "involved . . . the appearance of paper representing shares in an enterprise and, secondly, paper representing rights to income, especially in the form of state bonds and mortgage indebtedness" (2009, p. 379). Large sums of capital were raised from the publicly held stock company, which arose out of early war financing activities and the large colonizing companies of the 16th and 17th centuries (2009, pp. 379–380).

Western rationalism's economies continued to grow and to introduce systematizing mechanisms. The wholesaler became distinct from the retailer in the 18th century and soon introduced new commercial entities: wholesale trade, the auction, consignment trading, and buying on commission, for example. The standardization and quantification of units increasingly allowed speculation on, and exchange of, commodities. Futures trading, and especially the building of the railroads, unchained the "speculative urge." Soon various goods, grains, and colonial products were "drawn into the circle of exchange speculation in the nineteenth century." The appearance of newspapers and commercial organizations facilitated the growth of speculative and wholesale trade. Finally, the construction of turnpikes and railroads boosted economic growth enormously (1927, pp. 292–294, 297).

Let us summarize briefly before moving to modern Western rationalism. Despite the concatenating influence of facilitating groups and the conducive social contexts provided by Western rationalism, *modern* capitalism had not yet appeared.[5] Exclusive reference to political, economic, scientific, and organizational constellations fails, Weber holds, to account for its rise. And neither types of law nor types of rulership rooted in formal rationality had yet crystallized. Both will facilitate greatly the growth of modern capitalism by providing predictability to economic transactions and allowing long-range calculations and planning, he insists. Far from linear, twists and turns characterized modern capitalism's advance.

The Protestant ethic, which introduced a methodical-rational organization of life oriented toward world mastery, assisted the transformation of England's political capitalism into modern capitalism. This element, Weber maintains, proved pivotal for the suppression of the practical-rational way of life, the shattering of the traditional economic ethic, and the birth of a modern economic ethic. His exhaustive comparative investigations yielded a clear conclusion: This-worldly asceticism alone managed to do so. The systematic ethical action of Puritanism organized the believer's life comprehensively *and* produced a vocational ethos. Weber's "empirical experiments" isolated ascetic Protestantism's singularity *and* its long-range roots.

Ancient Christianity had confirmed the "worldly" direction for salvation striving established by Judaism's monotheism: The believer's *conduct* proved decisive for redemption. Henceforth, the faithful in the West could attain certainty of their salvation *only* through daily activity. For this reason, Weber insists, the action of the devout can never be comprehended as exclusively utilitarian in nature. Instead, it implied a salvation-relevant, value-grounded, and nonempirical dimension—and thus an *intensification* of conduct, Weber insists. Despite the significant historical presence of sects that cultivated mysticism throughout Western history, a complete "world rejection"—a "world fleeing" search for an "escape from the senseless mechanism of the 'wheel' of existence"—could not move into the mainstream of the Western religious tradition (1958, p. 373; see 1946c, p. 286).

These conclusions can also be rendered in a slightly different vein. On behalf of a quest to acquire salvation certainty, Puritanism's this-worldly ascetics, as the Hindu and Buddhist mystics, aimed to substitute a conscious and methodical directing of life toward the supernatural realm for a dependence on utilitarian action and the random flow of practical rationality. However, unlike mysticism, and also unlike ancient Judaism, early Christianity, and medieval Catholicism, this-worldly asceticism awarded psychological premiums to *manifold* ethical action *in* everyday life. A comprehensively *disciplined believer* completely scornful of "irrational" sorcery, attributing intense meaning to economic activity, and systematically focused on work and profit, now marched onto the West's historical stage (2009, pp. 266–267).

Far more capable of calling forth significant social transformations than great political actors, powerful economic elites, and technical inventions, Puritanism's "practical-ethical" faithful formulated cohesive congregations throughout several societies in the 16th and 17th centuries, Weber maintains. Comprised of extremely dedicated believers, their churches and sects influenced societies far and wide, pushed social change, and rejected age-old traditions. They also assisted the birth of modern capitalism, he contends.

Placed on the defensive, mercantilism was largely banished in the 18th century. Weber stresses, of course, the capacity of the ascetic devout to *direct* energy vigorously toward wealth, profit, and work in a vocational calling. The search by the faithful for signs of their salvation status, the ways heretofore purely utilitarian activities became sanctified, the newfound clear conscience of the entrepreneur in search of profit (see 2009, p. 342), and the necessity to testify to belief through ethical conduct proved sociologically significant, he insists.

By rationalizing action radically and introducing *practical-ethical* action, ascetic Protestantism disrupted and replaced both the *practical-rational* organization of life and the traditional economic ethic. Patterned action more methodical and intense than utilitarian calculations had been required to do so. This *directed* life endowed the organization of labor in factories with a systematic aspect, promoted the introduction of new technologies into the workplace, and facilitated the birth of a broad-based middle class of entrepreneurs and industrious workers, Weber contends.

The conflict between mercantilism's political capitalism and the Puritan ethos, and the subsequent victory of Puritanism, were pivotal episodes in the history of modern capitalism's unfolding in England, according to Weber. The patrimonial empires proved unable to sustain an entrepreneurial spirit, although capable of awakening one. A *modern* economic ethic, which stimulated unceasingly the expansion of the market in a variety of ways, appeared only with ascetic Protestantism. Western rationalism's various groups now gradually became more tightly interwoven and nourished each other reciprocally—weakening market-irrational substantive rationalities. The free market expanded and the preconditions for a "maximum degree of formal rationality of capital accounting" began to fall into place (see 1968, pp. 161–164). Calling forth formal rationality, configurations of groups in several major life-spheres lent strong support to modern capitalism's development, Weber emphasizes. Modern Western rationalism then embarked on the stage of history.

Modern Western Rationalism's Concatenating Groups: Logical-Formal Law, the Modern State, and Bureaucratic Rulership

According to him, if to congeal and endure, modern capitalism required a further array of groups arranged in a supportive conjunctural constellation. As a result of unique juxtapositions, 18th- and 19th-century developments introduced predictability and stability into the marketplace. Its capacity to give birth to high degrees of capital accounting is sustained in this epoch by a modern type of law, a modern state, and bureaucratic rulership. Formal rationality grounded all these central components of modern Western rationalism.

Modern capitalism "operates best" wherever embedded in a legal order that functions in a calculable manner in reference to rational rules. Objective regulations, statutes, and laws universally applied provide systematized and unambiguous procedures. This type of legal order offers, for example, a secure method for transferring legal claims and a firm basis for the constant expansion of market exchanges (1927, p. 343; 1968, pp. 1394–1395). Indeed, according to Weber: "The tempo of modern business communication requires a promptly and predictably functioning legal system, i.e., one which is guaranteed by the strongest coercive power" (1968, p. 337; see also p. 1095). Hence, as the market expands, modern capitalism:

> favored the monopolization and regulation of all "legitimate" coercive power by *one* universalist institution with a monopoly over the legitimate use of force (*Zwangsanstalt*)—the state—and the disintegration of all particularist, status-determined and other coercive structures based mainly upon economic monopolies. (1968, p. 337; translation altered; emphasis in original)

In addition to the modern state, modern Western rationalism is significantly constituted from bureaucratic rulership. It also offers a supportive milieu to modern capitalism's formal rationality, Weber contends. While not necessarily highly efficient, the modern bureaucracy nonetheless far surpasses feudal, patrimonial, and charismatic forms of rulership in sheer organizational capacity, the performance of tasks, and formal rationality.[6] A standardized execution of duties and an orientation to rules, prescriptions, and regulations characterizes action within bureaucracies rather than an orientation—favoring or disfavoring—to persons (see above, p. 54).[7]

This organization's modes of procedure, which ultimately provide rationally debatable "reasons" for administrative acts, enable business to take place at an impersonal level and in a predictable fashion (1968, pp. 956, 1095). The stability and continuity indispensable for economic planning and the operation of large industrial enterprises is provided. Moreover, the status ethic of the manager—disciplined, organized, and reliable—further sustains modern capitalism's demand for calculability. The "matter of factness" (*Sachlichkeit*) of the professionally trained experts, their view of knowledge as "useful" in a technical sense, and their formal rationality "tend already . . . in the direction of the private economic rationalism of the middle class strata" (1968, p. 847; translation altered). "In its modern stages of development," Weber maintains, "capitalism requires the bureaucracy" (1968, p. 224; see pp. 956, 1095).

Modern Western Rationalism and Modern Capitalism's Autonomy

Called Western rationalism by Weber, configurations of groups in the Middle Ages commenced the meandering pathways that engendered modern capitalism's origin and sustained its development. For the West's uniqueness and track, pivotal were above all groups that carried the growth of citizenship in politically independent cities, guild-based city economies, Christianity's ethos of universal compassion, the religious congregations and guilds that cultivated confraternization, Roman law and Canon law, feudalism's notion of contract, the weakening of magic and insider-outsider dualisms anchored in clans, tribes, and ethnic groups, and the office charisma developed by the Catholic Church.

Weber saw these various groups as interacting off each other and forming configurations of groups. Contexts crystallized from patterns of subjective meaning held by people in groups that juxtaposed interests, values, emotions, and traditions. Both alliances and antagonisms across groups were regular. However, out of these dynamic groups Western rationalism eventually acquired an internal coherence and a developmental direction— one that would offer to capitalism constellations of multiple groups largely conducive to its growth. Again, Weber insists that a linear line of "progress" cannot be ascertained.

Capitalism experienced significant circumscription in the 15th, 16th, and 17th centuries owing to the centralizing powers of absolutist patrimonial empires, feudalism's status-based conventions and opposition to the unfolding of a middle class outlook, and Catholicism's traditional economic ethic. Nonetheless, on the basis of a favorable configuration of interacting "world *and* religion" groups, capitalism resumed its expansionary journey in the 18th century.

Multiple elements interacted, indeed in supportive ways: innovations, modern science, the methodical application of new technologies, the organization of a workforce into factories, and the introduction of new commercialization mechanisms. Clusters of groups congealed in ways that gave vibrancy to, and sustained, Western rationalism's trajectory. Along this winding pathway from capitalism to modern capitalism the presence of a distinct and large group systematically in pursuit of profit and motivated to labor in a methodical manner provided a significant impulse, Weber contends: ascetic Protestants. Sects endowed the Puritan ethic in the United States with an unusual dynamism and served as its effective social carrier. Several generations later, businessmen's clubs and a variety of civic associations cultivated a secular spirit of capitalism.

Only cognizance of a variety of "world and religion" patterns of action, as manifest in multiple cohesive groups, allows consideration of the full configuration of groups—Western rationalism's deep context—that gave rise to, facilitated, and nourished capitalism along its long journey, Weber insists. It eventually expanded, carried by additional arrays of facilitating groups, in the 18th and 19th centuries: modern law, the modern state, and the modern bureaucracy.

This multidimensional context—*modern Western rationalism*—lent powerful support to the economy's growth. Entrepreneurs and businessmen were assisted in respect to the fulfillment of indispensable tasks: to calculate actual costs in reference to the free market and to introduce technical efficiency. Along this uneven terrain, capitalism eventually became transformed into modern capitalism. According to Weber, the twists and turns indigenous to both capitalism's expanse and metamorphosis into modern capitalism become apparent only if researchers acknowledge the amenable *configurations* of groups that constitute Western rationalism and modern Western rationalism.

In his many investigations of Western rationalism, as well as in his comparative research into the rationalisms of China, India, the Middle East, and the ancient West, Weber analyzed how powerful groups opposed to the efficient functioning of the market's laws gradually declined *only in the West*: for example, feudalism's aristocracy, Catholicism's traditional economic ethic, and the "adventure capitalists" who carried mercantilism. Only then could the "free market," an impersonal "spirit of calculation," a technically refined formal rationality, and capital accounting become widespread, he held.

The rules of commercial accounting and efficient management began in the 19th century to dominate action oriented to the market in several Western nations, Weber argues. Rather than by reference to an ethos anchored in ideals of universal compassion and ethical action, decision making in the economy life-sphere more and more occurred exclusively by reference to the laws of the market and struggles over economic and political interests, Weber contends. With "market freedom," capitalism now pursued unhindered its *own* laws: those of the marketplace. And noncompliance with its formal rationality implied direct consequences: "The growing impersonality of the economy on the basis of association in the marketplace follows its own impersonal lawfulness, disobedience to which entails economic failure and, in the long run, economic ruin" (1968, p. 585; translation altered; see 2009, pp. 426–427).

This reconstruction of capitalism's expansion and transformation has revealed Weber's sociology as an empirical sociology of groups that form configurations of groups and, in the process, delimit deep contexts. It rejects both unilinear and monocausal views of history, as well as all depictions of the West's pathway as one of metaphysical and unceasing progress. Crucial crossroads, even disjunctures, appeared frequently, he maintains.

At times, Western rationalism's constellations of supportive groups failed to push the unfolding of the economy toward modern capitalism. At other times a qualitative leap in this direction was sustained by concatenating groups. At still other times a course taken proved only much later, once a variety of groups had shifted and new configurations had formed, a spur to modern capitalism.

Even initiatives favoring capitalism's growth conveyed by powerful carrier groups often faded from the landscape—crushed, at least temporarily, by centralizing and bureaucratizing tendencies. Not least, the *sheer tension* between ethical standards articulated by groups in the religion domain on the one hand and daily life's a-ethical practical rationality as well as the formal rationality dominant in the rulership, economy, and law arenas on the other hand *itself* placed dynamic—and unpredictable—thrusts into motion, Weber emphasizes (2009, pp. 86–88; see 1946b, pp. 328–330; 1968, pp. 578–579; Kalberg, 2012, pp. 43–72).

This extensive discussion has sought to convey how, in Weber's post-*PE* writings, groups formed configurations of groups in the West that provided deep contexts—Western rationalism and modern Western rationalism—*favorable* to capitalism's development and its transformation into modern capitalism. However, three further goals have also been central in the above analysis: It sought to demonstrate Weber's multicausality, to convey his conjunctural causality, and to examine the many ways that constellations of groups from the *distant* past for him repeatedly cast long shadows—indeed, even into the immediate present. Western rationalism's origins must be located in part even in the ancient world. These themes must be briefly reviewed.

Weber's Multicausal, Comparative, and Configurational Methodology Revisited

This reconstruction from disparate threads has attempted to capture the broad multicausality at the foundation of Weber's comparative-historical sociology. Causality perpetually "shifts" across a range of groups, above all ones oriented to the economy, rulership, religion, law, family, clan, and status-honor arenas, although also across groups that have arisen from discrete historical occurrences, Weber contends. A "final resting point"—whether, for example, the economy or the religion sphere—can never be identified (1968, p. 341; 1988, p. 456; 2009, pp. 215–216). Hence, his analysis of the rise of modern capitalism rejected, as noted, the Marxian formula articulated by his colleague and friend, Werner Sombart: The modern economic ethic is best understood as an outgrowth of capitalism's development (2009, pp. 86–88). "Economic forms," Weber emphasized repeatedly, prove incapable of giving birth to economic ethics.

Nonetheless, whether manifest as guild-based capitalism, the putting-out system, or mercantilism, these forms *must* be included in any analysis that purports to explain modern capitalism's origin and expansion, he holds. And the *economic and political interests* of persons in the major groups oriented to an economic form, as well as their pursuit of sheer power and the causal power of their carrier groups, must also be acknowledged. However, the "other side" must not be lost in the process, Weber also insists. As mentioned, the development of technological innovations utilized by market-based capitalism, for example, was accelerated by the religious beliefs of ascetic Protestant scientists.

His multicausal, context-specific, configurational, and comparative methodology maintains that *both* "internal" and "external" causes must be scrutinized. It also contends that *reciprocal* interactions across values, economic and political interests, and traditions must be acknowledged in all analyses that seek to establish causality. Religious congregations in the cities of the Middle Ages, for example, overcame traditional insider-outsider dualisms and turned believers effectively, as members of a *new* community *of belief*, toward universal values. This transformation then assisted confraternization elsewhere: Guilds and commerce could now include heretofore excluded groups. However, Weber takes his analysis also in the reverse causal direction: Guilds recruited members on the basis of skills rather than ethnic or clan criteria—and hence facilitated Christianity's attempt to introduce universalistic ethics. Again, no "final resting point" can be identified.

His search to demarcate configurations of groups that formulated many deep contexts and his investigation of the long-range developments specific to Western rationalism and modern Western rationalism that gave birth to, and sustained, capitalism and modern capitalism resulted from his highly comparative methodology. Large-scale comparisons to China, India, and the Middle East, he maintains, alone delineate the uniqueness of Western rationalism's contours and trajectory. How did capitalism's course in other civilizations vary from its course in the West? Weber's fine-grained, multicausal investigations repeatedly explore the ways constellations of interacting groups successfully formed contexts of groups—ones in reference to which the economy developed at varying speeds and in singular directions.

Variations of great magnitude have been revealed, indeed to such an extent that a widely held view of Weber's analysis can now be discredited. According to this position, China and India would early on have pursued the West's economic modernization path if only an "equivalent" for the Protestant ethic had appeared (see 2009, pp. 215–216). However, his multicausal, context-sensitive, configurational, and groups-based analyses all teach that the investigation of such large questions requires utilization of a far more sophisticated research design. It must attend, in comparative perspective, to the causal potential of *multiple* groups and their unique interactions.[8]

Weber's explorations reveal many civilizational differences. Western rationalism's structural heterogeneity must be recalled. Regular antagonisms across the rulership, law, economy, and religion spheres became intense and widespread. First apparent during the Middle Ages, they assumed a qualitatively broader and more enduring form than appeared in Chinese rationalism or the rationalism of India (see below, pp. 131–162). However, rather than calling forth unceasing fragmentation and debilitating polarization, this heterogeneity introduced a societal dynamism. It distinguished Western rationalism and proved crucial both for its transformation into modern Western rationalism and for capitalism's metamorphosis into modern capitalism, Weber maintains.

He knew that his hope to define the substance, contours, and parameters of Western rationalism and modern Western rationalism and then to offer an explanation for the growth in the West of capitalism and modern capitalism, as well as to chart their specific trajectories, required rigorous comparative procedures. Weber's studies of the rationalisms of China and India served this purpose. He emphasized their distinctiveness vis-à-vis Western rationalism and modern Western rationalism.

We turn first to China. For Weber, albeit singular, this civilization's rationalism, like Western rationalism and modern Western rationalism, was constituted from arrays of groups that formed configurations of groups and hence viable social contexts. In a manner more succinct than do Weber's texts, this chapter conveys the ways in which Chinese rationalism, owing to its substance, contours, and parameters, *failed* to provide constellations of groups that facilitated the growth of capitalism and modern capitalism. In the end, pivotal groups in China's classical era formulated multiple and powerful obstacles against capitalism's expansion, ones that outweighed the thrusts placed into motion by groups favoring its growth.

Study Questions and Thoughts to Ponder

1. Please define "capitalism" and "modern capitalism."

2. Why did the economic ethic of Puritans stand opposed to mercantilism?

3. Note at least three elements, in addition to the Protestant ethic, that must be present, according to Weber, for the transformation of capitalism to modern capitalism to occur.

4. Both values and interests play parts wherever a civilization develops from capitalism to modern capitalism. Give examples of each.

5. Christianity's universalism played an important part in the West's Middle Ages as a predecessor to modern capitalism. Trace out its influence.

6. What features made the city of the West's Middle Ages unique?

7. Discuss the impact of technology and/or scientific innovation in general on the development of modern capitalism. Does it constitute an independent causal variable?

8. Far from a linear course, the rise of modern Western rationalism, Weber maintains, must be characterized as involving "twists and turns." Note examples that demonstrate this nonlinear trajectory.

9. We must acknowledge, according to Weber's analysis, that *many* groups played parts in calling forth modern capitalism. Is this *broad* multicausality really necessary?

10. According to Weber, Western rationalism forms a facilitating context conducive to capitalism's expansion and modern Western rationalism forms a facilitating context conducive to modern capitalism. Please explain.

11. Discuss the role of *practical* rationalism in Weber's analysis of the development in the West from capitalism to modern capitalism.

12. Discuss the role of *formal* rationalism in Weber's analysis of the development in the West from capitalism to modern capitalism.

Notes

1. *Today* these major aspects of Western civilization do not seem unique to it. We must at this point keep in mind that Weber is writing during a period when Asian economies in certain respects lagged behind those in the West. Furthermore, it must be stressed that his project aims to explain why these features developed *earliest* in the West. His position does not imply that the development of these, and other, major features of Western civilization remain impossible outside the West.

2. The terms—"follow their own laws" and "autonomous"—are translations of *Eigengesetzlichkeit*. They will be used synonymously.

3. It must be stressed that Weber's salient definitions and causal analyses are scattered widely in fragments throughout his three-volume treatises, *E&S* and EEWR, and his *General Economic History* (1927). This chapter undertakes a reconstruction.

4. This economy is also referred to as the "domestic system" and "cottage industry."

5. The above discussion, as noted, has attempted to draw attention to major groups rather than to be comprehensive.

6. The secondary literature has too often argued that Weber viewed this form of rulership as "efficient" as such. His orientation instead is toward the question of the organization of labor and the bureaucracy's technical superiority (the performance of administrative tasks) *in comparison to* the other types of rulership (see pp.). He is well aware of "red tape."

7. It should be again recalled that Weber is here constructing an ideal type. See Glossary.

8. Weber's studies manifest a comparative thrust not only in respect to this overarching theme. He seeks to isolate and explain the uniqueness of the route toward modern capitalism followed in the West *and* to define precisely the ways in which the pathways followed by several Western nations varied. A homogeneity of development is not evident. Despite significant "Western" similarities, Weber identified separate routes toward modern capitalism in Germany, France, England, and the United States. This complex analysis cannot be explored here (see Kalberg, 2012, 2014b, and forthcoming).

The Sociology of Civilizations II: The Rationalism of China

C entral to Weber for an understanding of the "particular rationalism" unique to classical China[1] is the sustaining strength of clan ties and the absence of politically autonomous cities. In direct contrast to the medieval West, patrimonial princes and literati officials stood opposite the clan. As a consequence of its support by Confucianism and an entire host of magical spirits, together with multiple further groups, Chinese rationalism was constituted from constellations of groups that effectively opposed the widespread development of both capitalism and modern capitalism.[2] This civilizational rationalism—and the extent to which patterned action becomes rationalized—can be reconstructed in a detailed manner. A number of Weber's texts will be utilized.[3]

The Stratification Configuration: The Clan, Magical Spirits, Patrimonial Rulership, and the Literati

In a succinct passage, Weber calls attention to the unusual strength of the clan in China:

> The clan, which in the Western Middle Ages was practically extinct, in China was completely preserved in the administration of the smallest political units

as well as in the operation of economic associations. Moreover, the clan developed to an extent unknown elsewhere, even in India. (1951, p. 86)

The cohesion of the clan, and the prestigeful position of its elders, continued unbroken for thousands of years. Family piety itself, "by far the strongest influence on man's conduct," contributed to the cohesion of the clan and the strength of traditional action (1951, p. 236). Even more important for its extreme durability were ancestral spirits. The attribution of power to them, especially to the spirits of one's own ancestors, comprised the "most fundamental belief of the Chinese people" (1951, p. 87). Their favor could be gained through sacrifices. As a consequence of their strength, the clan overcame numerous threats to its survival by rulership and economic organizations (1951, p. 87).

The clan's "strong counterbalance from below" clashed directly with "patrimonial rule from above" (1951, p. 86). "Patrimonial bureaucracy," China's major form of rulership, constituted a mixture of the bureaucratic and patrimonial forms.

Unlike the modern bureaucracy, a functional differentiation of jurisdictional spheres and offices advanced only to a limited degree. Neither the bureaucracy's conception of organizational structure, as designed to serve the sole purpose of efficiently fulfilling a goal, nor its notion of an officialdom narrowly educated to perform prescribed tasks in a "vocation," took root in China. The administrator under this form of rulership—a specialist who viewed his task as simply a means toward an organizational goal—opposed the ideals of Chinese officialdom. To this proud stratum, education sought to enhance one's cultural level, to refine a person into a "gentleman," and to cultivate a "universal personal self-perfection" rather than to impart professional qualifications and specialized competencies. This particular character of Chinese officialdom, as well as its ideal of social welfare, "accounts for the specifically anti-bureaucratic and patrimonialist tendency of this administration" (1968, p. 1049).

On the other hand, because it rejected personal discretion and status distinctions based on blood descent as means to decide how offices should be filled, China's patrimonialism appeared highly modern. The objective administration of an examination system comprised the single means for the attainment of office:

China was ... that country which had oriented status privileges most exclusively toward a conventional and officially patented literary education; to this extent it was formally the most perfect representative of the modern, pacified, and bureaucratized society whose monopolies of benefices on the one hand and specific status structure on the other rest everywhere on the prestige of patented education. (1968, pp. 1049–1050)

Moreover, as in the modern bureaucracy, the bureaucracy in China, reacting against widespread belief in an irredeemable difference between the noble clans and the people, upheld the principled equality of persons (1951, pp. 43, 146).

This form of legitimate rulership in China accommodated to traditions as well as clan elders and, at the same time, managed to recruit a stratum of officials to serve as administrators. Directly dependent on rulers and serving their interests, this stratum—the classically educated literati, or Mandarins—succeeded in preventing the development of territorial lords and feudal barons independent of the power of the patrimonial ruler (1968, p. 1048). Furthermore, the literati demonstrated charisma not only by correctly performing ceremonial tasks, but also by appeasing restless spirits and ensuring the harmonious course of government (1951, p. 132).

Once entrenched as a cohesive and ruling stratum in the period of nationwide pacification that followed the Warring Kingdom era (475–221BCE), officialdom remained in place even when the charisma and magical powers of particular officials were repudiated by an evil event or natural catastrophe. Similarly, the divine legitimation of a particular emperor might be discredited if a disaster struck; however, as the supreme institution, the imperial power, endowed with magical qualities, was not called into question (1951, p. 143).

The stability of this form of rulership was further ensured by an ancestor cult: Strong premiums were placed on obedience to authority as a consequence of the belief in ancestors—and they became generalized to the ruler. The consequence was clear to Weber: a great docility by patrimonial subjects. The literati, although in principle scornful of magic as contrary to the dignity of an educated person, for their part lent their support to ancestor worship simply because they perceived it to be indispensable "for the undisturbed preservation of bureaucratic rulership" (1951, pp. 142–148, 213, 230).

This particular stratification configuration characterized China for nearly two millennia: Patrimonial rulers and officials stood directly opposite the clan immersed in magic. It distinguished this civilization from the ancient, medieval, and modern West, as well as from India. Moreover, both the values of the clan and patrimonial rulership were penetrated by Confucian values and thereby strengthened. Neither the feudal stratum, which suffered a dramatic loss of status and power with pacification after the Warrior Kingdom epoch, nor civic strata and guilds, which remained small, could establish the independent base of power that would allow these groups to serve as intermediaries between the small peasant on the one hand and rulers and their dependent officials on the other: "Not the organic status group structure, but the patriarchal family provided the dominant image for social stratification. The patrimonial bureaucracy could recognize no other autonomous social force" (1951, p. 143; see also p. 83; 1968, p.1047). In contrasting this configuration with England's, Weber emphasizes that the literati officials in China comprised a stratum dependent on rulers:

> In China the educated administrative officials face the elders of the clans and the guild associations, whereas in England the professionally trained judges face the educated honoratiores of the landowning gentry. The Chinese honoratiores are the educated who have been prepared for an administrative career through a classic-literary training; they are benefice-holders and aspirants to benefices, and therefore on the side of the patrimonial-bureaucratic power; by contrast, in England the core of the gentry was a free status group of large landowners, who were merely empirically trained on the job to rule over retainers and workers and who came to be humanistically educated. Such a stratum did not exist in China, which represents the purest type of patrimonial bureaucracy that is unencumbered (as far as this is possible) by any counterweight and that has not yet been refined into a modern specialized officialdom. (1968, p. 1062)

The Restriction of the Rationalization of Action: The Economy, Religion, and Law Domains

The capacity of the Mandarins and patrimonial rulers to defend their power and legitimate their rulership combined with the extreme strength of clans to block the rationalization of action in the economy, religion, and law domains.

The Clan Economy

Strengthened by the ancestor cult and Confucianism, the clan proved especially effective in determining the boundaries within which economic activity could develop. According to Weber, the "clan economy" constituted the "original Chinese economic organization" (1927, p. 22). In all economic relationships, the clan exercised a ubiquitous influence:

> The clan possesses schools and storehouses within its separate village, maintains the tillage of the fields, takes a hand in matters of inheritance, and is responsible for the misdemeanors of its members. The whole economic existence of the individual rests on his membership in the clan, and the credit of the individual is normally the credit of his clan. (1927, p. 45; see 1968, p. 380)

The clan's traditional economic ethic and orientation to an agrarian economy opposed strictly all thrusts toward a rationalization of action in the economy domain toward modern capitalism. This remained all the more the case as a result of the omnipresence of magic, since innovations were thought to provoke evil spirits. New fiscal practices in particular were believed capable of arousing the anger of magical forces (1951, pp. 95–96). Thus, monetary reform and other attempts to rationalize finance and the money economy repeatedly failed, as did many attempts to implement technological improvements.

In addition, the clan prevented the selection of labor on free market principles and on a competitive basis. The traditional character of this economy was also maintained as a result of the way in which it oriented action to ritualistic considerations, favors and privileges, and the income interests of the Mandarins. The clan also ensured that any surplus funds would be used normally to finance a family member's long period of preparation for his examinations and the subsequent purchase of an office (see below), rather than for reinvestment and profit.

All these factors also tended severely to restrict trade, as well as the formation of capital (1951, pp. 6, 13, 83, 95, 242). While a rudimentary putting-out system, as well as small artisan and merchant classes, did appear, a strong and self-conscious bourgeoisie in possession of an independent base of power failed to crystallize (1951, pp. 97, 136).

The extreme strength of clan piety determined that the cooperative (*Genossenschaft*), based on the extended family, would comprise classical China's fundamental form of economic organization (1951, p. 236). The clan remained so strong that the development from indigenous Chinese roots to impersonal, purposive, and purely functional forms of association and organization—formal rationality—was inhibited. The clan's "personalist principle" tied all economic organizations, including occupational associations, to kinship relations.

The clan's power even prevented the full development of independent guilds along the lines of those that arose prominently in the medieval West (see above, pp. 101–103). Even when living in urban areas, the "new citizen" retained close relations with his native area, clan, and temple, thus maintaining all ritually and personally important relationships (1951, pp. 14, 136–137). For this same reason, cities in the Western sense—an independent "community" endowed with purely instrumental and managerial forms of association and in possession of a charter that guaranteed its self-government "liberties" and functioning as an independent body—never developed beyond a preliminary form in classical China (1951, pp. 14–15). To Weber, "in China the great importance of the ancestral cult and clan exogamy resulted in keeping the individual city dweller in a close relationship with his clan and native village" (1968, p. 482). In the cities "all social action remained engulfed in, and conditioned by, purely personal, above all, kinship relations" (1951, p. 241; see also pp. 96, 236).

Lacking guilds and independent cities, no strong civic and bourgeois class could develop in China to serve as a carrier of economic activity oriented to formal rationality. Consequently, and despite considerable internal and foreign trade, capitalism in classical China remained, according to Weber, "political capitalism" similar to that of late Antiquity, Egypt, and the Islamic world (1951, p. 242).

Religion: Confucianism and Magic

Religion in China never stood in opposition to the dominant stratification configuration or the clan economy. Unlike Puritanism, Confucianism failed to give birth to an economic ethic capable of calling forth patterns of action antagonistic to China's clan-based economy. On the contrary, this religion's emphasis on familial piety as a central value opposed directly that which proved so central for the expansion of formal rationality in the economy sphere: the impersonal consideration of relationships.

Whereas religious duty toward his God compelled the Puritan to assess all human relationships in reference to the Deity's grand design and His expectations, the Confucian fulfilled his religious obligation "within organically given, personal relations." Piety toward "concrete, living or dead persons" comprised his duty, and no psychological premiums were attached to piety either toward an "idea" or toward the fulfillment of functional tasks: "For the 'Dao' was simply the embodiment of binding, *traditional ritual* and not 'action'" (1951, p. 236; emphasis in original).

Furthermore, lacking in Confucianism was an understanding of economic success as testimony to the believer's state of grace. Absent also was the notion of a religiously conditioned—and directed "from within"— methodical organization of life that aimed to alter the given course of affairs—namely, through "world mastery" on behalf of an all-powerful God's commandments. Instead, "adjustment to the world" characterized Confucian ideals. This utilitarian ethos lacked the Protestant ethic's methodical component despite the fact that it combined "sobriety and thriftiness ... with acquisitiveness and regard for wealth" (1951, pp. 243–244, 247–248). Also opposing the introduction of modern forms of economic organization was Confucianism's "gentleman ideal": For the Confucian, persons must not be "tools" and specialized training and vocational work never serve the literati's goal of universal self-perfection.

These basic tenets prevented Confucianism from setting into motion social action that challenged the clan and established a "community of faith" anchored in a congregation's opposition to the "community of blood." Thus, business confidence remained grounded in familial and semi-familial relationships rather than in either the ethical qualities of persons (as demonstrated in impersonal, vocational work) or interest-related calculations (1951, pp. 237, 246).

The religion of nonelites also failed to introduce either action oriented to economic organizations or an economic ethic. Innumerable spirits, the ancestor cult, and "a completely unsystematic pluralism of magical and heroistic cults" (1951, p. 143) characterized the relationship of the vast majority to the supernatural. Both the literati and administrators in the patrimonial bureaucracy, rather than confronting omnipresent magical forces and attempting to transform—on behalf of stability—their "irrationality," accepted this situation. Indeed, in the absence of a priesthood, the management of the diverse cults in possession of deified heroes came to be viewed as an affair of the state.

This task was regarded as important if only because the maintenance of magic, and the ancestor cult in particular, guaranteed obedience. It also allowed the patrimonial bureaucracy to oppose the development of an independent church and a congregational religion—developments that in Europe had led to an enduring tension between hierocratic and patrimonial powers (1951, p. 143; 1968, pp. 476–477). Without resistance—least of all by missionary prophets, as had taken place in ancient Israel—magical forces became ubiquitous. This occurred to such an extent that the rationalization of action oriented to the economy was precluded:

> The dominance of magic . . . is one of the most serious obstructions to the rationalization of economic life. Magic involves a stereotyping of technology and economic relations. When attempts were made in China to inaugurate the building of railroads and factories, a conflict with geomancy ensued. The latter demanded that, in the location of structures on certain mountains, forests, rivers, and cemetery hills, foresight should be exercised in order not to disturb the rest of the spirits. (1927, p. 361)

Magic not only surrounded the emperor and invested him with a "magical dignity," but also overwhelmed the small class of merchants and traders. It did so to such a degree that they failed to become carriers of an ethical religion, as occurred in the medieval West (1968, pp. 484, 1053). An "unbroken unity" of magic and a "purely magical world view" existed in China for centuries, according to Weber (1946b, p. 350).

Patrimonial Law

In light of Chinese patrimonial rulership, the traditional economic ethics of Confucianism and the popular, magic-based religions, the strength of the

clan and the clan economy, and the power of magic to intensify all traditions, a rationalization of action in the law domain and an independent
development of law could not take place. To Weber: "Chinese law shows in
a typical way the interaction of the rulership of patrimonial princes and the
maintenance of the family and kinship groups in their significance as guar-
antors of the individual's social status" (1968, p. 726).

The clan organized economic activities and became established as a local
authority capable, if need be, of standing against imperial rulership. It also
constituted itself as the fundamental juridical unit. Thus, an understanding
of the state as in possession of an authority based on law and independent
of the emperor and the clan could not develop. And neither private corpo-
rations nor voluntary associations could constitute themselves, as a result
of their insufficient autonomy from the clan, as social carriers of an independent body of law.

For the same reason, official law—to the extent that it acknowledged
municipalities at all—viewed them exclusively "as organizations for carrying
the family liability for taxes and charges" (1968, p. 726). Even the orientation of social action to natural law failed to appear: Its basic prerequisite—a
tension between "the world" and philosophical or religious postulates that
led to the idea of a natural, or "original," state of being—could not congeal
owing to the predominant this-world character of Confucianism, the values
of the clan, and patrimonial rulership (1951, p. 149). In view of these forces,
the concept of "juristic personality," which could be found in Western
Antiquity, was not surprisingly absent in China.

Advocacy in the Western sense also never arose. Patrimonialism's office
authority was too weak and secular law was too underdeveloped. Hence, a
stratum of jurists in possession of specialized legal training was not needed.
Consequently, action oriented to legally guaranteed liberties and a notion of
"fundamental freedoms of the individual" was lacking (see 1951, pp. 147–148,
101; 1968, pp. 726, 818). Moreover, Chinese law regarding business organizations remained underdeveloped. The legal ownership of collective property by
private associations, for example, was prohibited (1968, p. 727). Again, the
clan and patrimonialism proved instrumental in preventing a rationalization of
law-oriented action:

> Just as in Antiquity and in the Middle East, this underdeveloped state of the
> Chinese law of private associations and business organizations was caused by
> the continuing significance of the kinship group, within which all economic
> association is taking place, also by the obstruction of autonomous corpora-
> tions by political patrimonialism, and finally by the general reluctance to invest
> capital in anything other than fiscal enterprises and trade. (1968, p. 727)

The Emperor did offer administrative edicts, of course. However, they remained pedagogical in form, enamored by literary erudition, and imprecise as definitions of legal issues. Written by members of the literati, these codes of conduct expressed Confucian orthodoxy (1951, p. 102).

Basically, Weber views Chinese law as upholding age-old substantive notions of justice rather than procedural formalism. The typical Chinese judge exercised discretion to the extent to which a compelling magical aura or tradition did not surround a particular law within the imperial collection of laws and to the degree that local custom bore no direct connection to the given case at hand. In these cases, the judge based decisions on the one hand upon a judgment of the "concrete qualities" of the persons involved and, on the other hand, on the specific situation, rules of equity, and consequences. Unlike Islamism, no sacred book of laws existed.

"Legal" disputes involving property and income, for example, were settled either by reference to practical expediency or a "social-ethical concern for feeding the masses" (1951, p. 148; see also pp. 102, 149): "In the patrimonial state, the typical ramifications of administration and judiciary created a realm of unshakable sacred tradition alongside a realm of prerogative and favoritism" (1951, p. 100). To Weber, "a systematic, substantive, and thorough rationalization [of social action in the domain] of law was never attempted" (1951, p. 150).

He argues frequently that capital investment on a broad scale will not occur wherever a dependable state machinery offering predictability for economic activity is absent. And, lacking a legal framework to ensure regularity, orientations of social action toward the functional economic relations typical of the capitalist enterprise will not develop, Weber contends. Laws concerning private property and bankruptcy were also absent in China. In general, the rational and calculable administration and law enforcement—formal rationality—important as a foundation for the unfolding of industrialization and capitalism never arose in China (1951, pp. 100, 103; 1968, p. 380).

Chinese Rationalism: Limitations on the Rationalization of Action

This reconstruction of Chinese rationalism has been undertaken in reference to and configurations of groups and the societal domains and domain-specific ideal types of E&S. It has revealed that social action in classical China, unlike in the West, became rationalized to only a limited degree.

A universal organization rooted in traditional and affectual action—the clan—remained dominant, and the rulership, economy, religion, and law arenas failed to proceed along rationalization of action axes. Although Confucianism's values implied a specific substantive rationality, it never initiated a rationalization of action in these spheres. On the contrary, because only a strict support of proven magical means restrained the anger of spirits, an inviolable character became attached to the traditional economic ethic, the clan economy, and patrimonial rulership. As Weber notes: "In China, the pervasive factors were tradition, local custom, and the concrete personal favor of the official" (1951, p. 241).

Because it existed in a relationship of symmetry and harmony rather than antagonism, the value-rational patterned action indigenous to patrimonial rulership, the clan, and Confucianism became thoroughly interwoven. These groups strengthened one another in the process. For example, Confucianism emphasized the importance of familial piety, as did patrimonial rulership and the clan (1968, pp. 412, 575). This interlocking of domain-specific patterns of action repeatedly appeared in China.

It created an internally consistent configuration of values that stifled all impulses toward formal rationality in the economy, rulership, and law domains. With regard to China's major religion, Weber notes: "The whole of Confucianism became a relentless canonization of tradition" (1951, p. 164). Concomitantly, popular religious beliefs based in magic, as well as in Confucianism, placed premiums on docility among the masses and obedience to rulers. They also legitimated the social position and high prestige of the literati[4] and prevented the development of both an independent bourgeoisie and politically independent cities capable of facilitating the cultivation of notions of equality and citizenship. The Empire's failure to develop overseas trade and colonies (1951, p. 104), as well as an omnipresent traditional economic ethic and clan-based law, further hindered the unfolding of functional and impersonal capitalist relationships. For all these reasons, Chinese rationalism differed drastically from its modern Western counterpart:

> Only an ethic congruent with bureaucracy could be created, and this was limited solely by consideration of the forces of tradition in the clans and by the belief in spirits. Unlike Western civilization, there were no other specifically modern elements of rationalism standing either in competition with or in support of the bureaucracy. Western culture in China was grafted upon a base which, in the West, had been essentially overcome with the development of the ancient polis. (1951, pp. 151–152)

This configuration of groups, and the conducive contexts they formed for the crystallization of further groups and further contexts, was unique. In Weber's texts, *Chinese rationalism* captures this "characteristic individuality."

Although capitalism and modern capitalism were also obstructed by India's rationalism, each civilization constitutes a singular "mixture" of empirical patterns of action and constellations of groups, according to Weber. The next chapter reconstructs India's "individual constellation" following the same procedures utilized in this chapter: by reference to pivotal groups and configurations of groups specific to this civilization on the one hand and Weber's broad-ranging *E&S* theoretical framework on the other hand. His powerful concepts and procedures capture the uniqueness of both civilizational rationalisms in a precise manner.

Study Questions and Thoughts to Ponder

1. Weber distinguishes strongly between civilizations that originally call forth modern capitalism as opposed to civilizations that adopt, once in motion, modern capitalism. Is this distinction moot in our age of "globalization"?

2. Why does Weber insist on considering, in his analysis of the rise of the West, India and China?

3. Compare Confucianism to Puritanism (see the concluding chapter to Weber's book on China; 1951).

4. Assume China remained basically unchanged for 2,000 years. Following Weber, explain this situation.

5. According to Weber, in China a great deal of "overlapping" of the different life-spheres seems to have occurred. Please explain. Support or criticize this position.

Notes

1. The basic contours of "Classical China" endured for roughly 2,000 years from 100BCE until the Manchu dynasty fell in 1911. This is Weber's time frame rather than China today.

2. As emphasized in the last chapter, this is Weber's theme in his volumes on China and India, as is the investigation of "points of comparison" to the substance and trajectories of Western rationalism and modern Western rationalism. He seeks neither to write a "general history" nor an "economic history" of China (see 1951, p. 80).

Again, Weber is convinced that China can *adopt* capitalism. His query, however, concerns a different question, as noted: Why did China not call forth modern capitalism *earlier* than the West?

3. The reconstruction here draws not only on *The Religion of China* (1951), but also freely on those sections on China in *E&S* and Weber's *General Economic History* (1927). A great deal of synthesizing across these texts has been necessary in order to construct "Chinese rationalism."

4. Weber saw only one "major and permanent" opponent of the literati: sultanism and the eunuch system (1951, pp. 138–139). He views Daoism as a non-mainstream religion that lost out to Confucianism in the struggle to form the Chinese world view (see 1951, pp. 181–194, 202–205).

9

The Sociology of Civilizations III: The Rationalism of India

This chapter parallels the above discussion of China: it reconstructs a civilization's "particular 'rationalism.'" Although both India and China are "civilizations of the East," they diverge radically from one another. In combination with a close scrutiny of empirical patterns of social action and configurations of groups, Weber's broad-ranging concepts and research strategies identify these differences in a precise manner. Here we articulate the contours and direction of Indian rationalism.

As discovered above, classical China remained dominated by arrays of groups that placed patrimonial princes and literati intellectuals in direct opposition to clans deeply permeated by Confucianism and magic. Hence, it remained highly resistant to change. The overwhelming centrality of the caste order in India and its legitimating belief system—Hinduism—distinguished this civilization and obstructed the rationalization of action in the economy, law, and rulership domains. With the orientational assistance of the societal domains and domain-specific ideal types constructed in *E&S*, this civilization's rationalism can be reconstructed.[1]

The Centrality of the Caste
Order, the Brahmins, and Hinduism

Caste in India implied a ritualistic estrangement of groups from each other owing to firm rituals. This occurred to such an extent that *fraternization* and social mobility were prevented. Both constituted preconditions for the creation of significant networks of trade, the efficient organization of labor, the development of merchant cities, and the Western concept of citizenship, Weber holds.

These developments, so significant for the rupture of traditional forms of rulership and the power of the clan in the West, were successfully repelled by the caste order. As India's single institution empowered to legitimate social status and bestow economic advantages (1958, p. 20), the caste system assimilated all opposing social forces. Firmly rooted throughout Indian rationalism in its Middle Age epoch (700–1200CE), the caste order is defined by Weber largely through comparisons and contrasts to guilds.

The guilds of classical India (600BCE–700CE), as well as those in the cities of the medieval West, did not prohibit commensalism on the basis of ritual barriers; castes did so. This distinction was crucial according to Weber: only "factual barriers" separated one stratum from another in the West. Hence, even though the merchant and craft guilds at times opposed one another violently, no "magical distance" based on ritualistic taboos restricted connubium between occupations. In postclassical India (200CE and later), however, ritual and psychological resistances prevented, for example, artisans from different castes and crafts from working together in the same factory (1958, pp. 34–35; 1968, pp. 435–436).

Ritually inviolable principles estranged groups and precluded fraternization. A "deadly jealousy and hostility" resulted "precisely because the castes are completely oriented towards social rank" (1958, p. 38). Moreover, the hereditary nature of caste membership was permanent and supported by religious belief, while the relative degree of closure of the medieval guilds in the West depended on economically fluctuating conditions, Weber maintains. Finally, because the apprentice as a rule freely chose his master in the West, children could seek training in occupations other than those of their parents— and hence fraternization across guilds could occur in the West. An active "citizenry" capable of—legally or illegally—acting as a political force independent of the nobility eventually arose in the West from such fraternization (1958, p. 35; see chapter 7).

Once it became entrenched in India's Middle Age era, the capacity of the caste system to diffuse opposition to it became unlimited.[2] Rather than admit new social groups into an open arena free from ritual barriers, India's rationalism instead, dominated by castes and the common acceptance of them, simply created new castes or sub-castes that eventually co-opted groups originally formed in opposition to the caste system. Because legitimacy, social rank, and economic advantages could be established only from recognition as a caste, new groups actively sought a position *within* the caste order.

The caste system planted deep and firm roots in India and played a central part in its group constellations. These roots rested mainly on two pillars: the unequivocal support given to caste rigidity by a status group—the Brahmins—and by Hinduism.

The birth and endurance of the caste system would have been inconceivable without the pervasive influence of the Brahmins, a cohesive stratum (see 1958, pp. 130–131). These religious intellectuals and priests constituted the earliest caste and the social carriers of Hinduism, as well as Indian culture as a whole. Endowed with a charisma based on their training in, and sacred knowledge of, the ancient Vedic scriptures, they served as indispensable house priests, confessors, teachers, and spiritual advisors for all life's dilemmas.

In possession of a monopoly on all educational processes, only the Brahmins could offer instruction in the sacred formulae and magical practices that instilled charismatic and secret powers. Success in battle or in life depended on the correct performance of ritual; its violation accounted for failures, Weber sees. Originally sorcerers, holy singers, and the schooled sons of the military classes, this elite stratum of intellectuals and priests constituted the sole caste whose members could write (1958, pp. 61, 130, 140; 1968, pp. 427; 502). By the 6th century BCE the Brahmins had consolidated their powers as the possessors of spiritual authority and achieved the undisputed capacity to define, for recognition as a Brahmin, the educational prerequisites. Henceforth, they were properly defined as a caste rather than as a status group of cultivated intellectuals.

However, the position and power of a strong status group could not alone establish the caste system and ensure its long-term endurance, Weber insists. Its acceptance depended in particular on the existence of a legitimating belief system. Hinduism fulfilled this task. The two key teachings and "dogmatic doctrines" that formed this religion's substantive rationality— the *karma* doctrine of ethical compensation and the *samsara* belief in the transmigration of souls—placed strong and direct premiums on action that upheld the caste order.

According to the *karma* doctrine, eternal and automatically functioning processes keep full account of the acts of all individuals. No ethically relevant act can ever escape from this comprehensive and "universal mechanism of retribution," and each such act signifies distinct as well as unfailing consequences for the believer's destiny. The *samsara* doctrine asserts that the soul is forever subject to rebirth, and that guilt and merit in the world unfailingly determine a person's fate in all successive lives. Sickness and misfortune, for example, according to the doctrine of *karma* compensation, result solely from incorrect action in a prior life (1968, pp. 524–525, 553).

As a result of these doctrines, pious Hindus were perpetually engaged in a process of weighing merit or failings to assess their fate. The future lives of the soul, they knew, would be inevitably reincarnated into diverse animal, human, or even divine forms "in exact proportion to the surplus on one or the other side of the ledger." Rebirth into animal forms or into despised castes indicated simply atonement for offences in a previous existence. Those born into high castes were universally believed to have been compensated for living virtuously in their past lives (see 1968, p. 525). To Weber: "All salvation religions of Hinduism addressed one common question: how can persons escape from the wheel of rebirth and thereby ever new death? How is salvation possible from eternally new death and therefore salvation from life" (1958, p. 133)?

In the strict form they assumed in classical times, these doctrines admitted of no inner-worldly ritual deities or magical means that might allow escape from the eternal sequence of death, rebirth, and ethical compensation. Since persons determined their own futures, Hindus developed an accentuated awareness of caste-based responsibilities and learned to avoid violation of them. How did classical Hinduism in its historically most significant form—lay Hinduism—support the caste system?

Viewed in terms of its practical ethic, lay Hinduism placed psychological premiums with the weight of an ethical obligation on adherence to the caste system *as a whole*. This demarcation of ethical orientations meant that, within the separate castes, a vacuum existed within which caste-specific *ritualism* expanded unhindered. According to Weber, ritualistic rights, responsibilities, and duties according to caste, or *dharma*, constitute the "decisive criterion of Hinduism" (1958, p. 24; translation altered).

The everyday *dharma* of a caste was based on sacred tradition and mediated through the "literary and rationally developed learning of the Brahmins" (1958, p. 25).[3] If a Brahmin, his earthly tasks remained confined to learning the Vedas and otherwise following the correct ritual of his caste. Members of other major castes—the Kshatriya (warrior), Vaishya (merchant), and Shudra (craftsmen and workers) castes—also knew that the upholding of their traditional *dharmas* was most highly valued. They were also aware that an attitude of reserve and detachment from this-world must be cultivated.

The lay Hindu in classical times could discover no motive for a positive evaluation of earthly action except as related to *dharma*, Weber contends. Only those who practiced exemplary habits, were loyal to their caste by strictly adhering to caste *dharma*, supported prescribed traditions, and renounced all yearning to ascend in this life to membership in a better caste could hope for attainment of the salvation goal reserved for the laity: a fortunate rebirth. This held true for princes, warriors, judges, artisans, and peasants, as well as intellectuals, kings, robbers, and thieves, Weber notes. For these devout, distant from the virtuoso Brahmins, and knowing nothing of either escape from caste or salvation in this life, caste *dharma* alone mattered. Fulfillment of this ritualistic salvation path constituted the single means to acquire psychological assurance that death would involve a favorable reincarnation (1958, p. 326).

Even while acknowledging the unequal distribution of charismatic religious qualifications and institutionalizing them into castes, this "organic pragmatism" (*Heilspragmatik*) refused to permit the existence of unequal salvation chances, Weber holds. This remained the case even though equal opportunity could become a reality, for the vast majority of Hindus, only with rebirth (see 1946b, p. 338; 1958, pp. 144, 174–175; 1968, pp. 598–599). Moreover, since the "organic social ethic" graduated all religious demands to conform to varying religious qualifications, the expectations Hinduism placed on individuals never exceeded their capacity to fulfill them.[4]

Weber sees that the predominance of caste-specific *dharma* resulted in a fragmentation of Indian rationalism rather than the development of a caste-transcendent, ethical universalism capable of serving as a basis for intercaste fraternization. As the *karma* and *samsara* doctrines became firmly rooted, a perfect harmony between religious doctrine and caste particularism arose.

The influence of the entrenched caste order spread into the status, economy, religion, law, and rulership domains. Hence, it remained pivotal to Indian rationalism, Weber maintains. Although, due to a relative weakening of the clan, a certain potential crystallized for the development of viable cities and thus for an expansion of practical rationality in the economy domain, the caste order stood effectively against all impulses in this direction. It also restricted, as will become evident, all potential developments in opposition to the natural economy and to the traditional forms of law and rulership.

The Restriction of City Development

To some degree, as noted, the caste order succeeded in weakening the clan. Moreover, ascetic virtuosi, or *sramana*, who practiced asceticism and contemplation as means for the attainment of salvation, existed throughout India. Great prestige was awarded to these charismatic holy men if only because their feats of discipline were believed possible exclusively as a result of their possession of magical powers. This prestige also weakened familial bonds of piety and the sib group in general. Similar developments never took place in China:

> It is one of the most important and extraordinary of phenomena that the holy seeking of the *sramana* succeeded in breaking through the magical sib bonds of ancestor worship. This is to be explained only by one circumstance: that no one doubted the magical powers which the ascetic possessed. In India, and this is the most important contrast to China, the prestige of the sramanistic magical charisma outweighs the duties of piety to the family. (1958, p. 174)

Weber understood the weakening of sib bonds generally as of enormous significance. This development provided a strong precondition for the unfolding of cities and the expansion of practical and formal rationality in the economy, law, and rulership domains on the one hand and for the possibility of citizenship on the other hand. Nonetheless, city *communes* failed to arise in India. Instead, the strength of the caste order combined with the continued power of familial ties to hinder the development of the city in the Western sense—namely, as a polis or commune with an armed population and an organized citizenry that opposed the estrangement of groups from one another and facilitated open fraternization (1958, pp. 13–14; see chapter 7).

In this respect, the historical consequences of the suppression of the guilds by the Kshatriya nobles and the Brahmins in the late classical period could not be underestimated, according to Weber. With their subjugation, the possibility for the development in cities of a solidary, independent, and politically organized citizenry, as well as artisan and bourgeoisie classes, to oppose the kings was eliminated. And the subsequent unhindered unfolding of the caste order and the steady growth of rulership in patrimonial bureaucracies headed by kings and princes precluded the extension of a politically cohesive fraternization across a broad cross-section of the citizenry. Hence, royal officials and Brahmins increasingly monopolized administrative powers. All this increased the strength of castes. Weber stresses the great historical significance of the displacement of the ancient guilds in India by a caste order:

> The uniqueness of the development of India lay in the fact that these beginnings of guild organization in the cities led neither to the city autonomy of the Western type nor, after the development of the great patrimonial states, to a social and economic organization of the territories corresponding to the "territorial economy" of the West. Rather, the Hindu caste system, whose beginnings certainly preceded these organizations, became paramount. In part, this caste system entirely displaced the other organizations; in part, it crippled them; it prevented them from attaining any considerable importance. (1958, pp. 33–34)

Thus, although urban industry, craft guilds, and guild confederations remained visible, they failed to launch the development of autonomous cities. Rather, racial and ethnic segregation, and then caste-specific and ritually inviolable *dharma*, became paramount and blocked the unfolding of a Western-style city commune (1958, pp. 36–39, 128; 1968, pp. 1229, 1260). Taboos, magical barriers, and caste ritual prevented intergroup association, even more so than in China:

> In India ... the endogamous and exclusive caste with its taboos ... has prevented any kind of fusion of city dwellers into an association of burghers [citizens] based on religion and secular equality before law, connubium, commensality, and solidarity against non-members. Because of taboo-protected caste closure, this applies to India even more than to China. (1968, p. 1241)

In those settlements in India which approximated cities "only clan associations and sometimes also occupational associations were vehicles of organized action, but never a collective of urban citizens as such" (1968, p. 1233; see also, e.g., p. 1248; 1958, pp. 337–338). In addition, the flowering of Buddhism in the classical period, due to its absolute pacifism as well as the newly generated caste system, prevented a broad-based expansion of "citizen" military power. A fragmentation of the culture of India according to rituals for each vocation and ethnic group resulted.

Hence, a development in the direction of a caste-transcendent ethical universalism capable of serving as legitimation for intercaste fraternization could not spread widely. For the same reasons, cities similar to the inland industrial cities of the West could not unfold. Similarly, carrier groups for the rationalization of action in the rulership, economy, and law domains remained absent.

The Economy: Traditional Economic Forms and the Traditional "Spirit" of the Caste Order

The triumph of the Brahmin-Kshatriya coalition and Hinduism eventually led to the entrenchment of the caste system. Although great potential for change appeared as a result of economic development in the classical period, the unshakeability of the caste system eventually ensured the suppression of all those tendencies that pointed away from traditional, agrarian economies.

Weber notes that the pluralistic competition in the classical era among traders, nobles, and Brahmins for political and social superiority yielded heretofore unknown social privileges for the trader class. It also largely accounted for the creation of social egalitarianism. This milieu offered the opportunity to wield political authority to *all* peoples, even the lowly Shudra class of craftsmen and workers without rights to own property. More wealthy artisans could often socialize with the nobles, and city elders and Brahmins frequently advised the princes (1958, p. 88). Indeed, during the period of the burgeoning growth of the cities in the 7th and 6th centuries BCE, Weber describes the merchant and craft guilds of India as differing little from the guilds in the cities of the medieval West. However, largely due to their lack of an independent military organization and their sole dependence on financial resources, the potential power of the guilds in India remained limited (1958, p. 33).

Only the princes maintained a disciplined army. However, this situation could not last, Weber holds. As their reigns evolved into powerful patrimonial bureaucracies, their financial dependence on urban traders became less and less acceptable. The steady accumulation of power by the princes over the guilds became assured as soon as they devised an alternative means of monetary support for their administrations: the "substitutions of tax liturgies for capitalistic tax farming" and the reliance "upon rural organizations as sources for armies and taxes" (1958, pp. 128, 130). This occurred as well because the Brahmins' formulation of the *karma* doctrine of compensation, as well as their successful extension of the caste order, served to tame the citizenry.

The slow aggrandizement of the caste system placed a heavy damper on industrial development. Members of different castes, for example, could not be employed on the same shop floor, if only owing to the fact that intercaste contact (as would occur, for example, with the sharing of a water jug), was strictly prohibited. As well, because artisans from different castes could not work together, the production of commodities was precluded. The same barriers to commensalism, many of which were stereotyped and rigidified by magic and ritual, prevented the open social and economic contact necessary for the development of competition, selection according to capabilities, free trade, and social mobility (1958, pp. 111; 1968, p. 484).

The caste system also effectively blocked the introduction of technology simply because the employment of new procedures unregulated by caste ritual necessarily signified the danger of impurity and ritual degradation—and thus demotion into a lower caste (1927, p. 361). The same held for every change of occupation (see 1958, pp. 112–113; 1968, p. 436). Such a system, Weber argues, "is certainly not capable of giving birth to economic and technological revolutions endogenously, or even of facilitating the first germination of capitalism in its midst" (1958, p. 112; transl. alt.), let alone the systematic organization of work.

To him, the "spirit" of the caste system—that is, its traditional economic ethic—constituted the "core of the obstruction" to the development of modern capitalism in India (1958, p. 112). This "economic traditionalism" became visible blatantly in the caste system's glorification of the craftsmanship spirit—namely, its capacity to "enjoin pride . . . in the personal virtuosity of the producer as manifested in the beauty and worth of the product appropriate to his particular caste" (1968, p. 436). This ethic placed a far greater emphasis on the quality and perfection of the product than on possibilities to rationalize production methods or to "systematically [organize] a commercial enterprise along the lines of a rational business economy, which is the foundation of modern capitalism" (1968, p. 436; see also 1958, p. 111).

The caste order also severely restricted trade and the crystallization of a bourgeois class. The preservation of the clan-based economy and interethnic specialization was ensured as long as peasant villages and princely castles remained trade centers rather than cities and urban markets (1958, pp. 126–127). Without viable cities, the introduction of standardized coinage and monetary policies was precluded, as was a systematization of finance in the direction of formal rationality. Moreover, travelers were widely believed to have broken their caste *dharma*. This suspicion became transferred to traders and strengthened by general ritual beliefs that opposed geographical and occupational mobility, as well as by clear-cut restrictions against active trading with impure "barbarians" (1958, pp. 129, 341).

With the entrenchment of the caste order, economic conditions became stabilized. The success of any surviving freely mobile merchants now depended on their conformity to longstanding ritual practices. Accordingly, vocational associations became closed castes ordered by a Brahmin-prescribed ritual: "Individual acceptance for apprenticeship, participation in market deals . . . —these phenomena of the West either failed to develop in the first place or were crushed under the weight first of ethnic, later of caste fetters" (1958, p. 131).

Even the influx in the Indian Middle Ages of Greek, Roman, and Jewish merchants, and the granting of trading privileges to them, failed to counter the stereotypization of economic activity by castes and the view that occupational mobility violated important ritual. This same ritual stereotypization segregated occupations and further blocked the formation of a bourgeois class (1927, pp. 344–345; 1958, p. 103; 1968, p. 1229). According to Weber, the caste system is "completely traditionalistic and anti-rational in its effects" (1958, p. 111).

Capitalism arose in India only in its nonrational forms: as adventure capitalism, as capitalism on behalf of trade speculation or the financing of wars, and money-lending capitalism. Only "occasional economic activity of an irrational character" emerged rather than a "rational system of labor organization"

(1927, p. 334). To Weber, a traditional economic ethic anchored in magic and ritual constituted the strongest force against innovation.

Religion: The Traditional Economic Ethic of Hinduism and the Caste Order

Weber's investigation of the economic ethic of Hinduism in its elite and lay manifestations yielded no consistent patterned action. In combination with a constellation of groups, only such action was endowed with the potential to threaten the caste-based, traditional economic ethic at the core of India's rationalism. Even his detailed analysis of Hinduism's alterations—as it became transformed from a religion of virtuosi and intellectuals into one adapted to "mass religious needs"—failed to discover psychological premiums for action oriented to the economy and opposed to a traditional economic ethic.

To Weber, the economic ethics of Hinduism can be captured mainly by focusing on (a) the consequences for action of the "virtuoso" Brahmin's mystical salvation quest directed "away from the world" and (b) the purely ritual search for redemption pursued by the overwhelming majority of Hindus through "caste ethics." Such a discussion will answer whether this world religion placed psychological rewards on mundane ethical action, whether it did so in a methodical fashion, and whether, in particular, it placed incentives systematically on action oriented to the economy.

Because the virtuoso Brahmin devalued activity and sought to withdraw from it through methodical meditation, his salvation-striving never introduced an economic ethic. All activity, relationships, and attempts to change the world on behalf of values drew the mystic inexorably into the *karma* chain of insufferable rebirth; thus they led away from redemption. All such endeavors interfered profoundly with his aim of silencing the inner drives and extricating himself from worldly concerns: submersion into the All-One in an irrational ecstasy of unity could occur *only* if this virtuoso "turned away" from and "fled" the world. An elevated indifference to the world and a cultivation of an inner distance from all things worldly became central values to the same degree that systematic contemplation acquired acceptance as the classical route to salvation.

> The devaluation of the world, which each salvation religion brought with it, could here only become absolute flight from the world. Its highest means could be nothing other than mystic contemplation, not active ascetic conduct. . . . It would occur to no Hindu to see in the course of his economic professional

integrity the signs of his state of grace or—what is more important—to evaluate and undertake the rational constitution of the world according to empirical principles as a realization of God's will. (1958, p. 326)

Similarly, Weber argued that the attempts to escape from the eternal cycle of rebirth and death carried out by the redeemers and gurus of Hinduism's Restoration (*ca.* 300–800CE), whether more meditative or orgiastic-ecstatic, also failed to place psychological incentives on practical or economy-oriented action of any sort (1968, p. 630).

Wherever the sacred values and the redemptory means of virtuoso religion bore a contemplative or orgiastic-ecstatic character, there has been no bridge between religion and the practical action of the workaday world. In such cases, the economy and all other action in the world has been considered religiously inferior, and no psychological motives for world action could be derived from the attitude cherished as the supreme value. (1946c, p. 289)

Only the "ignorant" participated in trade, money-lending, or profitable pursuits of any form, since all were judged as activities devoid of relevance for salvation. Prevented by rigid ritual from using their learning on behalf of a vocation, the "knowing" person's activities instead involved teaching, sacrifice, and flight from the world through meditation. Furthermore, like members of all other castes, virtuosi Brahmins took pains to follow strictly their caste *dharma*. However, for them, doing so could not lead to salvation from endless reincarnation.

Conversely, for the laity adherence to caste ritual alone promised attainment of their salvation goal: rebirth into a higher caste. *Dharma*, the violation of which defined the only Hindu notions of "sin" and "evil," instructed lay believers in a comprehensive manner that regimented "from without"—to a degree scarcely conceivable to Westerners lives (1968, p. 530). It constituted their religiously sanctioned practical ethics. Nonetheless, the acknowledgment of ritual obedience as the exclusive means toward atonement itself ensured that actions awarded with psychological rewards would remain rigidly traditional and oriented to longstanding conventions and customs (1958, p. 337; 1968, p. 561).[5]

A small segment of each caste's practical ethics pertained to economic action, either directly or indirectly, Weber holds. However, to him this ritual bestowed premiums on either means-end rational action or rigidly traditional action rather than on either an Indian "spirit of capitalism" or action that aimed ethically to transform the world in a methodical fashion to conform to divine commandments. That both the virtuoso and lay Hindu "accepted this world as eternally given, and so the best of all possible worlds" (1968, p. 629), provided the most fundamental doctrinal presupposition for Hinduism's "organic, traditionalistic ethic of vocation, similar in structure to medieval Catholicism's, only more consistent" (1968, p. 599). Of greatest interest to Weber was the manner in which the artisan's traditional economic ethic "was necessarily heightened to the extreme by the caste order" (1958, p. 112) and by the religious legitimation it received from the *karma* and *samsara* doctrines.[6]

To the degree that they existed as different castes, particular crafts generally received a religious consecration. This constituted an acknowledgment of them as sacred vocations and convinced members that a special mission ordained by gods had been assigned to them (1968, pp. 436, 598). This confirmation by Hinduism integrated the devout thoroughly into a network of unquestioned ritual; it also instilled hope, owing to their beliefs in the transmigration of souls, that they might be reborn into a more elevated caste—but only if they faithfully executed their *dharma* (1968, p. 436). According to Weber, precisely this religious promise and mode of redemption had the effect of binding vocations in the most secure manner to caste and to existing stratification structures (1968, pp. 516, 599–560):

> The caste system tends to perpetuate a specialization of labor of the handicraft type, if not by positive prescription, then as a consequence of its general spirit and presuppositions. . . . Each caste nourishes its feeling of worth by its technically expert execution of its assigned vocation. (1968, p. 436; see p. 629)

Thus, far removed from lay Hinduism's economic ethic were ethical rewards on behalf of "economic rationalism," particularly of the type found in ascetic Protestantism. Without such incentives, even the extreme evaluation of riches and money in India, as in China, proved incapable of introducing a rational economic ethic (1968, p. 630):

> The unrestricted lust for gain of the Asiatics . . . is notoriously unequalled in the rest of the world. However, it is precisely a "drive for gain" pursued with every possible means including universal magic. It was lacking in precisely that which was decisive for the economics of the West: the displacement and rational immersion of the drive character of economic striving . . . in a system of rational, inner-worldly ethic of action. (1958, p. 337; transl. alt.)

The Puritan notion of a "calling," which involved a systematically rationalized fulfillment of vocational responsibility, contrasted "in principle" with "diametrically opposed . . . Hinduism's strongly traditionalistic concept of vocation," as it did, in other ways, with Confucianism (1968, p. 630).

Whether lay or virtuoso, the Hindu could never *guarantee his salvation* from the endless wheel of *karma* rebirth and compensation by methodical-ethical action in the world, economic or otherwise. And *signs* of his state of grace could not be derived, as occurred for the Puritan believer, from the integrity and success of his economic activity (1958, p. 326).

In sum, classical Brahminism, the popular sects in Restoration Hinduism, and the caste ethic adhered to by the vast majority of Hindus all failed to assign subjective meaning to a kind of action capable of rupturing ritual and magic. Nor could these groups introduce the methodical economic ethic identified by Weber as the spirit of capitalism.[7] Distinctly traditional orientations to law and rulership further characterized the rationalism of India.

Traditional Types of Rulership and Law

Although a vacillation between decentralized feudalism and centralized patrimonial rulership characterized much of the history of India, great kings and their officials gradually prevailed, beginning with the Maurya dynasty (300–200BCE), over innumerable petty kingdoms. They shattered the monopoly on offices held by the feudal knighthood. Indeed, the patrimonial monarchs slowly freed themselves from dependence on any single stratum, utilizing Brahmins and Shudras alike as scribes and bestowing a diverse blend of prebends and tax prebendaries throughout the population. They controlled the guilds as well, and the armed forces became transformed from people's militias and bands of knightly crusaders into a disciplined and organized military force staffed by officers. Moreover, tax collection became rationalized and clerical techniques became customary throughout the varied aspects of political administration. The village scribe became an "official" and an important authority in this "patrimonial bureaucracy" (1958, pp. 71–75).

> Kingly administration became patrimonial and bureaucratic. On the one hand, it developed a regulated hierarchical order of officials with local and functional competencies and appeals; on the other hand, however, administrative and court offices were not kept separate and jurisdictional spheres of a bewildering manifold of offices were fluid, indeterminate, irrational, and subject to chance influences. (1958, p. 67)

Thus, patterned action in Indian rationalism in the end failed to become oriented to a rational-legal rulership in which bureaucratic organizations prevailed. Similarly, the legal sphere never developed beyond traditional forms of law. Whereas secularization in the West placed sacred law in opposition to natural law, in India religious and ritualistic prescriptions remained all-encompassing, thus precluding a differentiation of the legal domain and the establishment of secular rules (1958, pp. 144–152). Rather, the law aimed to serve holy ends.

Even though officials appeared in India, a stratum of trained jurists or legal *honoratiores* never crystallized indigenously. The unity of the secular and religious administration of justice prohibited such a development. Unlike the West, a priesthood never stood independent and strong against the state in India. On the contrary, the Kshatriya rulers, their house priests, members of their courts, and Brahmin priests remained mutually dependent on one another. Indeed, the latter atoned for a wrong judgment—given by the king but only after consultation with his house priest—through fasting (see 1968, pp. 791–792, 810–811).

Not surprisingly, and despite long periods characterized by an absence of strong central authorities and thus the development of autonomous mercantile, occupational, and agricultural communities, procedural formalism never gained a foothold (1968, p. 727). An approximation of trial law developed in the guilds, but only in the most rudimentary sense. Because the town dweller in India was legally a member of a caste, the notion of a "citizen" in possession of autonomous rights could not appear (1968, pp. 1227–1228). Only status *dharma* was acknowledged: "The rights and duties of kings and other castes to themselves and to others" (1958, p. 145).

Hinduism's sacred books, the Vedas, contain "revelations" rather than "law," and the Dharma-Sutras and Dharma-Shastras, as compendia of dogmatics, ritual ethics, and legal teaching, constitute the authoritative source books for philosophers and legal scholars rather than documents utilized in legal practice (1968, p. 791). For this reason, legal erudition remained for the most part scholastic, theoretical, and systematizing; moreover, it was bound to sacred teachings rather than to the practice of law. Furthermore, as a consequence of the prevalent dogmatic objectives and the sheer centrality of caste throughout India, systematization carried out by priests as legal theorists exclusively concerned "the position of status groups and the practical problems of life" (1968, p. 792), as well as social convention and etiquette, rather than legal issues. As a result of all these factors, logical-formal law and formal rationality in the law domain—let alone natural law—could not unfold:

> The consequence is a casuistic treatment of the legal data that lacks definiteness and concreteness, thus remaining juridically informal and but moderately rational in its systematization. For in all these cases, the driving force is neither the practicing lawyer's businesslike concern with concrete data and needs, nor

the logical ambitions of the jurisprudential doctrinaire only interested in the demands of dogmatic logic, but is rather a set of those substantive ends and aims which are foreign to the law as such. (1968, p. 792)

Lawfinding in India represented that same characteristic intermixture of magical and rational elements which corresponds to both the peculiar kind of the religion and the theocratic-patriarchal regulation of life. The formalism of procedure was on the whole rather slight. (1968, p. 817)

The Rationalism of India:
The Endurance of Organic Traditionalism

The "particular 'rationalism'" of India has been reconstructed by reference to Weber's societal domains and domain-specific ideal types on the one hand and a close scrutiny of patterns of action distinct to India's history on the other hand. Above all, the combination of the caste system and its legitimating belief system—Hinduism—established insurmountable obstacles to the rationalization of action in the law, rulership, and economy spheres. Its *karma* and *samsara* doctrines called forth substantive rationalities in the religion arena, yet failed to place into motion a thrust toward formal rationality in the economy, law, and rulership realms. These realms rarely supported capitalism, and could not drive its transformation into modern capitalism.

The fusion of the caste order with a religion that upheld castes as eternal had a clear effect in India: support congealed for broad-ranging patterns of traditional action, all of which stood firmly in opposition to the rationalization of action and the growth of capitalism. Moreover, the predominance of caste-specific *dharma* resulted in a fragmentation regarding ritual for each vocation rather than the development of a caste-transcendent ethical universalism empowered to legitimate for intercaste fraternization. Hinduism's *karma* and *samsara* doctrines not only placed individuals into the caste order, but also, as a consequence of its eternal and closed character, deprived them of resentment—as well as the possibility of formulating an ethic of social revolution: "The existing order of the world was provided with an absolutely unconditional justification in terms of the mechanical operation of a proportional retribution in the distribution of power and happiness to individuals on the basis of their merits and failures in their earlier existences" (1968, p. 629).

To Weber, this "organic ethic of society" constitutes "an eminently conservative power . . . hostile to revolution" (1946b, p. 340). Only acceptance of caste status legitimated one's social and economic situation, whether high or low (1958, pp. 122–123, 1968, pp. 436–437, 493, 598–599). He discovered the diametrical opposite of Puritanism in Hinduism: "the firmest conceivable justification through religion of traditionalism" (2011, p. 265).

Once a juxtaposition of the caste order with Hindu religious beliefs had become securely established with the Hindu Restoration, all protests were successfully repelled. This remained the case regardless of the form they took. Some were led by the heterodox religious sects (see 1958, pp. 19–21), others by leaders possessing great charismatic powers (see 1958, p. 54),[8] and still others by those who introduced trade onto Indian soil (see 1958, pp. 54, 103). Overwhelmed by the enormous assimilative powers of the caste order, none of these groups posed a serious threat to this system. Securely entrenched, the caste system absorbed all protests and the Brahmins rewarded assimilation by bestowing legitimate social rank. Whether emanating from within or from without, patterned action never escaped the ubiquitous powers of the Brahmins and caste ranking (see 1958, p. 125).

The caste order, the Brahmin stratum, and Hinduism stood at the very center of India's "organic traditionalism" and prevented the rationalization of action in the rulership, law, and economy domains. Although the rationalism of India distinctly diverged from Chinese rationalism, both civilizations massively upheld traditional patterns of action. Moreover, both called forth arrays of groups that became formulated into configurations of groups in opposition to the growth of capitalism, as well as to the introduction of modern capitalism.

We have now concluded our discussions of the multiple groups that, according to Weber, comprised Western rationalism, modern Western rationalism, Chinese rationalism, and the rationalism of India. Each rationalism has been seen to be unique. Each constitutes a foundational building block in his sociology of civilizations.

Weber's concepts and research strategies can be utilized by sociologists today seeking to identify the major contours of a civilization's rationalism. His distinct mode of analysis unlocks central and distinguishing aspects of a civilization. What constellations of groups, he queries, comprise a civilization's "particular 'rationalism'"? How do they stand in relationship to capitalism and modern capitalism? Weber's approach opposes all linear, presentist, functional, narrative, and monocausal methodologies, as well as—as too diffuse and nonempirical—all evolutionary, differentiation, and universalization developmental schools.

His empirical, multidimensional, and interpretive sociology has yielded one immediately evident lesson: great variation exists across the civilizational rationalisms investigated here. The extent to which the rise and development of capitalism and modern capitalism is supported or opposed by configurations of indigenous groups diverges across civilizations significantly, Weber holds. By demarcating a specific rationalism, his constructs and rigorous mode of research "locate" a civilization in reference to this major theme. He teaches, in other words, that a civilization's construction of configurations of groups that facilitate or oppose capitalism and modern capitalism can be understood *only* by reference to his key multicausal and multidimensional concept: its rationalism.

This heuristic tool captures a civilization's complex contours and the "direction" of its development. Furthermore, as is now apparent, it articulates *arrays* of patterned action and their crystallization into cohesive groups and configurations of groups. These configurations then form delimited social contexts that facilitate or obstruct the manifestation of new groups—and eventually, when in combinations, facilitate or obstruct the development of capitalism and modern capitalism. Hence, any attempt to define a civilization alone by reference to the dominance of a particular arena (for example, the economy) or powerful status group (for example, intellectuals or the bureaucracy's functionaries) is rejected forcefully by Weber as too linear and monocausal.

The research procedures at the core of his ambitious cross-civilizational project directly assist fulfillment of his major aim: to offer a *causal* analysis of the West's particular contours and pathway of development. How do the multiple groups that comprise a civilization's rationalism inhibit or facilitate developments supportive of capitalism and modern capitalism? As is often asked today: how do *some* civilizations "take off"? What *sustains* those that remain dynamic over centuries? Weber sought, through interpretive, empirical, multicausal, and context-oriented procedures rooted in groups and configurations of groups, to provide explanations for the singular "rationalism" of each civilization he investigated, as well as for its developmental trajectory.

Further aspects of his systematic mode of analysis prove powerful in respect to his agenda. The influence of the past—and even the long term past—must be always recognized, he emphasizes, as well as the impact of groups oriented to religious beliefs. Furthermore, rather than oriented to "society," his procedures acknowledge and explore at the outset groups "located" within central life-spheres and developments within each arena. Finally, Weber stresses repeatedly how arrays of groups become aligned into configurations of groups. How then, he queries, do these configurations set boundaries that facilitate or obstruct the formation and expansion of new groups?

That is, as noted, these configurations formulate *contexts*—and *deep contexts*—that embed new patterns of action. They may influence the formation and substance of new groups and provide vitality to them. Again, if to appear, capitalism and modern capitalism require facilitating contexts, Weber insists: configurations of powerful carrier groups coalescing in ways *supportive* of the birth and growth of capitalism and modern capitalism. On the other hand, powerful carrier groups that place *barriers* against capitalism and modern capitalism also congeal regularly in all civilizations. Economic and political interests and the sheer power of groups and their carriers often come to the forefront. The *Weberian* mode of analysis implies a broad multicausality, empirical research, and a series of delineated constructs and procedures.

As we have seen, his investigations articulate in great detail the rationalisms of China and India. These studies, alike anchored in Weber's concepts and rigorous modes of research, isolate the uniqueness of Western rationalism and modern Western rationalism in illuminating and significant ways. For Weber, however, the widely held notion that the rationalisms of China and India serve exclusively to articulate "contrast cases" to the West omits too much. These constructs *also* demonstrate the capacity of Weber's sociology of civilizations to conceptualize the diverse ways in which a civilization's rationalism *may* be constructed and *may* develop. Indeed, his notion of a civilization's rationalism articulates a forceful manner of analyzing the multiple ways in which civilizations East and West create singular subjective meaning patterns.

Weber's approach to the study of civilizations constitutes only one example of the way in which his sociology oriented to a multicausal mode of analysis, multiple groups and their configurations, context-oriented procedures, societal domains, and ideal type models can be employed today. His now familiar constructs and research strategies provide clear guidelines for a wide variety of subjective meaning-based macro research projects. Only one example can be offered here. It indicates further the utility and range of Weber's concepts and procedures: his analysis of the singularity of the American political culture's manner of giving birth to a civic sphere and to innumerable civic associations. This is the focus of the following chapter.

Study Questions and Thoughts to Ponder

1. Weber calls Hinduism an "organic ethic of society." Please explain.

2. Weber sees in India "an extreme evaluation of riches and money." Why then was this civilization not the birthplace of a modern economic ethic?

3. The necessity of fulfilling the *dharma* of one's caste proved central to Hinduism. How does this notion relate to a positive or negative evaluation of social mobility?

4. "If the caste system had not been legitimized by Hinduism, it would have died out quickly." Debate this statement pro or con.

5. Discuss patrimonial rulership in India and its relationship to the caste system.

6. "If charismatic missionary prophets had appeared forcefully in India, the caste system would have collapsed quickly." Take a position on this statement.

7. How and why were cities in India different from the cities of the Western Middle Age?

8. "If India had developed Western cities, its developmental trajectory would have become similar to that of the West." Debate this statement.

9. "China and India did not develop modern capitalism earlier than the West for basically similar reasons." Debate this statement.

10. How can the cities of China be distinguished from the cities of India? Or were they similar?

11. The uniqueness of a civilization can be clearly defined, according to Weber, only after rigorous cross-civilizational comparisons. Do you agree with Weber?

12. Weber contends that each civilization calls forth unique patterns of subjective meaning. Debate the accuracy of this presupposition.

13. Is a multicausal methodology indispensable for all study of civilizations?

14. Chart the ways the West is unique. Or is it?

Notes

1. This reconstruction draws mainly on Weber's *The Religion of India* volume (1958), though also on *E&S* and, occasionally, *General Economic History* (1927). It captures a "classical India" (approx. 600–1800CE).

2. Weber's analysis of the rise and expansion of the caste system is reconstructed at Kalberg, 2012, pp. 165–178.

3. Whereas the *dharma* of the Protestant would involve baptism, church attendance, rest on Sunday, and a prayer of thanks before meals, the Hindu *dharma* implied caste-specific rituals (1958, pp. 24–25).

4. Consequently, no great psychological tension resulted of the type that repeatedly congealed in the Occident where the faithful were expected to order comprehensively their worldly actions to conform to an omnipotent God's ethical commandments. Weber succinctly summarizes the organic social ethic (see 1946b, p. 338).

5. Weber elaborates this point in reference to his central distinction between ethical and ritual action: "The catalogue of sins and penances in the Hindu sacred scriptures makes no distinction between ritual and ethical sins, and enjoins ritual obedience as virtually the sole method of atonement. As a consequence, the pattern

of everyday life could be influenced by these religions only in the direction of traditionalism. Indeed, the sacramental grace of the Hindu gurus even further weakened any possibility of ethical influence" (1968, p. 561).

6. Weber makes this point in comparative perspective as well: "Commercial capital, in its attempts to organize industrial labor on the basis of the putting-out system, had to face an essentially stronger resistance in India than in the Occident [West]" (1958, p. 112).

7. Although Hinduism attained clear hegemony in India's Middle Ages over Buddhism and Jainism, Weber by no means neglected these salvation religions (see 1958). However, he also failed to discover here a belief system that strengthened action in opposition to the traditional economic ethic.

8. The same fate awaited the sporadic attempts of great charismatic leaders to disrupt the caste system. Again, the caste order demonstrated its overwhelming powers to co-opt protest while preserving itself. It transformed individual charisma into clan charisma and subsequently into a legitimated new caste, possibly one with economic privileges: "No matter how often individual charismatic upstarts and their freely recruited followings shattered the firm structure of the sibs, the social process always resumed its firm course of charismatic clan organizations of tribes, phratries, and sibs" (1958, p. 54).

10

Applying Weber: The Birth and Growth of the American Civic Sphere

M ax Weber's several discussions of the American political culture identify particular elements as pivotal: a distinct, broad-ranging civic sphere and innumerable civic associations. This chapter takes as its task a reconstruction of his analysis of their origin and expansion. These features anchored and located the singular American mode of community building and establishment of social trust.[1] The reconstruction presented here illustrates the *usefulness* today of Weber's concepts and procedures as powerful explanatory aids for causal analysis.

Weber's analysis of the American civic sphere's sources and the origins of its civic associations focuses first on early strains of Protestantism. They formed crucial causal precedents, he contends, indeed in certain ways more so than economic interests, political power, the state, or differentiation processes. This chapter reconstructs central causes, as Weber sees them, behind the American civic sphere's unusual origin and the extreme growth of its civic associations.

Two further themes thread throughout his analysis. First, he discovers among the devout in the Colonial era both a "world-mastery (*weltbeherrschende*) individualism" and an intense commitment to a religious community, and a parallel dualism in the 19th century between a commitment to a world-mastery individualism and to a civic realm. Second, his analysis calls attention to an antagonism between a values-anchored, or *practical-ethical*, individualism and an interests-anchored, or *practical-rational* individualism.

The concepts and procedures familiar from the above chapters guide this reconstruction of Weber's analysis of the American political culture's unique origins and development.[2] His rejection of organic holism and typical focus on subjective meaning, long-range historical precedents, long-range legacies, the perpetual influence of the past on the present, the indispensability of social carriers, the ways in which multiple groups in coalitions form social contexts conducive—or not—to the recognition and influence of new groups, and the deep cultural roots of social action—all these pillars of Weber's mode of analysis remain at the forefront of this reconstruction. Comparative procedures also constitute, as discussed, a pivotal aspect of Weber's procedures. They are utilized in the concluding section. Here brief contrasts to the German political culture of Weber's time serve to demarcate further the singularity of the American political culture.

Weber discovers several long-range precursors to the American civic arena in the ascetic Protestant—or "Puritan"—sects and churches of the 17th and 18th centuries. He charts how a powerful commitment by believers to their religious community and to an ideal of trustworthiness appeared as legacies from the salvation paths carried by the Puritan churches and sects. The heritage they bequeathed to the 19th century shaped groups into configurations of *compatible* groups, he maintains. A social context was formed, one favorable to the birth and expansion of an American civic sphere and of innumerable civic associations.[3]

Long-Range Precedents for the American Civic Sphere I: Community Building in the Ascetic Protestant Sects and Churches in the Colonial Era

Weber contends that unusually intense belief in a Deity's Commandments and a vigorous penetration of daily life by religious values were widespread among ascetic Protestants in the Colonial epoch. This deep engagement in "the religious life" and its extremely disciplined organization—its asceticism—established highly cohesive communities.

A parallel development led in this era in the same direction, he holds. Puritanism demanded that the faithful toil together. Only by doing so can they fulfill their God-given purpose on Earth: to construct this Deity's affluent and just Kingdom in a manner that fosters unequivocal praise of His majesty and righteousness. Hence, intense faith combined in this era with loyalty to God's

Commandments and joint efforts to master large tasks. Viable bonds among believers and a "sect spirit" congealed (see 2011, pp. 158–170; 1968, pp. 549, 578–579, 1207–1209).

Furthermore, Weber maintains that a firm organization crystallized to cultivate and carry ascetic Protestantism's community-building capacities: the congregation.[4] This organized group assisted the creation among believers of *communities*; *all* in the sect could now become "brothers and sisters in the faith." Trust expanded in these congregations. New *family* relationships of helpfulness, allegiance, and ethical conduct, under the watchful eyes of God and the devout alike, were born among "the brethren."

Moreover, a practical mechanism ensured that only the sincere faithful would become members of this congregation, Weber argues: rigid investigative procedures guaranteed that exclusively persons of "good moral character" would be admitted to this devout community. Thus, membership in the sect *certified* righteous behavior, as well as a person's commitment to treat all as God's children—that is, in strict accordance with an ethos of equality and fair play (1968, p. 1205; 2011, pp. 209–226). Hence, good will and openness prevailed in congregations rather than fear and the sheer calculation of interests. Indeed, membership established in the larger community a reputation for honesty and candor even in business relationships, Weber contends (2005, pp. 284–288; 2011, 209–217).

In this way, carried and cultivated methodically by Puritan congregations, trust, ethical conduct, and good will broke from their accustomed location in the family bond. Attribution of these qualities now qualitatively expanded and became awarded to "unknown others"—as long as they were certified members of an ascetic Protestant sect. Ethical conduct now became, Weber insists, comprehended as an *impersonal and binding principle*—a firm *ideal* even for commercial relationships—rather than as a strong personal relationship or a longstanding tradition (see, for example, 1946, pp. 303–306, 312–313; 1985, pp. 7–9).

In addition, because constituting a new and extended *family*—or brotherhood and sisterhood—of certified believers, the sect congregation served as an effective training ground for the learning of behavior in conformity with this Deity's principles and values, as well as for the acquisition of group participation and social skills. Weber sees that the laity's involvement in the admission of new members proved pivotal at this point, as did the congregation's major role in selecting new ministers and in admonishing the "unworthy" to avoid communion—all to strictly insure, as God wished, "the purity of the sacramental community" (see 1968, p. 1208; 2005, pp. 219–221). This milieu of trusted believers itself facilitated further the cultivation of a notion of *service* to the group. Far removed from utilitarian and pragmatic concerns, this *religious life* oriented the devout intensely toward God's community, Weber holds (see 2005, pp. 277–290; 2011, pp. 209–216). To him: "[Puritan] individualism produced an eminent power to form *groups*" (2005, p. 284; translation altered).

Weber's essays on the Protestant sects illustrate frequently both the perpetual orientation to God by the faithful and the tight internal ties typical of these congregations. Only one example can be noted.

In the event of a change of residence, members of Puritan congregations were welcomed into a new sect or church on the basis of a "letter of introduction" from their home pastor. This document described the newcomer's devoutness and "good character." Acceptance and membership readily followed—and even immediate trust. A cornerstone element for values-based, community-building patterns of action had been established (see 1968, p. 1206; 2005, pp. 111–119, 277–289).

These firm groups imprinted early American society widely, Weber argues. A sincere dedication by believers both to high standards of ethical conduct *and* viable orientations to communities was evident, as was a radical extension of social trust. He maintains that community building in this manner formed a clear *precedent* for the creation and growth of—albeit less tightly knit— a further community in the 19th century: the secularized civic sphere (1968, pp. 1204–1207; 2011, pp. 209–233; see Kalberg, 1997, pp. 213–216; 2014).

However, a broader explanation for the origins and expanse of this sphere in American society requires attention to a further theme, Weber stresses. In unexpected ways, the particular *form of individualism* widespread in Colonial America and the early United States erected regular patterns of action and configurations of groups. These groups also contributed to the unfolding of the American civic sphere one century later. Weber's analysis again focuses on the contribution of dynamics emanating from the religion arena.

Long-Range Precedents
for the American Civic Sphere II:
World-Mastery Individualism in the Colonial Era

He insists that the heritage of ascetic Protestantism implied a rigorous cultivation of an initiative-taking, activity-oriented, and entrepreneurial individualism relatively unrestricted by age-old tradition (see chapter 2). Here interest-based utilitarianism came to the forefront. However, Weber viewed Puritanism as also capable of directing individualism away from this *practical rationality*: *this* individualism was characterized by a values-based, *world-mastery* individualism, he held. It set into motion pivotal precedents for the development of the American civic sphere. Weber's analysis must be reconstructed.

To an unusual degree, ascetic Protestantism opposed worldly pleasures. An especially vigilant watchfulness over all creaturely drives and desires was required of the faithful. Yet exercising the requisite discipline proved an onerous task. And the Protestant clergy could no longer directly assist the believer's salvation quest because the absolution of sins through Confession was now banned. The devout stood in a solitary relationship with the wrathful, omnipotent, and vengeful God of the Old Testament—and remained responsible solely to Him. Extreme anxiety was inevitable (see above, pp.xx. ; 1968, pp. 1198–1200; 2009, pp. 119–120, 134–135).

However, Weber stressed that Puritans were also required to focus their energy on God's Commandments and their special task: to create His just and abundant Kingdom on Earth. This obligation demanded that the faithful *act* with great discipline *against evil*. Even secular authority and popular opinion must be rejected wherever they oppose God's laws.

Hence, a strong impulse toward community activism was again set into motion, Weber contends. The reform of society now became more than a desired goal or utilitarian activity; it constituted instead a service to God and a sacred and encompassing duty placed on all believers. It must be undertaken on behalf of this Deity's Will. Withdrawal "from the world" was not permitted.

A world-mastery individualism congealed, Weber emphasizes—that is, a disciplined form of individualism anchored in religious doctrine and guided by values. The devout must, while living in a world of temptations, uphold with a robust energy their Deity's Commandments and oppose unjust traditions and activity. Only strong individuals were capable of consistently orienting their behavior to His values; they alone were endowed with the capacity to navigate innumerable obstacles and to meet this challenging goal (1968, pp. 1207–1209; 2005, pp. 284–286; 2011, pp. 122–123, 225–226).

Revisions announced by the Puritan Divines in the 17th century intensified this world-mastery individualism (see above, pp. 18–20). Weber saw that the devout could now "convince themselves" of their predestined status: wherever worldly success—defined as the capacity to labor methodically in a vocation (*Beruf*) and to acquire profit—is attained, the faithful can conclude that the energy of their omniscient and omnipotent God had been at work. And believers knew that nothing occurred by chance in this Deity's universe. He would offer such a positive "sign" only to the predestined, the devout were persuaded. "Psychological rewards" were bestowed in this manner upon systematic labor and the quest for wealth (1968, pp. 572–573,

1197–1200, 1203–1210; 2011, pp. 168–170; see the more detailed account above at chapter 2).[5] Rather than rooted in emotional relationships or sheer pragmatic calculations, Puritanism's world-mastery individualism placed abstract principles at the core of the believer's life and obligated all to honor them in a strict manner.

Remarkably, these revisions by the Puritan Divines laid down patterns of action that would prove amenable, one century later, to the growth and expansion of an American civic sphere, Weber insists. Although the faithful were charged with the task of creating "evidence" of their membership among the saved, the means of doing so—methodical work in a calling— never served exclusively utilitarian and egocentric motives. Instead, in light of the obligation to create the just and humane earthly Kingdom that extolled their Divinity's majesty, the labor required of all believers occurred *on His behalf* and as a means to create His community. Now intensified, the work of all Puritans became oriented beyond the random, practical-rational flux of daily life and toward an ethical goal: the improvement of God's Kingdom. Rather than utilitarian and mundane, activity "in the world" now acquired an *ethical* element.

Weber emphasizes that a religion-based orientation to systematic work, and its relocation as a calling at the center of life, in this way strengthened the commitment of the devout *to a religious community*. Regular labor, occurring on behalf of a purpose divorced from all accumulation of material goods, now tied the faithful into a constellation of fixed sacred aims. In doing so, it assisted the creation of cohesive, value-oriented groups. Indeed, because undertaken by *all* ascetic Protestant believers, systematic labor in a vocation nourished social trust and community building. Not surprisingly, in Puritan communities methodical labor itself became elevated a level of prestige heretofore unknown.

A *symbiotic dualism* now became apparent to Weber. A world-mastery individualism, anchored in the capacity of the self-reliant devout to shape and reshape their salvation destinies through labor and the acquisition of wealth, became accentuated. However, the same salvation quest pushed the faithful toward engagement in their communities and social reform—because God commanded believers to construct a just and affluent Kingdom that would praise His glory. Weber sees a "community-forming energy" imparted by the ascetic Protestant sects "to an Anglo-Saxon World" (2011, pp. 230–231). Hence, *ethical* conduct characterized both the lonely salvation-seeking activity of believers *and* their commitment to a religious community. *Practical-ethical* action "in the world," Weber holds, now acquired an intensified energy and direction that separated it clearly from all practical-rational action.

Owing to Puritanism's clear sanctification of trade, profit, and systematic labor, its fostering of a disciplined relationship between believers and God's Commandments, and its cultivation among the devout of loyalty to a religious community, a constellation of values assumed the form of *ethical ideals* for interpersonal interaction and even for commercial relationships: good will, trust, candor, honesty, and fair play. As these community-building values became secure in the religion and economy domains, and then expanded widely, they established configurations of groups and firm precedents. A social context of groups conducive to the birth and expansion of an American *civic sphere*, as well as to the growth of innumerable *civic associations*, appeared. They became manifest widely one century later. Their expansiveness proved unusual, Weber argues.

From Ascetic Protestantism to the 19th Century's Civic Sphere

Weber perceived a weakening of the sect spirit's vibrancy amid the 19th century's rapid urbanization and industrialization. Nonetheless, major elements endured. To him, Puritanism's capacity to call forth values-oriented behavior, social trust, community-building activities, *and* a world-mastery individualism gave rise to a unique political culture. Its arrays of groups ultimately fostered the birth and growth of a broad civic sphere and civic associations. The sect spirit cast a long shadow, Weber holds. How did this occur?

The expansion in the 17th and 18th centuries of practical-ethical patterns of action in sects and churches into the economy and political arenas was accompanied by a continuous tension, according to Weber: means-end rational action and sheer instrumental calculation—that is, practical-rational activity—held sway in these arenas. Nonetheless, wherever strong carrier congregations appeared, practical-ethical action *could* penetrate even into these spheres, he maintains. Given the disciplined and patterned orientation of Puritans *toward* the world, their values significantly influence activity in the economy and political domains. They did so long before the onset of industrialism. As *secular legacies*, they survived into the industrial era.

Weber contends that they played a strong role in giving birth in the 19th century to a civic sphere. This development confronted "the world" to such a degree that elected officials and businesspersons at times felt obliged to uphold the civic arena's high ethical standards. To the extent that this occurred, action patterns were introduced oriented to community building and social trust parallel in form—albeit secular—to those earlier patterns introduced by Puritanism. Moreover, Weber views the civic *sphere* as comprised of constellations of groups favoring the establishment and expansion of civic associations. How does he explain this transformation?

New civic associations formed throughout the 19th century. Their birth and expansion occurred in part as a consequence of the conducive social context established by ascetic Protestantism, according to Weber. He offers several examples to explain how this occurred.

The sect, on the basis of "balloting" membership procedures, maintained a severe exclusion-inclusion distinction. Weber discovers parallel procedures in the Lyons, Rotary, and Kiwanis civic clubs widely dispersed across the 19th-century American landscape. Furthermore, members of these and other civic-oriented groups reciprocally monitored behavior, as had sect members earlier, and likewise punished harshly whenever an offense took place. As held for the Puritans, high ethical standards *must* be consistently upheld because recognition and prestige in the community was at stake (see above, pp. 24–25). Finally, expulsion procedures from civic associations were strict. As also apparent in the sects, they involved a severe social stigma. Banishment from the entire community likely followed (2011, pp. 211–217, 220–221, 227; see above, pp. xx).

To Weber, legacies of ascetic Protestantism—now manifest in the 19th century as community norms of civic participation, "service," and "citizenship," as well as ideals of civic ethics—proved conducive to the formation of these civic associations. Various action patterns established in the earlier era served as amenable precursors that facilitated the acknowledgment and acceptance of these new groups on a broad scale. "The old 'sect spirit,'" Weber contends, "holds sway with relentless effect in the internal character of these [civic] organizations" (2011, pp. 231–232). Members of civic groups wore their membership pins permanently: they served as secular "badges" of respectability and decency, he contends. In this manner, certification of unknown others as trustworthy and as "gentlemen" occurred through membership (1968, p. 1207; 2011, pp. 227–228, pp. 221–222).

> Today, large numbers of "orders" and clubs of all sorts have begun to assume in part the functions of the religious community. Almost every small businessman who thinks something of himself wears some kind of badge in his lapel. However, the archetype of this form, which all use to guarantee the "honorableness" of the individual, is indeed the ecclesiastical community. (1985, p. 8; original emphasis; see 2011, pp. 216–217, 223–224)

To Weber:

American democracy is not a sand pile of unrelated individuals, but a maze of highly exclusive yet absolutely voluntary sects, associations and clubs which provide the center of the individual's social life. (2011, pp. 216–217; see 1968, p. 1207; 2005, p. 286)

All civic groups both cultivated the legacies of Puritanism and rigorously organized the behavior of members. Those values originally anchored in the religion arena and linked to the question of salvation continued to guide action. Indeed, the earlier moral posture endured and now legitimated secular ideals. Hence, behavior in conformity with Puritanism-influenced expectations and standards was sustained, and the "upright" posture and "respectable demeanor" conveyed "fairness" and "trustworthiness" (2005, pp. 111–119; 277–290; 2011, pp, 209–226). Characterized by norms and standards earlier upheld and cultivated in the sect, a community-building civic sphere more and more crystallized:

It is obvious that in all these points the modern functions of American sects and sect-like associations . . . are revealed as straight derivatives, rudiments, and survivals of those conditions which once prevailed in all asceticist sects and conventicles. (2011, p. 223)

The tremendous flood of social groups, which penetrate every nook and cranny of American life, are constituted according to this "sect" model. (2009, p. 204)

"Community service" and membership in "service clubs" now indicated firm ethical conduct and the presence of "good moral character" rather than "God's presence within." "Civic ethics," cultural ideals, and social trust became rooted in a demarcated civic sphere separate from the market, political parties, the state, and all world-view ideologies rooted in socialism and communism (1968, pp. 1204–1210; 2009, pp. 185–204; Kalberg, 2014b).

At the end of the 18th century, numerous groups allied through the possession of a Puritan heritage formed social contexts conducive to the birth of a civic sphere and further civic associations. According to Weber, they experienced forceful growth throughout the 19th century and became carriers of social trust and community-building processes originally established by—and carried by—ascetic Protestant congregations. As a consequence in part of a common foundation in Puritanism's world-mastery asceticism and cohesive carrier congregations, civic values and a values-based individualism endured and became intertwined.

This interweaving took place in a manner that *intensified both* elements. Importantly, according to Weber, a thick civic realm proved capable of encompassing and directing even entrepreneurial individualism. Manifest as civic ethics, this civic sphere now demarcated and defended a values-based domain of activity antagonistic to all utilitarian, self-interested action patterns oriented exclusively to instrumental gain. Conversely, world-mastery individualism, because it supported high intensity activity on behalf of the civic sphere's universal values, principles, standards, and rights, perpetually rejuvenated the civic realm.

In turn, reinvigorated civic ideals again placed high expectations on persons to align action patterns with the ethical values of the civic sphere. Even world-mastery individualism, Weber holds, remained locked within the civic arena's ideals. To the same extent, this sphere opposed all practical-rational individualism, utilitarian and interest-based calculations, and egocentric striving. A mutually sustaining *dynamic* developed in this manner from this strong individualism-civic sphere dualism. A symbiosis was apparent (see Kalberg, 1997, pp. 209–216; 2014).

Let us review Weber's argument. To him, ascetic Protestantism in the 17th and 18th centuries required that the devout contribute to God's just Kingdom. This sacred duty established strong social trust and community-building ideals in sects, and congregations crystallized as their social carriers. Amid 19th-century industrialization, urbanization, and secularization, these profoundly religious organizations and their indigenous values-based legacies ironically formed arrays of groups that delineated social contexts conducive to the birth and growth of *secular* civic associations. Weber views this favoring milieu as their significant precursor (2011, pp. 211–213). In this manner he comprehends religious values and religious organizations as at the core of the expansive and vigorous group-formation dynamic distinct to the American political culture.

To him, appearing in the 19th century, innumerable civic associations formed a *thick* civic arena. They became deeply and widely embedded in the American political culture. Eventually cultivated and reinvigorated by further secular carrier groups—families, neighborhoods, and schools—practical-ethical patterns of action now acquired a solid foundation for the expansion of public ideals of universal justice, fair play, social trust, and equal opportunity—despite their empirical abuse and violation on a regular basis. With inestimable consequences for the political culture of the United States, ethical action became *diffused* throughout numerous carrier groups now embedded across American society's political, social, educational, economic, and family arenas.

Owing to their quasi-sect features, and the quasi-religious context within which they originated, American civic groups oriented the behavior of members in the 19th century *to a constellation of values* in an unusually intense fashion, Weber holds. As the civic sphere expanded, practical-ethical action regularly challenged utilitarian and pragmatic activities. At times, civic values and civic groups permeated and altered even the political and economy realms (2011, pp. 211–213), thereby strengthening the American political culture's specific version of social trust and community building. Indeed, these groups often articulated and carried cohesive community service ideals, codes of ethical conduct, and "mission statements." Whenever empirically expansive and pulsating, the American civic sphere relegated the state and its laws to the level of distant secondary and tertiary mechanisms of community building and social trust.

In stark terms, Weber's analysis reveals the uniqueness of both the American Colonial and 19th-century political cultures. The capacity of the civic sphere to generate a sustaining community-building energy and to call forth a symbiotic dualism between this sphere and world-mastery individualism is emphasized. The high salience of these major components of the American political culture led to a specific conclusion: ethical conduct acquired an unusual *location*—namely, beyond its traditional anchorage in the private sphere yet independent of the state's authority (see Weber 1985, pp. 10–11; 2005, pp. 277–289). This distinct location was visible even in the Colonial period.

Weber insists that the origins and growth of the civic sphere and its associations cannot be understood by exclusive reference to, for example, the development of the state or the economy, or to the pursuit by individuals of purely economic and political interests. As little have they appeared as a consequence of differentiation and value-generalization processes putatively indigenous to industrialization.

Albeit strongly cognizant of the civic sphere's ethical element in the 19th century, Weber never views ethical conduct as dominant. Rather, its fragile nature is invariably apparent to him: it is locked perpetually in a relationship of antagonism—if not open conflict—with practical rationality. Thus, a state of tension infused the American political culture: its "individual" and "civic" components, although both were grounded in common religious legacies and inextricably intertwined, strained in opposite directions and clashed repeatedly.

His fears must be acknowledged. When supported by strong carrier groups, American practical rationalism subjugates orientations to ethical values within the civic sphere. To Weber, this sphere then loses its independence, as well as its ethical component, and expands or contracts depending exclusively on domination constellations, the irregular flow of power, and instrumental alignments (see Kalberg, 2014, pp. 47–58).

Weber's analysis oriented to interpretive understanding, subjective meaning, and the interlocking of the past and the present has unveiled significant causal factors. Indeed, he weaves often occluded historical precedents and legacies into the core of his argument. For him, values and beliefs from the distant past prove influential, as do their social carriers: Puritan sects and churches in the 17th and 18th centuries and civic associations in the 19th century. In other words, Weber's analysis attends on the one hand to the manner in which the subjective meaning of persons in groups establishes firm patterns of action—including value-based and belief-based regularities—and, on the other hand, to the particular groups that served as the bearers of these patterns of action. If carried by powerful and enduring organizations, these regularities of action cast their imprint through the centuries. As precedents and legacies, they did so even when monumental transformations—secularization, urbanization, and industrialization, for example—led to an alteration of their social carriers.

Weber announces a further conclusion with great vehemence. It rests on his rejection of those theories that chart the routes taken across nations to "modern" political cultures as homogeneous and parallel. The political landscape of his nation, he insists, and his era—late 19th- and early 20th-century Germany—diverged qualitatively from the American political culture. Lacking both powerful sects and a strong civic sphere in its historical heritage, social trust and community-building values originated in a singular manner and assumed a quite different societal location. Weber's analysis reveals in particular that the state in Germany and in the United States played very different roles.

The remainder of this chapter reconstructs Weber's analysis, albeit in a severely abbreviated form. Only several central elements can be highlighted. Moreover, this discussion exclusively serves an heuristic purpose: through contrasts and comparisons, it casts a further beam of light onto the American political culture—and thereby identifies more clearly its content, parameters, trajectory, and particularity.

At this point we are again following Weber's comparative methodology. Now familiar to us, he utilizes comparative procedures to demarcate cross-nation differences and to challenge those theories that discover homogeneous and parallel historical developments. An examination of the distinct part played by the state in the formation of community building and social trust in Germany must serve as our point of departure.

Germany's Political Culture: A Contrast Case

Germany's political culture in the latter half of the 19th century diverged qualitatively from the American political culture of the same period.

What were its sources? How do identification of its contours assist demarcation of the American political culture's boundaries? Weber's analysis must be reconstructed.

Absent in America, feudalism's conventions and customs remained powerful in Germany throughout the 19th century. They penetrated deeply into its rapidly changing political and economy spheres. Although grounding *patterns* of social activity, and hence insulating German society against social chaos, these hierarchical conventions and customs constrained practical rationalism's sheer interest-based relationships only partially, according to Weber (see 1994, pp. 80–129).

Germany's major religions—Lutheranism and Catholicism—also failed to do so in a penetrating manner, he argues. Lacking this-worldly asceticism, these religions never instilled among the faithful an ethos of *extreme* self-reliance and discipline, as did Puritanism in the American Colonies (2011, pp. 104–105; see above, pp. 19–25). Thus, absent in Germany was a set of values capable of *intensely and comprehensively* influencing the believer's routine activity—namely, to such a degree that practical rationalism in the political and economy spheres was confronted directly and circumscribed by practical-ethical action. During the Bismarckian-Wilhelmine era (1871–1917), many Germans believed that capitalism, urbanization, and secularization would soon shatter the old *Gemeinschaft* and cause unparalleled social and political disorder (see 1968, pp. 1381–1462; 1994, pp. 80–129).

Germany's elites concluded that a restriction of practical rationalism must occur in a broad-ranging manner, especially in light of the widespread social disorder in the 1870s and 1880s. Owing to the absence of multitudes of *civic* associations capable of serving as powerful social carriers of an expansive civic sphere,[6] expectations and hopes congealed around the state. It was broadly perceived as the only institution in possession of sufficient authority to modulate the effects of great societal transformations and to prevent social chaos. A mobilization of the full resources of the state appeared both urgent and the single viable alternative (see 1968, pp. 1381–1462; 1994, pp. 80–129).

A variety of "protection and care" measures aimed to assist a population widely understood as structurally disadvantaged and potentially disruptive became defined as both appropriate and necessary. The *ethical* obligations of the German state involved (a) a directing role in managing the economy and promoting a regulated market that offered high degrees of employment security, including unemployment, accident, and health insurance; (b) the implementation of an array of social equity, social welfare, and social cohesion measures in general that included state obligations in respect to retirement pensions, wealth redistribution through taxation, and various social welfare benefits; (c) the construction and implementation—through a court system—of a comprehensive legal code; and (d) guarantees of formal equality before the law.

Hence, reforms initiated by the state were broad. In these ways it extended its influence throughout German society and became rather than churches, sects, and civic associations as in the United States the carrier of community building and social trust, as well as the indispensable bulwark against practical rationalism. This outcome was strengthened by a quasi-sanctification of the state that arose on the one hand from the legacies of a highly authoritarian version of feudalism and on the other hand from Lutheranism's direct legitimation of secular authority (2011, pp. 104–105).

Thus, the German state possessed legitimacy on a sustained basis to combat advanced industrialism's social problems and to confront dangers that might destabilize the economy, the political order, and the society in general. Powerful obstacles to this unfolding social welfare state failed to appear, and confidence was lacking in the capacity of individuals to adapt to the severe dislocations implied by modern capitalism without state assistance. Far more than in the United States, the state in Germany became with industrialism a central fulcrum and major point of reference. Indeed, the fulfillment of its appropriate and necessary tasks was widely viewed as an *ethical* obligation.

Two important consequences followed, Weber emphasizes. First, unlike in the United States, in Germany practical-ethical action became focused around the state. Second, the legitimacy of the political realm became more closely tied to the state's success in combating the social disorder believed to be indigenous to capitalism, secularism, and urbanism. Whereas in the American case, broad arrays of civic associations—each articulating ethical ideals in tension with practical rationalism—composed a *diffuse and extended arena*, the state more so constituted and monopolized this arena in industrializing Germany. Although significant in scale, Weber saw that political parties and unions failed to compete with the state's overwhelming power and authority.

As a consequence of these diverging views of the state and varying locations of ethical action, Weber concludes that the political cultures of industrializing Germany and the United States must be understood as substantively dissimilar. He views this heterogeneity as strong despite all structural constraints common to industrialization and urbanization processes. *Distinct* features are central to the composition of each political culture.

Albeit reconstructed here in a highly foreshortened manner, Weber's comparative case has served an important purpose: his analysis of the

German political culture has thrown into relief many components pivotal in the American political culture. Six elements are readily apparent: its civic-oriented individualism, unique location for practical-ethical action, extended civic sphere, "small state" contours and posture of hostility toward the state, and singular locating of practical-ethical action.

At this point, Weber's emphatic opposition to all theories that view political cultures as developing in response to a "general evolution" is again apparent. However, he is often misunderstood on this point: too many commentators comprehend him as a theorist of a linear "bureaucratization process" that assumes similar contours—even of political cultures—across all modernizing nations. Such an interpretation of Weber neglects his repeated demarcation of significant cross-nation variation. This chapter has called attention to the capacity of his concepts and comparative procedures to delineate the divergent origins and unique features of the political cultures of two "highly advanced" industrial nations: the United States and Germany. Weber's concepts and procedures have rendered several qualitative differences starkly manifest.

Above all, views of the state, religious traditions, and the location of practical-ethical action have varied. Perhaps most striking in the American case was the presence and forceful impact of a sect tradition and its legacy: a wide-scale civic sphere. Its absence in the German case is also now vividly apparent. In addition, Weber's comparative analysis has unveiled singular elements in respect to the state: the "strong state" in Germany, which undertook wide-ranging measures to manage and guide the economy and political arenas, throws the American "weak state" into stark relief. Perhaps the pervasive influence of the civic sphere and civic associations significantly pushed the American state away from broad efforts to administer the economy and the parameters of the political arena. Conversely, perhaps their absence in Germany rendered industrialization and democratization "from above" more likely.

Again, Weber's rigorous mode of analysis has enabled a highly differentiated charting of the ways in which political cultures arise and diverge in different nations. His comparative analysis has revealed that central features of political cultures—community building and social trust—are *located* differently. This chapter has illustrated the capacity of Weber's concepts and procedures to offer a differentiated analysis of this delimited theme.

We must now turn to an examination of the strengths and weaknesses of his sociology.

Study Questions and Thoughts to Ponder

1. Despite significant differences, as charted in part in this chapter, between the German and American political cultures, both evidence among their citizens a high respect for law. Having studied this chapter, what reasons can you offer for this similarity?

2. Explain the differences between practical-ethical and practical-rational action.

3. Weber emphasizes throughout his sociology the significant impact, if social carriers are strong, of the past on the present. What role did legacies from the Colonial era play in the formation of the American civic sphere in the 19th century?

4. Has the section in this chapter on the German political culture cast a beam of light on the uniqueness of the American political culture? If so, how? What aspects of Weber's research procedures have assisted your understanding of the differences?

5. Weber sees American civic associations as deeply embedded in major components of American society past and present. Reconstruct his argument.

6. Inventory major aspects of Weber's research procedures that have been utilized in this application of Weber.

7. Weber's analysis of the origins of the American civic sphere and the birth and expansion of civic associations on American soil can be called a "deep culture" and a "deep context" analysis. Explain how.

8. What set of factors grounded the commitment of Puritans to their communities? Or was the commitment strong given the obligations of Puritans to act in ways that guaranteed their own salvation?

9. Has the section in this chapter on the German political culture cast a beam of light on the uniqueness of the American political culture? If so, how? What aspects of Weber's research procedures have assisted your understanding of the differences?

10. Weber sees American civic associations as deeply embedded in major components of American society past and present. Reconstruct his argument.

Notes

1. A nation's "political culture" refers to the sets of values that underlie and underpin a nation's social policies and the direction of its social change.

2. This chapter is a reconstruction in the modest sense. In reference to these concepts and procedures, it systematizes numerous and scattered passages in Weber's major works on the American political culture.

3. Thus, the reconstruction offered in this chapter examines the American political culture's major contours until 1900. For a reconstruction that moves up to the present, see Kalberg, 2014.

4. Weber saw *American* individualism (unlike the more inward-looking German individualism) as fundamentally located in groups, even in those groups—especially sects—that expect strict adherence to firm norms. Rather than losing the capacity for decision-making when in groups, Americans "hold their own," he contends, on the basis of defined standards, values, and goals. To him, here ascetic Protestantism's influence is evident (see Weber, 2005, pp. 277–290; see above, pp. 23–25).

5. Weber's extremely complex analysis has been noted here only in abbreviated form (see Kalberg, 2012, pp. 18–19; 2014).

6. This is not to say that associations (*Vereine*) did not exist in Germany. This view has been appropriately discredited. Rather, *Vereine* were unpolitical (hiking, chess, choral, etc.), and political parties were polarized. Thus, and also as a consequence of the authoritarian character of this protection and care state, a strong civic sphere could not develop.

11

An Assessment

Magical and religious powers, and the belief in them anchored in ethical notions of duty, have been in the past among the most important formative influences upon the way life has been organized.

(Weber, 2011, p. 246)

Large questions about the contours of the modern world and its origins drove Weber's sociology.

- What is the fate of ethical action, the unique individual, compassion in the society dominated by advanced capitalism, and the personality unified by a constellation of noble values?
- What does the rise of modern capitalism imply for the "type of human being" who will live within this "new cosmos"?
- What defines the particularity of the West?
- How have we arrived at our present situation?
- What are the parameters for social change in the modern West?

Weber's sociology was also driven by queries focused on the possible ways, viewed through a sweeping comparative-historical lens, configurations of groups—and the social contexts they form—influence subjective meaning. What sets of patterned action in groups lead persons to attach meaning to specific activities? How can social scientists understand the subjectively meaningful action of persons in other civilizations and epochs *on their own terms* rather than by reference to a hierarchy of Western values?

This concluding chapter holds Weber's project up to the light. What are the merits of his comparative-historical and interpretive approach? His macrosociology stands apart from all structural-functional neo-Marxian schools and narrative. What weaknesses and strengths are apparent?

Weber's Weaknesses

Although impressive in many ways, Weber's approach is not without weaknesses. Its sheer complexity and frequent lack of clarity has led often to the charge of inconsistency. For example, while subjective meaning stands at the center of his sociology, the language utilized in his comparative-historical works frequently leaves the impression that his focus is on structural forces.

The translations comprise a long-standing problem just in this respect. Readers of Weber in English have frequently accused him of becoming a structural sociologist in violation of his own methodological premises. Some major terms in the German original—for example, *Handlungsorientierungen* (action-orientations) and *Regelmäßigkeiten des Handelns* (regularities of action, patterns of action)—only rarely appear in the English translations. However, Weber himself is in part to blame. For example, on behalf of consistency, he should use phrases such as "action oriented to feudalism" or "action oriented to Puritan doctrine." Abjuring such awkward phraseology, he generally prefers simply "feudalism" and "Puritanism."

Substantive criticisms have cut to the core of Weber's works. Many interpreters have found a concept at the foundation of Weber's sociology—the ideal type—troublesome. Guidelines for its formation and application have remained imprecise, it is argued. These same opponents have generally rejected Weber's view that sociological generalization is appropriately limited to the conceptual level only.

Many in the Durkheimian tradition have faulted his orientation to subjective meaning as such and questioned the viability of an approach that takes motives as pivotal. A number of more recent sociologists insist that interaction, creativity, identity formation, and narrative accounts must constitute the fundamental level of analysis. Moreover, while subjective meaning rooted in means-end rational action may be identifiable, the critics contend that values-based and emotions-based subjective meanings will always remain amorphous and problematic. Indeed, some have questioned whether, for sociologists, an analytic armament that includes traditions, emotions, and values is at all necessary. Persons act by reference on the one hand to pragmatic interests and on the other hand to external constraints and power, they maintain.

Organic holists have regularly attacked Weber's elevation of multiple ideal types to the center of his research procedures and lamented both the absence of their major explanatory concepts—society, institutions, and socialization—and his indifference to "the problem of social order." Many of these same commentators have viewed his definition of sociology's aim— to offer causal explanations of unique cases—as exceedingly modest. In rejecting Weber's view of theory as an endeavor in the service of heuristic ends only and hence as always provisional, and in opposing also his value-relevance axiom, they seek to establish sociology as a discipline empowered to articulate the general "laws of social life." They also endow the social sciences, *contra* Weber, with the task of offering predictions about the future.

Marxists and neo-Marxists have argued vehemently against Weber for generations. They stress the principled incapacity of his methodology to formulate clear-cut mechanisms for social change, let alone avenues of emancipation from modern capitalism. Hence, it is argued that Weber's works in the end remain too beholden to the status quo. His critics from the Left also insist that this "bourgeois" character of his sociology is apparent in its putative idealism, its failure to elevate material interests to the level of a preeminent causal force, its unwillingness to recognize the "laws of history," and its rejection of the clear dominance throughout history of a single class.

Weber's Strengths

Sociologists today only rarely ask questions of the magnitude apparent in Weber's comparative-historical works. Very delimited themes guide research and broad queries are pushed aside into the misty, nonscientific realm of social philosophy. Yet Weber's studies remain throughout anchored deeply empirically. Indeed, he "translated" his large questions and themes into rigorous concepts, research strategies, modes of analysis, and methodological axioms. Had he failed to do so, his writings would be understood as exclusively a set of commentaries on the rapidly changing era in which he lived—and only intellectual historians and historians of sociology would study them. A *Weberian sociology* would not exist.

Weber created a rigorous and distinct approach that combined empirical description, theoretical generalization, and the interpretative understanding of subjective meaning. Distinguished by its exceptional comparative and historical breadth, his sociology investigates the patterned social action of persons in groups and seeks to explain it by reference to values, traditions, interests, and emotions. It attempts to offer causal analyses of unique cases and proceeds by reference to ideal types, societal domains, configurations of groups, social contexts, and the exploration of subjective meaning.

His various studies emphasize that the past is ineluctably intertwined with the present. They assert that patterned orientations of social action in the religion, economy, status honor, rulership, law, and family and clan domains must be acknowledged in every case as potentially of causal significance for the formation of groups. Power, social carriers, historical events, competition, conflict, and technology must also be recognized as viable causes of meaningful action. Hence, patterned action in groups cannot be comprehended by reference *alone* to "material" *or* "ideal" factors, and least of all by reference to transcendent forces, mysterious causes, or "ultimate" determinants. And while economic and political interests possess a strong grip on everyday activities, persons are also capable of orienting their social action to values, conventions, customs, habits, status honor, and emotions, Weber holds. At times this occurs, he recognizes, even when a chosen activity flies in the face of the person's economic well-being or pleasure-maximizing considerations.

Despite his adherence to a broad and dynamic multicausality, Weber remains fully cognizant that *some* civilizations *may* become, in certain epochs and as a result of multiple and identifiable patterns of action, more closed or even ossified. Nevertheless, he scorns organic holism and takes omnipresent conflict and power for granted. However, he also sees that regularities of action—continuities and patterns—arise repeatedly and throughout all corners of every group configuration. They do so on the basis of values, traditions, interests, and even emotions. In this way, Weber's sociology takes cognizance of societies and civilizations as ordered variously along a spectrum anchored at one end by more "closed" configurations of groups and on the other side by more "open" and dynamic configurations of groups.

Furthermore, his analysis of rulership and obedience manifests a similar capacity to conceptualize cases in a manner that acknowledges movement across an entire spectrum. Weber is convinced that persons in groups throughout history have repeatedly viewed rulership as legitimate, even at times when it was perceived as oppressive. They have therefore rendered obedience. Nevertheless, they also from time to time form groups that deny legitimacy to established ruling groups and overthrow them—only soon thereafter to erect further rulers. To him, social change that involves complex conflicts and both merging and antagonistic groups is inevitable, even though it never flows at the same tempo or follows, in the longer term, lawful, evolutionary, and differentiation pathways.

Finally, Weber's approach to the conundrum of meaningful action is likewise multidimensional. It is conceptualized as occurring in four types of social action and formulated in a vast variety of ways. Pivotal to him, values *do* exist, as do internally consistent constellations of values. Some address broad, even ultimate questions; Weber emphasizes that world views have congealed in all major civilizations. Other approaches seldom note their capacity to set the *tracks* within which *certain* social action becomes defined as viable.

In studying relationships, groups, epochs, nations, and civilizations of interest to them, Weberian sociologists take as their task the interpretive understanding of how persons formulate meaning in widely varying social contexts and orient their action accordingly. By utilizing multicausal explanatory procedures, they seek to comprehend the configurations of regular action that give birth to new patterns of social action and the groups that sustain them, and the further configurations of regular action and groups that lead to their alteration. Multiple groups and cross-group relationships also stand at the fulcrum of Weber's sociology. Chapters 7–10 sought to illustrate these features of his research procedures.

His sociology of comparative civilizations stands at the core of most of his empirical investigations and deserves special attention in this concluding chapter. Again, in what ways can the West be said to be unique and how can its singular development be explained? His civilizations project—its questions, scope, tenor, and aims—constitutes a distinct contribution to macrosociology. A brief review of its themes and procedures will reveal its unusual accomplishments.

Weber acquired, through *PE*, his EEWR studies, and *E&S*, essential insight, clarity, and knowledge regarding the overarching tracks within which each major civilization developed (see 2009, pp. 241–242). The tracks in the West, for example, were formed in Antiquity and the cities of the Middle Ages; they were sustained by a series of subsequent "world and religion" developments. In the 20th century, these tracks became manifest in the wide expansion of an impersonal formal rationality in the domains of law, rulership, and the economy and of a theoretical rationality in the domain of knowledge.

Profound ramifications followed regarding the *type of human being* who *could* live under modern Western rationalism, Weber insisted repeatedly. What were its singular features, he queries, vis-à-vis the rationalisms of China, India, the Middle East, and the Western ancient and medieval civilizations? And what constellations of groups and group interactions over two millennia causally explain its rise? As we have discovered, his sociology addresses overarching queries in a systematic manner. In offering answers to these questions on the basis of broadly multicausal analyses, Weber's multidimensional and nonevolutionary empirical investigations even today stand alone in the field of comparative-historical sociology.

His sociology of civilizations directly poses even more queries. What regular orientations of social action—means-end rational, value-rational, affectual, and traditional—became meaningful in pivotal carrier groups in each of the major civilizations? How can large-scale causal explanations be offered for each historical trajectory? What possibilities, given its contours and parameters, does modern Western rationalism allow for viable social change? To Weber, the search for answers to these questions required urgent attention: he viewed compassion, ethical action, and the autonomous individual as highly endangered in the modern West by the dominance of formal, practical, and theoretical rationalization processes. These queries stand at the core of his comparative-historical and interpretive sociology of civilizations.

Casting their focus exclusively on *PE* and a few rigorous concepts in *E&S*, the vast majority of Weber interpreters neglect his large-scope agenda, wide-ranging comparative themes, and rigorous mode of civilizational analysis. Here his methodology and expansive works stand nearly alone. They reveal, for example, as noted in Chapter 7, that any examination of the West's particular historical development must address its "structural heterogeneity." *In comparison to* China, India, the Middle East, and the ancient West, a higher degree of pluralistic conflict between the economy, religion, law, rulership, social honor, and family and clan domains distinguished the Western contours and the Western pathway, he holds. The resulting tensions across relatively independent spheres called forth a comparative openness and societal flexibility that facilitated further cross-domain conflict. Indeed, the West's competing spheres introduced a degree of dynamism that Weber sees as both specific to this region and eventually conducive to the introduction and expansion of modern capitalism (see 1968, pp. 1192–1193).

Throughout this sweeping analysis, he never loses sight of his large-scale questions. Repeatedly, whenever the civilizational rationalisms indigenous to China, India, and the West appeared to acquire cohesion to such an extent that stagnation loomed, Weber reformulated a central question: would ethical *values* retain a capacity to orient patterned action? If so, the utilitarian and random push and pull characteristic of raw interests and power would then be counterbalanced. Perhaps this would take place to such an extent that patterned action in groups would become significantly *directed* by ethical ideals. Persons would then become accountable to values and practice an *ethic of responsibility*. Of critical importance to Weber, the ethical ideal itself, to the extent that "the individual places himself under [this] common norm," places a thrust toward community into motion (1946b, p. 342).

As we have seen, Weber sought to define the major contours of a variety of civilizations through interpretive, empirical, multicausal, comparative, and context-sensitive procedures. He attempted also to chart the singular empirical trajectories followed by various civilizations in the economy, ruler-ship, law, and religion domains. In doing so, he wished not only to under-stand the uniqueness of the West—the causes behind its origins and development and the direction of its specific course—but also to compre-hend the ways in which persons living in diverse epochs, and amid the inter-play of patterned action in varieties of groups, create subjective meaning in their lives.

However, he pursued as well a further central task: to define the concepts and research procedures indispensable to the formation of a rigorous comparative-historical and interpretive sociology of civilizations. Indeed, as now apparent, he offers arrays of concepts and strategies that can be employed by sociologists oriented *today* to the goal of interpretive under-standing and engaged in cross-civilizational research. Only comparative and multicausal investigations that recognize the interweaving of the past with the present can support his quest to demarcate systematically the many ways in which patterns of social action, situated in configurations of groups, erect unique "meaning complexes." And only such studies can explain the modern West's singularity and the causes behind its historical trajectory to the present.

The strengths and weaknesses of Weber's expansive sociology will be debated for many years to come. Even as an array of his essays continues to be widely discussed, the opposition by many comparative-historical schools to core features of his approach will endure. Others will continue to defend Weber's concepts, procedures, and remarkable agenda. As the microchip and globalization revolutions reach deep into the 21st century and continue to bring distant peoples into direct and sustained contact, a place remains for a comparative-historical sociology of civilizations that unlocks near and far a civilization's unique rationalism, pathway, and pre-dominant subjective meanings.

12

Further Readings

Commentaries On Max Weber's Oeuvre

The beginning reader will require assistance in working through Max Weber's diffuse and challenging writings. Only a tiny segment of the vast commentary on his works, and only a few major arenas of the reception, can be noted here.

The classic introduction by Reinhard Bendix remains the best overview (1962), although it lacks a discussion of Weber's methodology. The collection of essays by Bendix and Guenther Roth (1971) constitutes an ideal companion. Roth's introduction (1968) to *Economy and Society* provides an indispensable guide to this volume. See also *Max Weber's 'Economy and Society': A Critical Introduction*, edited by Charles Camic, Philip S. Gorski, and David M. Trubek (2005).

Many anthologies collect Weber's works. Among them, three stand out. All offer fine cross-sections of Weber's corpus: see *From Max Weber*, edited and translated by Hans H. Gerth and C. Wright Mills (1946); *Weber: Selections in Translation*, edited by W. G. Runciman and translated by Eric Matthews (1978); and *The Essential Weber*, edited by Sam Whimster (2004).

A reader edited by the author, *Max Weber: Readings and Commentary on Modernity* (2005), collects his writings on America and a variety of themes salient to social scientists today: the Protestant ethic thesis, inequality, authority in the modern epoch, ethical action, race and ethnicity, the workplace and the "work ethic," the nation and the state, and the value of modern science. It also includes selections from recent scholars who *apply* Weber's concepts and procedures to a variety of research topics. A further reader edited by the author places together in one volume central essays on Weber's pivotal theme: the uniqueness of the West and the development of modern Western rationalism (see *The Protestant Ethic and the Spirit of Capitalism with Other Writings on the Rise of the West*, 2009).

Any study of Weber's multiple writings on the influence of religion on economic development must begin with *The Protestant Ethic and the Spirit of Capitalism*, as well as his essays on the American sects (2009, 2011). Two edited volumes are invaluable guides; see Hartmut Lehman and Guenther Roth, *Weber's Protestant Ethic: Origins, Evidence, Contexts* (1993); and William Swatos and Lutz Kaelber, *The Protestant Ethic Turns 100* (2005). Indispensable also are the in-depth discussions offered by Gordon Marshall (1980, 1982), David Little (1969), Benjamin Nelson (1973a), Lutz Kaelber (2005), and Donald Nielsen (2005). A wide-ranging reader edited by S. N. Eisenstadt (1968) investigates "the Protestant ethic thesis" in comparative perspective. The powerful influence of the Protestant ethic and the Puritan sects on the formation of the American *political* culture has been examined, following Weber, by Ralph Schroeder (1998), Sung Ho Kim (2004), Terry Maley (2011), and Stephen Kalberg (2014).

Widely viewed as the most enduring controversy in the social sciences, the debate regarding "the Weber thesis" extended throughout the 20th century. The early criticism of *PE* in the years 1907 to 1910, and Weber's replies, have been collected; see David Chalcraft and Austin Harrington, *The Protestant Ethic Debate* (2001). In recent years, James Henretta (1993), Margaret Jacob and Matthew Kadane (2003), Lutz Kaelber (2005), and Anne Kelly Knowles (1997) have completed studies supporting Weber. The major axes of this debate have been summarized by Kalberg (2011, pp. 50–58).

A number of works influential in post-war sociology have been directly inspired by *PE*, including those by Philip Gorski (2003), Michael Walzer (1965), Robert Holton (1985), David Zaret (1985), Lutz Kaelber (1998), Colin Campbell (1987), David Landes (1999), Ilana Silber (1995), and Mary Fulbrook (1983). *PE* has been described by Daniel Bell as "probably the most important sociological work of the 20th century" (1996, p. 287). The quality of the older and the more recent translations of *PE* into English have been discussed in a special issue of *Max Weber Studies* (Chalcraft & Whimster, 2001).

Weber's major methodological reflections can be found in an older volume, *The Methodology of the Social Sciences* (1949), translated and edited by Edward A. Shils and Henry A. Finch, and in the introductory chapter to *Economy and Society* (1968, pp. 3–62). A recent compilation collects his scattered methodological writings into one volume (see *Max Weber: Collected Methodological Writings* [2012]; translated by Hans Henrik

Bruun and edited by Bruun and Sam Whimster). However, these writings should be attempted only with the guidance of Albert Salomon (1934), William Outhwaite (1975), Thomas Burger (1976), Martin Albrow (1990), and Fritz Ringer (1997). The research procedures and comparative strategies utilized by Weber in his comparative-historical works have been addressed by R. Stephen Warner (1970), Mary Fulbrook (1978), Neil Smelser (1976), Guenther Roth (1971a, 1971b, 1971c, 1976), and Stephen Kalberg (1994, 2012).

Weber's most stimulating discussions in his Economic Ethics of the World Religions series are found in the chapters "Confucianism and Puritanism" (2009, pp. 275–289) and "The General Characteristics of Asian Religions" (1958, pp. 329–343). His systematic analyses of the potentially broad influence of religion-oriented action are found in "The Social Psychology of the World Religions" (1946c) and the "Sociology of Religion" chapter in *Economy and Society* (1968, pp. 399–634). The volume edited by Thomas Ertman (2016) collects commentary by prominent area specialists on Weber's analyses in his books on China (1951), ancient Israel (1952), and India (1958). Benjamin Nelson's examination (1973b) of Weber's preface (*Vorbemerkung*, 2011, pp. 233–250) to his collected essays on the sociology of religion appropriately situates these volumes and highlights Weber's themes: the uniqueness of the West and the causes behind its singular development.

Weber's sociology of civilizations has been explored by Karl Löwith (1982), Benjamin Nelson (1974, 2011), F. H. Tenbruck (1980), Randall Collins (1986, 1999), Andreas Buss (2003, 2015), Johann Arnason (2003, pp. 86–104), Wolfgang Schluchter (1981, 1996), Toby Huff and Schluchter (1999), Stephen Molloy (1980), Martin Fuchs (2016, 2017), Bryan S. Turner (1974, 1992), and Kalberg (2012, pp. 13–42, 145–192; 2014a, 2014b; 2017; and forthcoming). Weber's most sweeping and profound analysis of modern Western rationalism can be found in his "Religious Rejections of the World" essay (1946b). Robert Bellah offers an illuminating commentary (2006, pp. 123–149). On the modern West, see also *Max Weber, Rationality and Modernity*, edited by Sam Whimster and Scott Lash (1987).

Many authors have written on Weber's personal life. See, for example, Marianne Weber (1975), Gerth and Mills (1946, pp 3–46), Roth (1993, 1997, 2001, 2005), Paul Honigsheim (1968), Lewis A. Coser (1971, pp. 234–243), Lawrence Scaff (2011), and Wolfgang Mommsen (2000). His political writings, many of which have been collected in *Weber: Political Writings* (1994), edited by Peter Lassman and Ronald Speirs, have been also frequently addressed and debated. See J. P. Mayer (1956), Karl Loewenstein (1966), Anthony Giddens (1972), David Beetham (1974), and Mommsen

(1985; 1986, pp. 3–43, 53–120). Fritz Ringer (1969) offers an excellent portrait of the German university during Weber's time, and the volume edited by Mommsen and Jürgen Osterhammel (1987) discusses Weber's relationships to his many colleagues. H. Stuart Hughes (1958) and Coser (1971, pp. 234–260) situate Weber's thought and methodology within the major intellectual currents of his time, as do, in a broader sense, George Mosse (1964) and Leonard Krieger (1973).

On the wide impact of Weber's works throughout the 20th century, see Scaff (2014) and Joshua Derman (2013). The journal *Max Weber Studies*, edited by Sam Whimster, is devoted exclusively to an examination of his works and their influence. See also *The Max Weber Dictionary*, edited by Richard Swedberg (2004). The recent *Anthem Companion to Max Weber*, edited by Allan Sica (2017), offers interpretations of a wide range of central themes in Weber's work.

This highly abbreviated discussion must suffice. The remainder of this chapter provides two selections from two of Weber's most famous essays, "Science as Vocation" and "Politics as a Vocation." They were, throughout the 20th century, perhaps the two most widely assigned essays to students in America in social science classes. A brief introduction is first required.

"Science as a Vocation" and "Politics as a Vocation": An Introduction

In 1917, students in a progressive student group at the University of Munich (The Bavarian Union of Free Students) invited Weber to offer two lectures in their lecture series titled "Intellectual Work as a Vocation." "Science as a Vocation" was delivered on November 7, 1917, and "Politics as a Vocation" on January 28, 1919. Published in 1919, both became standard readings by the 1950s in university courses throughout the world.

Approximately 80 to 100 students, many of whom had recently returned from the front lines of World War I, attended the "Science as a Vocation" lecture. With defeat, the German nation, and particularly the younger generation, was searching for guidance in respect to both the future course of the nation and meaningful pathways for their lives. Students looked to Max Weber for leadership.

He completely disappoints his audience in this regard. Rather than placing the social sciences high on a pedestal and charting out a lofty capacity to provide values, modes of conduct, and even a new world view, to shape a new and more just society, and to offer direction to students in the midst of major personal crises, Weber depicts the social sciences as involving limited tasks and as possessing a modest usefulness. His dual aim in doing so is apparent.

First, he wishes to carve out and defend an open space for an individual autonomy uninfluenced by a caste of scientists pronouncing "expert opinion." Weber seeks, in other words, as also in "Politics as a Vocation," to foster individualism and a sense of personal responsibility among German youth. Second, he attempts to define distinct boundaries for the social sciences and to establish on a firm foundation the independent legitimacy of this domain. He wishes to do so to protect its impartial research procedures against pressures emanating from the state and from political interests in general. Weber emphatically insists that the social sciences must be clearly and strictly separated from politics. How does he pursue these aims?

He first argues that professors in university classrooms in front of captive audiences must not offer to students value judgments, personal views, and political opinions "so long as [they wish] to remain teacher[s] and not to become demagogues." He then holds that the social sciences, although constituting a modern "world view," must not be perceived as empowered to prescribe ethical values, as do religious world views. They are simply incapable of doing so, according to Weber. Furthermore, they *should* not do so, for an intrusion of conclusions from science into the realm of the individual's autonomy would thereby occur.

Hence, excluding in principle political views, personal opinions, and ethical prescription, the legitimate domain of social science is circumscribed, according to Weber. What, then, constitutes its value and usefulness in the modern epoch? What *viable meaning* can individuals today attach to the activity of the social scientist? Weber examines each query and demarcates clear and meaningful, but limited, tasks for social scientists. They can, he contends, practice their profession *as a calling*.

The second selection is from "Politics as a Vocation." It first compares the modes of conduct of political leaders and state civil servants. Leaders, Weber holds, far more effectively announce and cultivate values, take responsibility for their actions, and fight for ideals. These endeavors are indispensable, he insists; he fears that rulership by administrators and functionaries will quickly banish them. However, political leaders too easily fall victim to "vulgar vanity." They must, he admonishes, serve a cause of their own choosing that internally motivates them, *and* they must possess three qualities: passion, a feeling of responsibility, and a sense of proportion. Moreover, on the basis of their values, leaders should stand against the formal rationality of functionaries, managers, and technocrats. Powerful parliaments, where political positions can be aggressively articulated, assist the cultivation of leadership skills and an "ethic of responsibility," he argues. Weber then defines, with examples, this ethic and its counter-part: the "ethic of conviction." In many modern social contexts this ethic proves ill-suited, he contends.

The role of ethical action in respect to the use of violence by the state now becomes Weber's theme. It is repeatedly addressed with deep concern and a sense of urgency. He charts the dilemmas surrounding the responsibility of politicians for the consequences that follow whenever violence by the state takes place. In a world of inevitable paradoxes, "diabolical powers," and irreconcilable conflicts, these consequences are normally unforeseen, Weber holds. "It is *not* true that good can follow only from good and evil only from evil," he insists. Nonetheless, in such a "world of irrationality," responsibility must be taken, he maintains.

As in "Science as a Vocation," Weber's focus on the parameters of ethical action is evident throughout "Politics as a Vocation." Whether a person *can* be truly *called* to the vocation of politics involves, to him, above all a sense of responsibility for the consequences of actions and acknowledgment of the complex ethical issues intimately connected to the use of violence.[1]

Reading 1: "Science as a Vocation"

From "Science as a Vocation," in *From Max Weber: Essays in Sociology*, 1946, H. H. Gerth and C. Wright Mills (Eds. and Trans.); revised by Stephen Kalberg. New York, NY: Oxford University Press, pp. 145–153.

It is said, and I agree, that politics is out of place in the lecture hall. It does not belong there from the point of view of the students. If, for instance, in the lecture hall of my former colleague [and German militarist] Dietrich Schäfer in Berlin, pacifist students were to surround his desk and make an uproar, I should deplore it just as much as I should deplore the uproar which anti-pacifist students are said to have made against [the pacifist] Professor Förster, whose views in many ways are as remote as could be from mine. . . .

To take a practical political stand is one thing, and to analyze political structures and party positions is another. When speaking in a political meeting about democracy, one does not hide one's personal standpoint; indeed, to come out clearly and take a stand is one's damned duty. The words one uses in such a meeting are not mechanisms for scientific analysis; rather, they are means of canvassing votes and winning over others. They are not plowshares to loosen the soil of contemplative thought; they are swords against the enemies. Such words are weapons. It would be an outrage, however, to use words in this fashion in a university lecture hall.

If, for example, "democracy" is under discussion, one considers its various forms, analyzes the way they function, and determines what results for the conditions of life the one form has as compared to the other. Then one confronts the forms of democracy with non-democratic forms of a political order. One then attempts to find the point in reference to which students can define *their* ultimate ideals and, in reference to them, take a stand. The true teacher will be wary of imposing from the podium any political position on the student, whether it is expressed or suggested. "To let the facts speak for themselves" is the most unfair way of arguing a political position vis-à-vis a student.

Why should we abstain from doing this? I stated in advance that some highly esteemed colleagues are of the opinion that this self-restraint can't be carried through consistently. They also argue that, were it possible, it would constitute an imaginative means of avoiding declaring oneself.

Now one cannot demonstrate scientifically what the duty of a professor is. One can only demand that he have the intellectual integrity to see that it is one thing to state facts and to determine mathematical or logical relations or the internal structure of cultural values, and it is quite another thing to answer questions regarding the *value* of a culture and of its particular contents, as well as questions concerning how one should *act* in a cultural community and in political organizations. These are quite *heterogeneous* problems. If he further asks why he should not deal with both types of problems in the lecture hall, the answer is: because the prophet and the demagogue do not belong on the academic podium.

To the prophet and the demagogue, it is said: "Go your ways out into the streets and speak openly to the world." That is, speak in that forum where criticism is possible. In the lecture hall the professor stands opposite an audience obligated to remain silent as long as he is speaking. I hold this situation to be irresponsible. It exploits the circumstance: here, for the sake of their advancement, students must attend a course, yet no one is there to oppose the instructor with criticism. Rather than to imprint his personal political views upon students, the task of the teacher is to serve them through his knowledge and scientific experience.

It is certainly possible that the individual professor will not entirely succeed in eliminating his personal sympathies. He is then exposed to the sharpest criticism in the forum of his own conscience. However, this failure does not refute my position; further errors—such as erroneous statements of facts—are also possible. Yet they also prove nothing against my position: they fail to confront the lecturer's duty to search for the truth. I also reject, in the very interest of science, this mixing of political views and the scientist's impartial procedures. I am ready to prove that, from the works of our historians, a full understanding of the facts *ceases* whenever the man of science introduces his personal value judgment. But this goes beyond tonight's topic and would require lengthy elucidation.

I ask only: In a course on the forms of church and state or on religious history, how should a devout Catholic on the one hand and a Freemason on the other ever be brought to evaluate these subjects alike? This is out of the question. However, through his knowledge and methods the teacher must desire and must demand of himself to serve the one as well as the other.

Now you will rightly say that the devout Catholic will never accept the view of the factors operative in calling forth Christianity that a teacher free of dogmatic presuppositions presents to him. Certainly! The difference, however, lies in the following: Science "free from presuppositions," in the sense of a rejection of religious bonds, does not know of the "miracle" and the "revelation." If it did, science would be unfaithful to its own "presuppositions." The believer knows both: miracle and revelation. And a science "free from presuppositions" expects from him no less—and no more—than an acknowledgment: *if* the process can be explained without reference to supernatural interventions, which an empirical explanation has to eliminate as causal factors, then it has to be explained in the same way as science. The believer can do this without being disloyal to his faith.

But has the contribution of science no meaning at all for a man indifferent to facts as such and caring only about the practical standpoint? Perhaps science nevertheless contributes something.

The primary task of a useful teacher is to teach his students to recognize *inconvenient* facts (*Tatsachen*)—I mean facts that are inconvenient for their party opinions. And facts exist that are extremely inconvenient for every party opinion, for example, for my own opinion. I believe that the professor accomplishes more than a mere intellectual achievement if he compels his audience to accustom itself to the existence of such facts. I would be so immodest as even to apply the expression "moral achievement," though perhaps this may sound too grandiose for something that should go without saying.

Thus far I have spoken only of *practical* reasons for avoiding the imposition of a personal point of view. But these are not the only reasons. The impossibility of "scientific" intercession on behalf of a practical standpoint—except in discussing the means for a firmly *given* and presupposed end—rests on reasons that lie far deeper.

"Scientific" intercession is meaningless in principle because the various value spheres of the world stand in irreconcilable conflict with each other. The elder Mill, whose philosophy I will not praise otherwise, was on this point right when he said: If one proceeds from pure experience, one arrives at polytheism. This is shallow in formulation and sounds paradoxical, yet there is truth in it. If anything, we realize again today that something can be sacred not only in spite of its not being beautiful, but rather *because* and *in so far* as it is not beautiful. You will find this documented in the fifty-third chapter of the book of Isaiah and in the twenty-first Psalm.

And, since Nietzsche, we realize that something can be beautiful not only in spite of the aspect in which it is not good, but rather in that very aspect. You will find this expressed earlier in the *Fleurs du mal* [The Flowers of Evil] as Baudelaire [1824–1876] named his volume of poems. It is commonplace to observe that something may be true although it is not beautiful and not holy and not good. Indeed, it may be true in precisely those aspects. But all these are only the most elementary cases of the struggle between the gods of the various life-spheres and values. How one might wish to decide "scientifically" the *value* of French and German culture I do not know. For here, too, different gods struggle with one another, now and for all times to come.

We live as did the ancients when their world was not yet disenchanted of its gods and demons; only we live in a different sense. As Hellenic man at times sacrificed to Aphrodite and at other times to Apollo, and, above all, as everybody sacrificed to the gods of his city, so today our behavior also manifests an internal genuine flexibility. This remains the case even though, unlike for the ancients, [our world] has become disenchanted and stripped of the mythical. Fate, and certainly not "science," holds sway over these gods and their struggles. One can only understand *what* is divine for one arena or for the other—or better, what divinity is in the one or in the other sphere.

With this understanding, however, the matter has reached its final conclusion so far as it can be discussed in a lecture hall and by a professor. Yet, of course, far from being concluded is the mighty problem of *life* contained therein. However, here powers other than university lecturers have their say.

What person will take upon himself the attempt to "refute scientifically" the ethic of the Sermon on the Mount? For instance, the sentence, "resist no evil." Or the image of turning the other cheek? And yet, viewed from the vantage point of daily life, it is clear that this is an ethic of undignified conduct. Here a choice must be made between the religious dignity that this ethic confers and the dignity of manly conduct that preaches something quite different: "resist evil—lest you be co-responsible for [the world's] preponderance of violence." According to the ultimate standpoint, one is a devil and the other a God. The individual must decide which is God for him and which is the devil. And so it goes throughout all the spheres of life.

The splendid rationalism of the rigorously ethical conduct of life, which flows from every religious prophecy, has dethroned this polytheism in favor of the "that which is necessary." And then, confronted with the realities of outer and inner life, found compromises and relative judgments of the type we all know from the history of Christianity to be necessary. Many old gods, disenchanted and therefore in the form of impersonal powers, are ascending from their graves. They strive to acquire a controlling force over our lives and again they resume their eternal struggle with one another. Hard for modern man, and especially for the younger generation, is to measure up to this situation on a *daily* basis. The ubiquitous chase after "experience" arises out of this weakness—for it is weakness not to be able to look directly at the fate of our times with its stern seriousness. However, it is our fate in our present civilization to again become conscious of these struggles after our eyes have been blinded for a thousand years—blinded by the allegedly or presumably exclusive orientation towards the impressive moral fervor of Christian ethics.

But enough of these questions that lead far away. Those of our youth are in error who react to all this by replying with a single answer: "Yes, but we happen to come to lectures in order to experience something more than mere analysis and statements of fact." The error is that they seek from the professor something different from what stands before them: they crave a *leader* and not a *teacher*. But we are placed at the podium solely as *teachers*. And these are two different things, as one can readily see. Permit me to take you to America. There one can often observe such matters in their most massive originality.

The American boy learns unspeakably less in school than the German boy. In spite of an incredible number of examinations, his school life has not had the significance of turning him into an absolute creature of examinations, such as has the German school. For in America that which presupposes the examination diploma as a ticket of admission to the realm of civil service perquisites—the bureaucracy—is only in its beginning stage.

The young American has no respect for anything or anybody, for tradition or for public office—unless it is for the personal achievement of individual men. *This* is what the Americans call "democracy." However inconsistent this reality may be vis-à-vis the subjective meaning of the Americans, this subjective meaning is prevalent—and this is what matters here. Hence, the American's conception of the teacher who faces him is: he sells me his knowledge and his methods for my father's money, just as the greengrocer sells my mother cabbage. And that is all.

To be sure, if the teacher happens to be a football coach, then he can make a claim to being something more: namely, in this field, a leader. But if he is not this (or something similar in a different field of sports), he is simply a teacher—and nothing more. And no young American would think of a teacher who will sell him a *Weltanschauung* [world view] or authoritative standards for the guiding and organizing of his life. Now, when formulated in this manner, we should reject this. But the question is whether there is not a grain of truth contained in this portrayal of the American sensibility, which I have deliberately stated in extreme with some exaggeration.

Fellow students! You come to our lectures and demand from us the qualities of leadership. However, at least ninety-nine of one hundred professors do not, and must not, claim to be football coaches in respect to the guiding and organizing of life, or even to be "leaders" in matters of conduct. Please consider that the value of persons does not depend on whether or not they possess leadership qualities. In any case, *the* qualities that make people excellent scholars and teachers are not the same qualities that make them leaders able to give directions in the realm of practical life-orientations or, more specifically, in the arena of politics.

It is pure accident if a person also possesses these qualities. Indeed, it is cause for concern if every teacher at the podium feels himself confronted with students expecting these qualities. It is still more worrisome if it is left to every university instructor to set himself up as a leader in the lecture hall: those who most frequently think of themselves as leaders often qualify least as leaders. But irrespective of whether they are or are not, the university lecture setting simply offers no possibility to *prove* oneself as a leader. The professor who feels called upon to act as a counselor of youth and to enjoy their trust may prove himself a man in personal interactions with them. And if he feels called upon to intervene in the struggles of world views and party opinions, he may do so in the market place, in the press, in meetings, and in associations wherever he wishes. But, after all, it is somewhat too convenient to demonstrate one's courage by taking a stand in those [lecture hall] situations where the audience and possible opponents are condemned to silence.

Finally, you will ask: "If this is so, what then does science actually and positively contribute to practical and personal 'life?'" Now we are again back to the problem of science as a "vocation."

First, of course science contributes knowledge of how, with technology, human beings acquire, through calculation, control over life, both the external objects and the activities of people. Well, you will say, that, after all, amounts to no more than the greengrocer of the American boy. I fully agree.

Second, science can contribute something that the greengrocer cannot: methods of thinking and the tools and training for thought. Perhaps you will say: well, that is no vegetable, but it amounts to no more than the means for procuring vegetables. Well and good, let us leave it at that for today.

Fortunately, however, the contribution of science has not yet reached its limit. We are in a position to help you to attain a third objective: to gain *clarity*. Of course, it is presupposed that we ourselves possess clarity. As far as this is the case, we can make clear to you the following:

In practice, you can take this or that position when concerned with a problem of value—for simplicity's sake, please think of social phenomena as examples. *If* you take such and such a stand, then you have to use, according to scientific experience, such and such a *means* in order to carry out your conviction practically. Now, these means are perhaps such that you believe you must reject them. Then you simply must choose between the end and the inevitable means. Does the end "justify" the means? Or does it not? The teacher can confront you with the necessity of this choice. He cannot do more—as long as he wishes to remain a teacher and not to become a demagogue. He can, of course, also inform you: if you want such and such an end, then you must take into the bargain the subsidiary consequences. According to all experience, they will occur. Again we find ourselves in the same situation as before.

These are problems that can also emerge for the technician, who in numerous instances has to make decisions according to the principle of the lesser evil or of the relative best. To him, one thing—the main thing—is usually given: namely, the *end*. However, this is *not* the case as soon as truly "ultimate" problems are at stake. With this situation, at long last, we come to the final service that science as such can render to the aim of clarity. At the same time we come to the limits of science.

We can, and we should, state: In terms of its *meaning,* such and such a practical stand can be derived with inner consistency—and hence integrity—from this or that ultimate *weltanschauliche* position. Perhaps it can only be derived from one such fundamental position, or maybe from several; however, it cannot be derived from these or those other positions. Figuratively speaking, when you decide to adhere to this position you serve this god and you *offend the other* god. And if you remain faithful to yourself, you will necessarily come to certain final and meaningful *conclusions* that subjectively make sense. This much, in principle at least, can be accomplished. Philosophy, as a special discipline involving the essentially philosophical discussions of principles in the other sciences, attempts to achieve this.

Thus, if we are competent in our pursuit (which must be presupposed here), we can force the individual—or at least we can help him—*to give to himself an account of the ultimate meaning of his own conduct.* To me, this appears as not so trifling a thing to do, even for one's own personal life. Again, I am tempted to say of a teacher who succeeds in this: he stands in the service of "moral" forces; he fulfils the duty of bringing about self-clarification and a sense of responsibility. And I believe he will be more able to accomplish this the more conscientiously he avoids the desire personally to impose upon, or suggest to, his audience his own stand.

This proposition, which I present here, always takes its point of departure from the one fundamental fact that, so long as life takes itself as its own resting point and is understood by reference to itself, it knows only of an unceasing struggle of these gods with one another. Or, literally, the ultimately *possible* standpoints toward life are irreconcilable, and hence their struggle can never be brought to a final conclusion. Thus it is necessary to make a *choice* between them.

Whether, under such conditions, science is a worthwhile "vocation" for somebody, and whether science itself can be viewed as having an objectively valuable "vocation"—again, these are value-judgments about which nothing can be said in the lecture hall. To affirm the value of science is a *presupposition* for teaching. I personally, through my own work, answer in the affirmative. And I do so from precisely the standpoint that hates intellectualism as the worst devil, as the younger generation does today—or usually only presumes it does. For these youths the maxim holds: "Mind you, the devil is old; grow old to understand him." This does not mean age in the sense of a birth certificate. It means that if one wishes to banish this devil, one must not flee from him, as so many like to do nowadays. Above all, one has to see the devil's ways to the end if one wishes to see his power and his limitations.

Science today is a "vocation" organized into *specialized fields* in the service of self-clarification and knowledge of actual relationships. It is not the gift of grace of seers and prophets dispensing sacred values and revelations, nor does it partake of the contemplation of sages and philosophers about the *meaning* of the world.

This, to be sure, is the inescapable condition of our historical situation. We cannot evade it as long as we seek to remain true to ourselves. And again Tolstoi stands upright inside of you and queries. Who is, as science does not, to answer the questions: "What shall we do?" "How shall we arrange our lives?" Or, in the words used here tonight: "Which of the warring gods should we serve? Or should we serve perhaps an entirely different god? Who is he?" The answer can be given only by a prophet or a savior.

Reading 2: "Politics as a Vocation"

From "Politics as a Vocation," in *From Max Weber: Essays in Sociology*, 1946, H. H. Gerth and C. Wright Mills (Eds. and Trans.); revised by Stephen Kalberg. New York, NY: Oxford University Press, p. 95.

According to his particular vocation, the genuine government civil servant—and this is decisive for the evaluation of our former regime—should not be engaged in politics. Rather, he should participate in "administration," above all *without regard to political parties*. This also holds, at least officially, for the so-called "political" functionaries in so far as the *raison d'état*—that is, the vital interests of the ruling order—are not in question. He shall administer his office *sine ira et studio*: "without anger and prejudice." Hence, he shall not do precisely what the politician, the leader as well as his following, must always and necessarily do: namely, *fight*.

To take a stand and to struggle with passion—*ira et studium* [anger and zeal]—is the politician's element. Above all, this is the element of the political *leader*. Compared to that of the civil servant, his action is subject to a quite different—indeed, exactly the opposite—principle of *responsibility*. The honor of the civil servant is found in an ability to execute conscientiously the order of superior authorities exactly as if it agreed with his own conviction. This holds even if the order appears wrong to him and if, despite the civil servant's complaint, the person in authority insists on the order. Without this moral discipline and renunciation, in the highest sense, the whole apparatus would fall to pieces.

However, the honor of the political leader and leading statesman lies precisely in an exclusive *personal* responsibility for what he does; he cannot and must not reject or transfer this responsibility. It is in the nature of officials of high moral standing to be poor politicians and—above all in the political sense of the word—to be irresponsible politicians. In this sense, they are politicians of low moral standing, such as we [in Germany] unfortunately have had again and again in leading positions. This is what we have called *Beamtenherrschaft* [civil-service rule].

From "Politics as a Vocation," in *From Max Weber: Essays in Sociology*, 1946, H. H. Gerth and C. Wright Mills (Eds. and Trans.); revised by Stephen Kalberg. New York, NY: Oxford University Press, pp. 114–117.

[What] inner enjoyments can [a] career [in politics] offer and what personal conditions are presupposed for one who enters this profession?

Well, first of all the career in politics grants a feeling of power. The knowledge of influencing men, of participating in power over them, and, above all, the feeling of holding in one's hands a nerve fiber of historically important events can elevate the professional politician above everyday routine—even when he is placed in formally modest positions. But now the question for him is: Through what qualities can I hope to do justice to this power (however narrowly circumscribed it may be in the individual case)? How can he hope to do justice to the responsibility that power imposes upon him?

With these queries we enter the field of ethical questions, for that is where the problem belongs: What kind of person must one be to be permitted to place a hand on the wheel of history? One can say that three preeminent qualities are decisive for the politician: passion, a feeling of responsibility, and a sense of proportion.

This means passion in the sense of *matter-of-factness:* a passionate devotion to a "cause" and to the god or demon who governs it. Nonetheless, however genuinely felt, mere passion is not enough. It does not make a politician unless this passion, as service to a "cause," also makes *responsibility* to this cause the guiding star of action. And, for this, a sense of *proportion* is needed. This capacity, namely, with inner concentration and calmness, to let realities work upon him is the decisive psychological quality of the politician. Hence, his *distance* to things and people. "Lack of distance" *per se* is one of the deadly sins of every politician.

For the problem is simply how can warm passion and a cool sense of proportion be forged together in one and the same soul? Politics is made with the head, not with other parts of the body or soul. And yet devotion to politics, if it is not to be frivolous intellectual play but rather genuinely human conduct, can be born and nourished from passion alone. However, that firm taming of the soul, which distinguishes the passionate politician and differentiates him from the "sterilely excited" and the mere political dilettante, is possible only through habituation to detachment in every sense of the word. The "strength" of a political "personality" means, in the first place, the possession of these qualities of passion, responsibility, and proportion.

Therefore, daily and hourly, the politician inwardly has to overcome a quite trivial and all-too-human enemy: a quite vulgar vanity. This is the deadly enemy of all matter-of-fact devotion to a cause, and of all distance— in this case, of distance towards one's self.

Vanity is a very widespread quality and perhaps nobody is entirely free from it. It is a sort of occupational disease in academic and scholarly circles. Nonetheless, precisely with the scholar, vanity—however disagreeably it may express itself—is relatively harmless in the sense that it does not, as a rule, disturb the scientific enterprise.

The case is quite different for the politician. The striving for *power* is unavoidable in his daily endeavors. Therefore, the "power instinct," as one is inclined to express it, belongs indeed to his normal qualities. The sin against the lofty spirit of the politician's vocation, however, begins where this striving for power ceases to be *objective*: instead of exclusively entering the service of "the cause," it becomes a purely personal self-intoxication. Ultimately, in the field of politics there are only two kinds of deadly sins: lack of objectivity and—often but not always identical with it—irresponsibility. Vanity, or the need personally to stand in the foreground as clearly as possible, strongly tempts the politician to commit one or both of these sins.

This is more truly the case to the extent that the demagogue is compelled to count upon "results." He therefore is constantly in danger of becoming a performer (*Schauspieler*), of taking lightly responsibility for the outcome of his actions, and of being concerned merely with the "impression" he makes. His lack of objectivity tempts him to strive for the glamorous semblance of power rather than for actual power, and his irresponsibility suggests that he enjoys power merely for power's sake and without a substantive purpose. Although—or rather just because—power is the unavoidable means of all politics and striving for power is one of its driving forces, there is no more harmful distortion of political force than that which occurs when the parvenu-like braggart acquires power, when a vain self-reflection in the feeling of power occurs, and wherever, in general, power *per se* is worshipped.

Although the mere "power politician" may achieve strong results, actually his work leads nowhere and is senseless. (Among [we Germans], too, an ardently promoted cult seeks to glorify him.) Here the critics of "power politics" are absolutely right. We can see, from the sudden inner collapse of typical representatives of this mentality, that inner weakness and helplessness lies hidden behind this boastful—but entirely empty—demeanor. It is a manifestation of an inadequate and superficially blasé posture toward the meaning of human conduct and has no connection whatsoever to the knowledge of tragedy with which all action—but especially political action—is truly interwoven.

The final result of political action often—no, even regularly—stands in a completely inadequate and often even paradoxical relationship to its original meaning. This point need not be grounded in detail here; it is fundamental to all history. However, because of this, service to a *cause* must not be absent if action is to possess internal substance.

Exactly *what* the cause, in the service of which the politician strives for power and uses power, looks like is a matter of faith. He may serve national, humanitarian, social, ethical, cultural, worldly, or religious ends. A strong belief in "progress"—no matter in which sense—may sustain the politician. Or he may coolly reject this kind of belief. Or he may claim to stand in service to an "idea." Conversely, he may reject this in principle and may want to serve external ends embedded in daily life. In all cases some kind of belief must always be *there*. Otherwise, it is absolutely true that the curse of human worthlessness burdens even the externally strongest political successes.

With this theme we are already engaged in the discussion of the last problem that concerns us tonight: the *ethos* of politics as a "cause." What calling can politics—quite independently of its goals—fulfill within the total ethical economy of the organization of life? What is, so to speak, the ethical locus where politics finds its home? Here, to be sure, ultimate *Weltanschauungen* clash. And between these world views one must in the end make a *choice*.

From "Politics as a Vocation," in *From Max Weber: Essays in Sociology*, 1946, H. H. Gerth and C. Wright Mills (Eds. and Trans.); revised by Stephen Kalberg. New York, NY: Oxford University Press, pp. 120–128.

We must be clear about the fact that all ethically oriented conduct may be guided by one of two fundamentally differing and irreconcilably opposed maxims: conduct can be oriented to an "ethic of conviction" or to an "ethic of responsibility." This is not to say that an ethic of conviction is identical with irresponsibility, or that an ethic of responsibility is identical with unprincipled opportunism. Naturally nobody says that. However, there is a deep chasm between conduct that follows the maxim of an ethic of conviction—that is, in religious terms, "The Christian does rightly and leaves the results with the Lord"—and conduct that follows the maxim of an ethic of responsibility. In this case one has to give an account of the foreseeable *results* of one's action.

You may demonstrate to a convinced Syndicalist who believes in an ethic of conviction that his activities will result in an increased likelihood of political reaction, an increased oppression of his class, and obstruction of its ascent—and you will not make the slightest impression upon him. If an action of good intent leads to bad results, then, in the eyes of those who uphold an ethic of conviction, they are not responsible for the evil. Rather, responsibility lies with the world, the stupidity of other men, or God's will who made them thus.

However, the believer in an ethic of responsibility takes account of precisely the average deficiencies of people. As [the German Idealist philosopher Johann Gottlieb] Fichte [1762–1814] has correctly stated, he does not have any right to presuppose their goodness and perfection, and does not feel in a position to burden others with the results of his own actions so far as he is able to foresee them. These results, Fichte maintains, are to be ascribed to my deeds.

Conversely, the believer in an ethic of conviction feels "responsible" only for seeing to it that the flame of the pure set of values is not extinguished; for example, the flame of protesting against injustice in the social order. To rekindle the flame ever anew is the purpose of his quite irrational—judged in terms of their possible success—activities. They are activities that can and ought to have only exemplary value.

This having been said, the problem is not yet exhausted. No ethics in the world can avoid the reality that the attainment of "good" ends in numerous cases depends upon a willingness to pay the price of using morally dubious means, or at least dangerous means. Moreover, this attainment involves the possibility, or even the probability, that evil ramifications must be tolerated. No ethical system has ever been able to specify when, and to what extent, the ethically good purpose "sanctifies" the ethically dangerous means and collateral effects.

Here, on the problem of the sanctification of the means by the end, the ethic of conviction must fail. . . . Those, for example, who have just preached "love against violence" call in the next moment for the use of force—for the *last* violent deed which would then lead to a state of affairs in which *all* violence is destroyed. In the same manner, our [World War I German] officers told the soldiers before every offensive: "This will be the last one; this one will bring victory and therewith peace."

The proponent of an ethic of conviction cannot deal with the ethical irrationality of the world. He is a cosmic-ethical "rationalist." Those of you who know Dostoyevski will remember the scene of the "Grand Inquisitor" [in *the Brothers Karamazov*, Bk 5, Ch. 5], where the problem is strikingly explained. If one makes any concessions at all to the principle that the end justifies the means, it is not possible to bring an ethic of conviction and an ethic of responsibility under one roof. Nor is it possible to decree ethically which end should cast a justifying halo around *which* means.

My colleague, Mr. F. W. Förster [the spokesman of the society for ethical Culture], who I highly esteem personally for his undoubted sincerity but who I reject unreservedly as a politician, believes it is possible to skirt around this difficulty by referring to a simple thesis: "from good comes only good; from evil only evil follows." At this point our entire dilemma ceases to exist.

But it is quite astonishing that such a thesis can come to light 2,500 years after the Upanishads. Not only the whole course of world history, but every frank examination of daily experience points to the very opposite. The development of all religions all over the world is determined by the fact that the opposite is true. The ancient problem of theodicy consists of the very question of how a power said to be at once omnipotent and kind could have created such an irrational world—namely, one of undeserved suffering, unpunished injustice, and enduring stupidity. Either this power is not omnipotent or not kind, or entirely different principles of compensation and reward govern our lives—principles we may interpret metaphysically or even principles that forever escape our comprehension.

This problem—the experience of the irrationality of the world—has been the driving force of all religious development. The Indian doctrine of karma, Persian dualism, the doctrine of original sin, predestination and the *deus absconditus* [hidden God]—all these have grown out of this experiencing of the world as irrational. Also the early Christians knew full well that the world is ruled by demons and that whoever engages in the arena of politics—that is, whoever uses power and violence as means—makes a compact with diabolical powers. And here it is *not* true that good can follow only from good and evil only from evil. Rather, often the opposite is true. Anyone who fails to see this is, indeed, a political infant.

Religious ethics have made their peace with the fact that we are placed into various life-spheres and that each is governed by different laws and in different ways. Hellenic polytheism made sacrifices to Aphrodite and Hera alike, to Dionysus and to Apollo. They did so even while recognizing that these gods were frequently in conflict with one another. . . .

As is known in Catholic ethics—to which otherwise Professor Förster stands close—the *consilia evangelica* [Catholic Church hierarchy] is a special ethic for those endowed with the charisma of a holy life. There stands the monk who must not shed blood or strive for gain, and beside him stand the pious knight and middle class citizens. Both are allowed to do so: the one to shed blood, the other to pursue gain. . . .

According to the presuppositions of the Christian faith, this could—and had—to be the case. Stemming from original sin, the wickedness of the world allowed the integration of violence into ethics with relative ease. It served as a disciplinary mechanism against sin and against the heretics who endangered the soul. However, the demands of the Sermon on the Mount—an acosmic ethic of conviction—implied a religion-based natural law of absolute imperatives. These imperatives retained their revolutionizing force and became manifest powerfully during almost all periods of social upheaval. In particular, they produced the radical pacifist sects, one of which in Pennsylvania experimented in establishing a polity that renounced violence towards the outside. This experiment took a tragic course inasmuch as, with the outbreak of the War of Independence, the Quakers could not stand up arms-in-hand for their ideals, which were those of the war.

However, [Lutheran] Protestantism absolutely legitimated the state as a divine institution and hence violence as a means. [This] Protestantism especially legitimated the authoritarian state. Luther relieved each person of the ethical responsibility for war and transferred it to the rulers. Hence, to obey the rulers in matters other than those of faith could never constitute guilt. In turn, Calvinism knew principled violence as a means of defending the faith. Thus Calvinism knew also the crusade, which was for Islam an element of life from the beginning.

One sees it is by *no* means the modern person born out of the hero worship of the Renaissance who calls forth the problem of ethics in politics. With highly differing success, all religions have wrestled with this problem—and, in light of our discussion above, it could not have been otherwise. It is the specific means of *legitimate violence*, when in the hand of human associations, that determines the particularity of all ethical problems in politics.

Whoever makes a contract with these violent means for whatever ends—and every politician does—is exposed to its specific consequences. This holds especially for the crusader, both the religious and revolutionary crusader alike. Let us confidently take the present as an example. He who wants to establish absolute justice on earth by *violence* requires a following, a human "machine." He must hold out the necessary internal and external—heavenly or worldly—rewards to this "machine"; otherwise it will not function. Under conditions of the modern class struggle, the premiums consist of the satisfaction of hatred and the craving for revenge. Above all, they consist of resentment and the need for pseudo-ethical self-righteousness: the opponents must be slandered and accused of heresy. The external rewards are adventure, victory, booty, power, and spoils.

For his success, the leader is completely dependent upon the functioning of his machine—and hence not on his own motives but on those of his followers. Therefore, he also depends upon whether or not the premiums can be *permanently* granted to the following, that is, to the Red Guard, the informers, and the agitators he needs. Under such circumstances, what he actually attains is therefore not in his hand; rather, it is prescribed to him by the followers' motives. If viewed ethically, they are predominantly base. Followers can be held in a tight rein only as long as an honest belief in the leader and his cause inspires at least some of them—yet this rarely occurs. If so, never the majority.

Even when subjectively sincere, this belief actually, in a very great number of cases, is nothing more than an ethical "legitimation" of cravings for revenge, power, booty, and spoils. We shall not allow ourselves to be deceived on this, for the materialist interpretation of history is no random taxicab; it does not brake before reaching the social carriers of revolutions.

Above all, the accustomed routine of *daily life* comes after the emotions-based revolution, the heroic believers, and the faith itself disappears—or, with even greater impact, the faith becomes part of the conventional phraseology of narrow-minded politicians and technicians. This development is especially rapid in the case of conflicts over faith because they are usually led or inspired by genuine *leaders*—that is, prophets of revolution. Here, as with every leader's machine, one of the conditions for success is—in the interest of discipline—a hollowing out and depersonalization: in short, a spiritual proletarianization. After coming to power, the followers of a crusader usually degenerate very easily into a quite well-known stratum—namely, one in search of spoils.

Whoever wants to engage in politics at all, and especially in politics as a vocation, has to be aware of these ethical paradoxes. He must know that he is responsible for what may *become of himself* under the impact of these paradoxes. . . .

Surely, politics is made with the head, but it is certainly not made with the head alone. In this the proponents of an ethic of conviction are right. One cannot prescribe to anyone whether he *should* follow an ethic of conviction or an ethic of responsibility, or when the one and when the other. One can say only this much: If in these times, which, in your opinion, are not times of "sterile" excitation—excitation is not, after all, genuine passion—if now *suddenly* the *Weltanschauungs* politicians crop up *en masse* and pass the watchword:

> The world is stupid and base, not I. The responsibility for the consequences does not fall upon me but upon the others whom I serve and whose stupidity or baseness I shall eradicate.

[If this occurs], then I declare frankly that I would first inquire into the degree of *inner character* backing this ethic of conviction. I am under the impression that in nine out of ten cases I deal with windbags who intoxicate themselves with romantic sensations and do not fully realize the responsibility they take upon themselves.

From a human point of view this is not very interesting to me; nor does it move me profoundly. However, it is immensely moving when a *mature* man—no matter whether old or young in years—is aware of a responsibility for the consequences of his conduct and really feels such responsibility with heart and soul. He then acts by following an ethic of responsibility and somewhere he reaches the point where he says: "Here I stand; I can do no other" [Luther, 1521]. This is something genuinely human and moving.

Every one of us who is spiritually alive must recognize the possibility of finding oneself at some time in this position. In so far as this is true, an ethic of conviction and an ethic of responsibility are not absolute contrasts; rather, they complement each other. Only when they appear in unison do they constitute a genuine man who *can* have the "calling for politics."

Now then, honored attendees, let us debate this matter once more *ten years* from now. Unfortunately, for a whole series of reasons, I fear that by then the period of reaction will have long since broken over us. It is very probable that little of what many of you, and (I candidly confess) I too, have wished and hoped for will be fulfilled—perhaps not exactly nothing, but what to us at least seems little. This will not crush me, but surely it is an inner burden to acknowledge it. Then, I wish I could see what "has become" of those of you who now feel yourselves to be genuinely "conviction" politicians and who share in the intoxication signified by this revolution [1918 in Munich]. It would be fine if all turned out in this way, for then Shakespeare's Sonnet 102 would hold true:

Our love was new, and then but in the spring,

When I was wont to greet it with my lays;

As Philomel in summer's front doth sing,

And stops her pipe in growth of riper days.

But such is not the case. Not summer's bloom lies ahead of us, but a polar night of icy darkness and hardness—regardless which group now externally triumphs. Where there is nothing, not only the Kaiser but also the proletarian has lost his rights. When this night shall have slowly receded, who of those for whom spring apparently has bloomed so luxuriously will be alive?

And what will have become of all of you internally by then? Will you be bitter or apathetic? Will you simply indifferently accept your world and occupation? Or will the third—and by no means the least often—possibility be your lot: mystic flight from reality for those who are gifted for it, or—as is both frequent and unpleasant—for those who torment themselves in order to follow this fashion?

In every one of these cases I shall draw the conclusion that they have *not* measured up. They have *not* measured up to their own deeds or to the world as it really is in its daily routines. Objectively and actually, although they thought they had, they have not experienced politics as a vocation in an internal sense. They would have done better by simply cultivating an ethos of plain brotherliness in person to person relationships and otherwise conscientiously undertaken their daily work.

Politics is a strong and slow boring of hard boards. It takes passion and perspective together. Certainly all historical experience confirms the truth: that people would not have attained the possible if time and again had they not reached out for the impossible. But to do that a man must be a leader—and not only a leader but as well a hero in the very unpretentious sense of the word. And those who are neither leaders nor heroes must arm themselves with the firmness of heart that can brave even the crumbling of all hopes.

This is necessary right now. They will not otherwise be able to attain even that which is possible today. Only he has the "calling" for politics who, when the world from his point of view is too stupid or too base for what he wants to offer, is certain that he will not crumble. Only he has the "calling" for politics who, in the midst of all this, is able to say: "In spite of all!"

Study Questions and Thoughts to Ponder

1. Discuss Weber's concern regarding the fate of ethical action in the modern world. Refer to "Science as a Vocation," "Politics as a Vocation," and arguments in at least two prior chapters.

2. The social sciences cannot provide values-based guidance for conduct and political policies, according to Weber. How does he then justify their usefulness? Please summarize Weber's position.

3. Discuss the restrictions Weber places on the social sciences. Why does he do so? Do you agree that his limitations are necessary?

4. Distinguish between the "ethic of responsibility" and the "ethic of conviction." Can Weber's distinction be defended?

5. Should politics and personal preferences be kept out of the classroom? Is it possible today to do so? What are Weber's reasons for wishing to do so?

6. Why does Weber insist that politicians possess a *calling* for politics?

7. Explain Weber's phrase: "the irrationality of the world." Do you agree?

Note

1. The translations by Gerth and Mills of both selections have been revised significantly by the author. Revisions have been based on the complete works (*MWG I/17*) edition (Weber, 1992). The "Science as a Vocation" section comprises approximately one-third of the original text (for a translation of further sections, see Weber, 2005; for a complete translation see Weber, 1946, pp. 129–156). The "Politics as a Vocation" selection constitutes approximately one-sixth of the original (for a complete translation see Weber, 1946a).

Glossary

This list includes (a) historical terms used by Weber that are often forgotten today and (b) terms that are key to his sociology. Italics indicate a cross-reference to another Glossary entry.

Adventure Capitalism. This type of *capitalism* has appeared universally. Since the dawn of history, entrepreneurs and speculators have financed wars, piracy, construction projects, shipping, plantations using forced labor, political parties, and mercenaries. These money-making enterprises are of a purely speculative nature and often involve wars and violent activities. Loans of every sort are offered. See *capitalism* and *modern capitalism.*

Affectual Action. One of Weber's *Four Types of Social (Meaningful) Action.* "Determined by the actor's specific affects and feeling states." See *means-end rational action, value-rational action,* and *traditional action.*

Affinity (elective, internal; *Wahlverwandtschaft*). A concept taken from Johann Wolfgang von Goethe (1749–1832). It implies an "internal" connection between two different phenomena rooted in a shared feature and/or a clear historical linkage (for example, between certain religious beliefs and a *vocational calling*). The causal relationship is not strong enough to be designated "determining."

Ascetic Protestantism (see *Puritanism; this-worldly*). This generic term refers to the Calvinist, Pietist, Methodist, Quaker, Baptist, and Mennonite *churches* and *sects.* Weber compares and contrasts the *vocational calling* of these faiths to each other and to those of *Lutheran* Protestantism and Catholicism. See *asceticism.*

Asceticism. An extreme taming, channeling, sublimating, and organizing of the believer's spontaneous human drives and wants (the *status naturae*) by a set of values. Western asceticism charted a *methodical-rational organization of life* in two "directions": *ascetic Protestantism* did so *in* the world (*this-worldly* asceticism) and medieval Catholic monks, living sequestered in monasteries, did so *outside* the world (*other-worldly* asceticism).

Associations (civic, social, voluntary; *Vereine*). Whereas Alexis deTocqueville saw the origins of American society's "innumerable" *civic associations* throughout American society in the "commercial passions," Weber locates their origin in *Puritanism*. These associations constitute to him secularized versions of the *sect*.

Autocephalous. Possessing an independent authority. In contrast to groups under the power of an external rulership (see *heterocephalous*).

Brahmins. The cohesive highest caste in India. These priests were the *carriers* of Hinduism.

Brotherhood and Compassion, Sociology of. Weber views each of the *world religions* as introducing, in different ways, a sociology of brotherhood and compassion. Variation occurs largely in reference to whether—and to what extent—*psychological premiums* are placed exclusively on elites (the *virtuosi*) or also on the laity. He foresees a weakening of brotherhood and compassion in the modern West amid *modern capitalism, bureaucratization, logical-formal law,* and a resurgence of the *formal* and *practical* types of *rationality.*

Bureaucratic (rational-legal) Rulership. Authority resides in a position in an organization and the rights it grants to incumbents rather than in persons or traditions. Hence, obedience to this rulership rests on belief in the appropriate procedural enactment of *impersonal* statutes and regulations. Attached to "the office," rulership remains even though people come and go. Historically unusual, this *type of rulership* has largely been found in the West in the past 150 years.

Bureaucratization. As industrial societies develop, Weber foresees a continuous expansion of large-scale organizations. He fears, in the process, the awarding of high social prestige to *specialists* (the bureaucracy's functionaries), the ascent of the specialist in general over "the cultivated"—or broadly educated—person, and a macro centralization of political power that will effectively preclude viable pluralistic *conflict* and democratization.

Caesaropapism. A secular ruler dominates over the realm of religion and constitutes its highest authority. The opposite of *hierocratic rulership.*

Calling (*Beruf*). Denotes a task given by God to the believer and the incorporation of a demarcated realm of work into the lives of the Protestant faithful in the 16th and 17th centuries. Despite a vast comparative-historical search in the EEWR volumes, Weber found this vocational calling only in Protestantism.

Calvinism. Founded by John Calvin (1509–1564), who formulated the *Predestination doctrine,* this version of Protestantism established a series of "Reformed" *churches* and *sects* rooted in this doctrine. These believers struggled intensely with the fatalism and despair that followed from the doctrine of Predestination.

Capitalism. Capitalism has existed in all the world's civilizations and in all epochs, according to Weber. It involves the expectation of profit and peaceful opportunities for acquisition. A calculation of earnings in monetary terms occurs at the beginning (starting balance) and end of the project (concluding balance), and in respect to the utility of all potential transactions. The origins of profits and losses are ascertained in a systematic manner. See *adventure capitalism* and *modern capitalism.*

Carriers. See *social carriers.*

Caste Order. In India. Persons are born into a specific caste and die in this caste. Mobility up or down is not possible. If caste *dharma* is fulfilled, a favorable (upward) rebirth occurs; if not, a rebirth into a lower caste or animal form takes place.

Charismatic Rulership. Obedience results from a consideration by "followers" or "disciples" of an individual as endowed with extraordinary, exceptional, and perhaps supernatural features. This type of rulership opposes all existing values, customs, laws, rules, and traditions.

Chinese Rationalism. A specific configuration of *societal domains* and historical developments. See *civilizational rationalism.* In its classical and enduring form, Chinese rationalism was dominated by the *literati* stratum, *patrimonial-bureaucratic rulership,* patrimonial law, Confucianism, an agrarian and *clan-based economy,* and strong families oriented to Confucianism and ancestor worship. This rationalism largely opposed the development and expansion of *modern capitalism.* Weber views the identification of China's unique rationalism as the first step toward the isolation of the causes behind its origin and development.

Church. Persons are "born into" a church and, hence, are obligatory members. Unlike *sects,* churches "lets grace shine over the righteous and unrighteous alike."

Civic Association. Prominent in the American 19th century as community service organizations (for example, the Rotary, Lions, and Kiwanis clubs). Secular legacies of the 18th-century Protestant *sects* cast their influence broadly. As in these groups, membership, which resulted from a favorable vote, conferred *status* and respectability. Their widespread proliferation led Weber to reject the view of American society common in Europe: as a *sandpile* of unconnected individuals.

Civic Individualism (practical-ethical individualism). A 19th-century *legacy* of *Puritanism.* Implies an orientation by Americans to a set of universal values located in a *civic sphere.* These values are understood to be *ethical*—that is, they set standards and ideals in reference to which persons feel an internal obligation. Hence, civic individualism involves a posture of activism in reference to a community's values. Weber sees this type of individualism as threatened in the 20th century by *practical rationality, formal rationality,* and *bureaucratization.*

Civic Sphere. A set of values separate from the private realm and the work sphere that set community standards toward which citizens are sincerely committed as *ethical* ideals. Distinct from the public sphere.

Civilizational Rationalism. To Weber, each civilization constitutes a differently formed and unique "rationalism." This term implies a value constellation endowed with a significant degree of internal coherence. It is formed mainly from singular configurations of the rulership, law, religion, economy, social honor, and universal organizations *societal domains* juxtaposed unique with historical developments. *Ideal types* assist identification of each rationalism's major contours. Some rationalisms erect a context of groups conducive to *modern capitalism;* others oppose its development. An amenable rationalism must crystallize if this type of capitalism is significantly to appear.

The Clan (*Sippe*). The extended family. Belongs, according to Weber's conceptual ordering (along with the family) to the *universal organizations* domain. Strong personal relationships of allegiance, compassion, and helpfulness are pivotal.

Clan Charisma. Exceptional, even supernatural, qualities are attributed not to a single person (such as a prophet) but to a group of related persons. This group shares a blood bond.

Commensalism. Interaction is possible among persons as a consequence of a similar social *status*.

Conflict. Weber rejects *organic holism* in favor of a methodology that places *subjective meaning, ideal types,* and *societal domains* at its foundation. This "lens" renders conflict highly visible. Moreover, he views values, interests, traditions, and charismatic leaders as very frequently standing in "relations of antagonism." Finally, *carrier* groups (*strata*, classes, and organizations) often oppose one another. Hence, conflict occurs regularly and broadly in Weber's analyses.

Confraternization (fraternization). Peaceful association of persons across groups with firm boundaries (whether familial, tribal, ethnic, or religious). A greater confraternization occurred in the cities of the Western Middle Ages. In this regard, guilds and religious congregations proved pivotal.

Deification of Human Desires (idolatry). The *Puritan's* loyalty must be exclusively to God and His Commandments. For Him, human wants and desires (personal vanity, sexual fulfillment, the enjoyment of love, friendship, luxury, etc.) must be tamed and remain subordinate to this noble and prior allegiance.

Dharma. In India. The Hindu's caste-specific obligations and rituals.

Disenchantment of the World (*Entzauberung;* demagification). This famous phrase from Friedrich von Schiller (1759–1805) refers, for Weber, on the one hand to a development within the domain of religion from ritual and magic to "*other-worldly* salvation religions." Here paths to salvation completely devoid of magic designate proper *ethical* conduct (see *Puritanism*). On the other hand this expression refers to a broad historical development in the West according to which knowledge of the universe is less and less understood by reference to supernatural forces and salvation doctrines, and more and more comprehended by reference to empirical observation and the experimental method of the natural sciences.

Dispassionate (*nüchtern*). A term Weber uses repeatedly to characterize the temperate and restrained *frame of mind* of Puritans. This disposition implies rigorous self-control and a capacity to organize life systematically around defined goals.

Domination. See *Rulership.*

Economic Ethic (*Wirtschaftsethik;* work ethic, work ethos). See *economic traditionalism* and *modern economic ethic.*

Economic Ethics of the World Religions. This is the title Weber gave to a series of studies on the world's great religions (1951, 1952, 1958). These investigations evaluate the presence or absence of economic ethics in Confucianism, Taoism, Hinduism, Buddhism, Jainism, ancient Judaism, and early and medieval Christianity. Unlike *The Protestant Ethic* volume, they address "both sides" of the causal nexus: "*world and religion.*"

Economic Form. In contrast to an *economic ethic,* an economic form refers to the way in which a company is organized and managed, the relationship of employers to workers, the type of accounting, the movement of capital, and so on.

Economic Rationalism. This term refers to the *modern capitalism* that developed in the 18th and 19th centuries in the West. It implies a *modern economic ethic* and the utilization of *modern science* on behalf of a systematic organization of labor and the entire production process. Hence, qualitative increases in productive capacity occur.

Economic Traditionalism (traditional economic ethic). A *frame of mind* in respect to work. Work is viewed as a necessary evil and only one arena of life, no more important than the arenas of leisure, family, and friends. "Traditional needs" are implied: work ceases when they are fulfilled. This frame of mind stands in opposition to the development of *modern capitalism.* ("Traditionalism," in Weber's time, referred to the conduct of activities in an accustomed, habitual fashion.)

The Elect. The *predestined* and those who have convinced themselves that they belong among the predestined.

Elective Affinity. See *Affinity.*

Enjoyment of Life (eudaemonistic view of life). The *methodical-rational organization of life* by *Puritans* and their disciplined orientation to work, when examined from the vantage point of every enjoyment of life, is irrational, Weber stresses.

Ethic of Conviction (*Gesinnungsethik*). Adherence to an ethical position in an absolute manner; that is, regardless of the possible negative consequences that might result from doing so. (Luther: "Here I stand, for I can do no other.") Good intent alone is central. Opposes the *ethic of responsibility.*

Ethic of Responsibility (*Verantwortungsethik*). An account is given to oneself of the foreseeable results of an action, and responsibility for them is accepted. Action is abandoned if assessment of its outcome reveals negative consequences. Opposed to an *ethic of conviction.*

Ethical Action. This action, rooted in values and involving an obligatory element viewed as an ideal, contains the potential to direct action. To Weber, an ethical standard is upheld and treated as a valid norm when persons believe in it and attribute validity to it. They then seek, in their own conduct, to act in a manner consistent with this standard. The "ethically correct" is then defined. Weber sees ethical action as weakened and circumscribed in the modern era to the extent that *practical* and *formal rationality* expand.

Ethical Neutrality. This term refers to the lecturer's classroom standards. Material must be presented in a fair, impartial, and balanced manner. Political and polemical statements are not allowed in the classroom.

Ethnic Group. Weber contends that this concept is of little utility to a social science that seeks to explain how *social action* arises and becomes patterned in a manner that groups are formed. He views ethnicity as salient to the sociologist only when patterned action and groups form contexts that highlight ethnicity. He counsels caution and circumspection. See *race*.

Flight from the World (*Weltflucht*). The Buddhist monk attempts, through rigorous meditation and by avoiding all ties "to the world," to silence the soul and to merge, in an acosmic unity, with his impersonal God. Considered irrational from the point of view of all *world-mastery* striving.

Formal Rationality. Omnipresent in *modern capitalism, logical-formal law, bureaucratic rulership,* and the modern *state,* this *type of rationality* implies decision making "without regard to persons"; that is, exclusively by reference to sets of universally applied rules, laws, statutes, and regulations.

Four Types of Social (meaningful) action. The foundational typology of action in Weber's sociology. He sees four types of social action: *means-end rational, value-rational, traditional,* and *affectual action.* Synonym: meaningful action.

Frame of Mind (*Gesinnung*). As captured by an *ideal type,* the singular temperament or disposition that Weber sees as specific to a demarcated group of people. He uses this term to refer to characteristic features of *Calvinists,* Catholics, Lutherans, *adventure capitalists,* feudal aristocrats, old family (patrician) financial magnates, persons in the middle class, and so on. The frame of mind in some groups may be more weighted toward values; in others it tends more toward endowing interests (adventure capitalists) or traditions rooted in conventions and customs (peasants) with greater meaning.

Fraternization. See *confraternization*.

Gemeinschaft. A community, generally small in size, where persons are intensely oriented to each other on the basis of emotions, traditions, and shared values rather than economic or political interests.

"Grinding Mechanism." See *steel-hard casing*.

Heterocephalous. Entities subordinate to an external rulership. In contrast to *autocephalous*.

Heterodox. A civilization's minor stream religion (for example, Daoism in China and Jainism in India). Opposed to *orthodox*.

Hierocracy (hierocratic rulership). The ecclesiastical power here penetrates into bureaucratic organizations. If a developed dogma and educational system rooted in religious doctrine is typical, this type of organization can be altered only under extreme circumstances. Its power rests on the principle that "God must be obeyed more than men." The hierocracy proves effective as a check against political power; indeed, secular rules and laws must be legitimated by priests. *Caesaropapism* contrasts directly.

"Hold Your Own." *Ascetic Protestant* believers, even in sects that monitor strictly their behavior, are still responsible directly to God. Individuals must *testify* through conduct to their own salvation. Despite temptation, the devout must "hold their own" in respect to His commandments.

Honoratiores. With the development of the economy, only the wealthy (landowners, patrician merchants) will possess the time and resources to fulfill local and regional administrative tasks. Thus, direct democracy will likely turn into rule by these "notables." The functionary in a bureaucracy generally carries out tasks in a manner technically superior (speed, precision, knowledge of the files, etc.) to the avocational and honorific service of honoratiores.

Ideal Type. Weber's major methodological tool. He creates in *PE,* for example, ideal types for an array of groups (Catholics, Lutherans, *Calvinists, adventure capitalists,* etc.). Each concept, by accentuating that which is *characteristic* from the point of view of a theme Weber has chosen and defined, seeks to capture that which is essential to a group.

Impersonal (abstract) Relationships. Weber sees such relationships, which are found in *modern capitalism* (for example, the relationship between mortgage holders and banks), *bureaucratic rulership,* and *logical-formal law,* as incapable—because lacking a personal element—of being regulated *ethically.*

Indian Rationalism. A specific configuration of *societal domains* and historical developments. In its classical and enduring form, it was dominated by *Brahmin* priests, feudal rulership, traditional law, Hinduism, *caste*-based stratification, an agrarian economy, and "organic traditionalism." This *civilizational rationalism* failed to facilitate the development and expansion of *modern capitalism.* Weber views the identification of India's unique rationalism as the first step toward the isolation of the causes behind its origin and development.

Individual Autonomy. Weber is worried that, in a modern world in which *modern capitalism, logical-formal law,* and *bureaucratic organizations* characterized by rigid hierarchies, specialized tasks, conformist pressures, and routine work dominate, individual autonomy and *ethical responsibility* will be eroded.

Interests. All groups possess "ideal and material interests."

Interpretive Understanding (*verstehen*). This is the term Weber uses to describe his own methodology. He wishes to understand the patterned actions of people in demarcated groups by reconstructing the milieu of values, traditions, interests, and emotions within which they live. He thereby fulfills a major goal: to comprehend how *subjective meaning* is formed.

Legacy (*Vermächtnis, Überbleibsel, Reste*). Weber argues that groups formed in the past—and at times the distant past—often influence the present, especially if strong and favoring social *carriers* for them congeal. Such influences are referred to as legacies.

Levelling. Weber sees a great social leveling as occurring wherever the *traditional types of rulership* with pronounced hierarchies (patrimonialism and feudalism) are replaced by bureaucratic rulership.

Life-sphere (*Lebenssphäre*). See *Societal Domain.*

The Literati (Mandarins). The cultural and political elite in China. Highly educated in the writings of Confucius. The administrators of provinces and the "*carriers* of Chinese culture."

Logical-Formal Law (modern law). Characterized by formal-legal equality and a rootedness in documents (such as a Constitution) and judicial precedent rather than sacred traditions, *charismatic* persons, or a *theocratic state*, logical-formal law is enacted and implemented impartially by *specialists* (legislators, judges). The *impersonal* execution of laws, by reference to systematic and universally applied procedures, is taken as an ideal.

The Lutheran Economic Ethic. Although Protestant and although Luther developed the notion of a *vocational calling*, Lutheranism never developed *asceticism*. Weber sees this *economic ethic* as remaining *traditional*.

Market-Irrational Substantive Rationality. Arises wherever groups carry constellations of values antagonistic to the open market are significant.

Meaningful Action. Synonymous with *social action*.

Means-end Rational Action (*zweckrational*). One of Weber's *four types of social action*. A calculation of interests is at the forefront, as are purely instrumental means on behalf of goals.

Methodical-rational Organization of Life (*methodisch-rationale Lebensführung*). Extremely systematic conduct grounded by adherence to a set of broad-ranging values. See *asceticism* and *organization of life*.

Middle Class (*bürgerlich*). PE offers an analysis of the religious origins of the ethos and *frame of mind* of a new class that placed steady work and the pursuit of profit at the center of life. Composed of both employers and workers, this middle class cultivated a set of values oriented to economic activity and "earning a living" that distinguished it significantly from the destitute urban poor, feudal nobles, patrician old-family capitalists, and *adventure capitalists*. This constellation of new values, Weber argues, played a role in calling forth *modern capitalism*.

Modern Capitalism. Weber sees *capitalism* as universal. He is interested in the origins of *modern* capitalism as it appeared in the West in the 18th and 19th centuries.

This capitalism involved the rational organization of free labor and the systematic pursuit of profit. He concludes that a *Protestant ethic* played a causal role in respect to the rise to modern capitalism.

Modern Capitalism's Substantive Conditions. To Weber, markets do not develop out of the "natural propensity" discovered by Adam Smith to "truck, barter, and exchange." Rather, many "substantive conditions" must have developed beforehand, such as rational modes of accounting and administration, enacted law "rationally interpreted and applied" by jurists, the concept of the citizen, *modern science* and technology, a *spirit of capitalism*, the separation of the household from the industrial company, and the absence of strict market monopolies. In the West, *modern Western rationalism* provided a supportive and facilitating context.

Modern Economic Ethic. Synonymous with *spirit of capitalism*.

Modern Science. Unlike science in Antiquity, the Middle Ages, and the 17th century in the West, modern science is unable to justify its own foundations, despite its state of high technological advancement. Hence, it remains incapable of answering Tolstoi's question: "How should we live?" Fearing a further threat to the *individual's autonomy* by yet another "caste of specialists," now in the name of science, Weber wishes to limit its legitimate goals to insight, clarity, knowledge, and rigorous procedures.

Modern Western Rationalism. The "rationalism" specific to the modern West. Through wide-ranging comparisons to the ancient and medieval civilizations of China, India, and the West, a further singular configuration of *ideal types, societal domains,* and historical developments is articulated. *Modern capitalism, bureaucratic rulership, logical-formal law, modern science,* and *the state* are central. Prominent also are the *formal, practical, and theoretical* types of rationality. This rationalism opposed traditional forms of law and rulership, the agrarian economy, and all anchoring of behavior in views of the supernatural realm and specific "salvation paths." It formulated contexts of patterned action that proved conducive to the development and expansion of *modern capitalism*. Weber views the identification of the modern West's unique features as the indispensable first step toward the isolation of the causes behind its origin and development.

Mysticism, world-fleeing. Through meditation techniques, the mystic devout seek salvation through a merging into an immanent and impersonal acosmic Being. Hence, action in the world possesses no salvation meaning; rather, a "flight from the world" and a "silencing of the self" through withdrawal and meditation is required of this believer. Mainly Buddhist. This "salvation path" contrasts directly in Weber's sociology to the *this-worldly asceticism* found among the *Puritans*.

The Nation. An "entirely ambiguous" concept, according to Weber. Rejecting common language, religious creed, and "common blood" as definitive features of nations, he instead emphasizes a "sentiment of solidarity" rooted in values.

National Character. Explanation of differences between groups by reference to national character was widespread in Weber's time. Because it failed to acknowledge the influence of particular religious, economic, rulership, social honor groups and so on patterned, Weber rejected this mode of explanation.

Notables. See *honoratiores.*

Objectivity. Social scientists never approach empirical reality in an "objective" manner, Weber argues. Rather, they bring to it sets of questions and interests related to their values (value-relevant). Hence, every approach to "the data" is "perspectival"—all the more as every epoch defines in its own way, in accord with its predominant concerns and currents of thought, certain aspects of empirical reality as "culturally significant." And even though new fashions, themes, and concerns render heretofore occluded aspects of social reality visible, other aspects, by the same token, always remain in the shadows. See *value-freedom.*

Office Charisma. An exceptional, even supernatural quality is attributed to an organization's office (bishop, cardinal). This occurs to such a degree that all office incumbents are perceived as possessing charisma.

Organic Holism. The view that societies are constituted from arrays of components, all of which are ultimately conjoined in an interlocking and symbiotic—or "organic"—fashion. Thus, they stand in relationships of cohesion and even harmony. In stark contrast to Weber's *ideal types*-based methodology and focus on *societal domains* rather than "society." The latter approach more readily acknowledges *conflict.*

Organization of Life (*Lebensführung*). This expression implies a conscious directing and leading of life. A systematic striving toward goals is also implied. Although for Weber the organized life is generally "internally" rooted in a set of values (even ethical values), this is not always the case (for example, interests anchor the "practical-rational" *Lebensführung*). This term contrasts in his writings to the undirected life that simply, like a natural event, flows on in time without guidance. Because Weber emphasizes in *PE* that Puritans must organize and direct their lives according to their beliefs and their quest for salvation, the phrase "organization of life" appears best to capture his meaning here. A synonym: organized life.

Orthodox. A civilization's mainstream religion. See *heterodox.*

Ossification. Dominated by extreme *bureaucratization,* ossified—or closed and stagnant—societies are ones in which social and political hierarchies become massive and rigid. Opposite of societal dynamism. Weber argues that highly stratified societies will not allow conflicts to surface over interests and values—and these are indispensable if political leadership, democracies, and a sense of ethical responsibility are to develop and endure. He fears that stagnant societies may be on the horizon in the West.

Other-Worldly. Salvation-striving can be, Weber maintains, "toward" the world or "away from" the world. This striving in the latter case is described as other-worldly. The world, as the proving ground for activity believed by the devout to lead to salvation, is devalued. A *flight from* the world and its meaninglessness occurs for both "other-worldly ascetics" (monks in cloisters) and "other-worldly mystics" (Buddhists engaged in a silencing of the self through meditation). See *mysticism*.

Other-worldly Asceticism. See *asceticism* and *this-worldly*.

Patrimonial-Bureaucracy. A "mixed" *ideal type* construct that combines elements of patrimonial rulership with elements of bureaucratic rulership. Found prominently in China, according to Weber.

Patrimonialism. One of Weber's "traditional" *types of rulership*. Rulers (monarchs) acquire hegemony over large territories and seek, through their "officials," to administer them. They do so through personal relationships rather than through *impersonal* regulations, laws, and statutes. In these organizations, officials regularly abandon their loyalty to the ruler and contest his *power* and *authority*. Unless the ruler remains strong, tensions are inherent and tendencies toward decentralization and fragmentation are regular.

Patterns of Action. Weber's sociology is anchored not only in the subjective meaning of individuals, ideal types, societal domains, and interpretive understanding, but also in the patterns—or regularities—of social action of persons. As patterns become more regular, groups are formed. Each group, given facilitating contextual occurrences, becomes a carrier of values, interests, emotions, or traditions.

Power. In direct contrast to rulership, power implies to Weber sheer coercion, or "the likelihood that one person in a social relationship will be able, even despite resistance, to carry out his or her own will" (1968, p. 53; translation altered).

Practical-Ethical Individualism. See *civic individualism*.

Practical Rationality (practical rationalism; practical-rational individualism). The random flow of daily interests is here central, and the individual's adaptation—through means-end rational calculations—to them. Directly contrasts to all *substantive* rationality, according to which the random flow of interests is confronted and ordered by groups *carrying* patterned orientations of action to values.

Predestination (doctrine of). Prominent especially among *Calvinists*. God has willed a very few to be saved; the vast majority are condemned. His reasons are indecipherable and unknowable; no human activity can change a believer's "predestination status." The logical consequence of belief in this doctrine among the devout was fatalism and despair. Later revisions by theologians and ministers (*Puritan Divines*) gave birth to *the Protestant ethic*.

The Protestant Ethic. The source of the *spirit of capitalism* in *PE*. Sixteenth- and Seventeenth-century interpretations of the Calvinist doctrine of *Predestination* by the *Puritan* Divines eventually allowed believers to convince themselves of their favorable salvation status if they successfully oriented their action to methodical work, economic competition, profit, and the attainment of wealth.

Providential (to sanctify). Rendering with religious (salvation) significance an activity heretofore purely utilitarian (work and profit, for example).

Psychological Motivations (*Antriebe*). Weber is concerned throughout *PE* with the motivation behind action, particularly action directed toward work, wealth, and profit as it originates—or doesn't—from religious beliefs. The important psychological motivations behind religion-oriented action never derive, he argues, from the *ethical* conduct implied by *salvation doctrines* or that which is officially taught in manuals. Rather, central are the motivations that arise from combinations of belief and the regular practice of the religious life (as transmitted by the clergy to believers through pastoral care, church discipline, and preaching). See *psychological rewards*.

Psychological Rewards or Premiums (*psychologische Prämien*). "Salvation premiums" are defined through belief and the practice of religion. They are awarded to particular activities, such as good works, the accumulation of wealth, and the *organization of life* in accord with God's laws. They assist those among the faithful who perform these activities to convince themselves of their membership among the saved.

Puritan Divines. These ministers and theologians in 17th-century England jointly revised John Calvin's *Predestination doctrine* in ways that permitted believers to perceive certain "signs" of God's favor (for example, a capacity to work intensely could be understood as God's strength within, and great wealth could be viewed as coming from His hands)—and hence to conclude that they belonged among the saved (for God would convey these signs only to *the elect* few). These adjustments, which led to a focus among believers on methodical work and a systematic search for profit, gave birth to *the Protestant ethic*.

Puritanism (see *ascetic Protestansism, this-worldly*). Weber's usage follows the everyday language of the 17th century. This "amorphous term" refers to the *ascetic Protestant* movements in Holland, England, and North America oriented toward *this-worldly asceticism*. All Puritans *organized their lives* around work and a this-worldly, morally rigorous, asceticism. Puritanism, Weber argues, provides the most consistent foundation for the idea of a *vocational calling* found in *the Protestant ethic*. Remarkably, because oriented to salvation in the next life rather than exclusively *this-worldly* goods or interests, the intense activity of Puritans must be understood as *in* the world but not *of* the world.

Race. Weber opposes the notion that reference to innate and inheritable qualities can be helpful in sociological analysis. "Racial theories" anchored in inherited instincts, he argues, are hypothetical and methodologically weak. *Social action* that appears to be oriented to race is, on closer inspection, Weber holds, actually a consequence of the juxtaposition of other (for example, economic, political, status groups patterns of social action). See *ethnic group*.

Rational. A systematic, rigorous, disciplined element to action.

Rationalism. See *civilizational rationalism*.

Rationality (types of). See *formal rationality, practical rationality, substantive rationality,* and *theoretical rationality.*

Rationalization. Weber is using this term in accord with the usage of his time. Implied is a systematizing of one's actions that, in going beyond a *utilitarian adaptation* to the "random flow of life," calls forth action in conformity with a constellation of values. This may even occur to the point of the introduction of a *methodical-rational organization of life* grounded in a comprehensive orientation to a constellation of values. Such extreme continuity of action proved stronger against the *traditional economic ethic* than utilitarian action. *Ascetic Protestant* believers rationalized their *this-*worldly activities in the most rigorous fashion.

The Rationalization of Western Civilization. This expression implied to Weber a civilization in which systematic work, a modern *economic ethic,* cities characterized by the presence of autonomous governing units, *logical-formal law, bureaucratic rulership,* impersonal judiciary codes and civil servants to implement them, a modern bureaucratic *state, modern science,* advanced technology, and so on are prominent. It does not imply the "superiority" of the West.

Rational-legal Rulership. See *bureaucratic rulership.*

Religious Reward. See *Psychological Rewards.*

Routinization. The patterned action of persons in groups can be conceptualized, according to Weber, as moving across a *four types of social action* spectrum. Action oriented originally toward values that becomes calculating and exclusively means-end rational has become "routinized."

Routinization of Charisma. *Charismatic* figures (prophets, political leaders) act rigorously in reference to constellations of values, as do their immediate followers. However, their message loses in the next generations its intense orientation to values and may become oriented to a significant extent to political and economic interests alone, Weber argues. To this extent "routinization" occurs.

Rulership, types of (*Herrschaft*). Often translated as "authority" or "domination." Why do people obey commands? In contrast to sheer *power,* rulership implies to Weber that persons attribute, for a variety of reasons, legitimacy to commands and requests for obedience. Hence, a voluntary element is characteristic; that is, a belief that the rulership in the end is justified. Weber identifies three types of rulership: *traditional* (patriarchalism, feudalism, patrimonialism), *charismatic,* and *rational-legal* (*bureaucratic*).

Salvation Doctrine. A religion's formal prescriptions in respect to the question of salvation and the appropriate means for its attainment. However, Weber emphasizes that his interest concerns the *psychological premiums* placed on the believer's conduct, and these are often not manifest from a religion's salvation doctrine. See *psychological rewards* and *psychological motivation.*

Sanctified (Sacrosanct). See *Providential*.

Sandpile. American society should not be perceived as a "sandpile" of atomized individuals, Weber contends—that is, as persons lacking substantive group ties. Rather, the "tremendous flood of *civic* and social associations that penetrated from the beginning all corners of American life" pulled individuals securely into groups.

Sect. As opposed to a *church*, an exclusive and tightly knit group that admits new members only on the basis of *ethical action*. Hence, all members are "certified" as of "good character." The monitoring of behavior by sect members to ensure compliance with high ethical standards is intense. Ethical conduct constitutes a means of testifying to one's salvation "before men." See *church*.

Social Action. Synonymous with "meaningful action." Foundational to Weber's sociology is his aim "to offer an interpretive understanding of social action." Unlike "reactive" or "imitative" action, social action implies a subjectively meaningful component that "takes account of the behavior of others." This aspect can be understood by the researcher. Weber identifies (as *ideal types*) four "*types of social action*": *affectual, traditional, means-end rational, and value-rational*. Among other major goals, *Economy and Society* seeks to chart out the social contexts that call forth meaningful action in a variety of *societal domains*.

Social Carrier (*soziale Träger*). Values, emotions, and interests are important causes forces of historical change for Weber, but only if they are "carried" by charismatic leaders as well as by demarcated and influential groups: classes, strata, and organizations. For example, in *PE* Weber wishes to define the groups that carried specific types of vocational ethics—and hence rendered them influential. Further, secular groups may carry (as legacies) values originally grounded in the sphere of religion (and vice-versa). A central concept in Weber's sociology.

Societal Domains (*gesellschaftliche Domäne;* life-spheres [*Lebenssphären*]*;* societal orders, arenas, and realms [*gesellschaftliche Ordnungen* and *gellschaftliche Bereiche*]). To Weber, *social action* arises mainly within the law, economy, rulership, religion, *status groups,* and *universal organizations* (the family and the *clan*) domains. Each constitutes a demarcated realm characterized by definable constellations of *subjective meaning* that are captured by *ideal types*. His comparative-historical analyses are organized around these spheres (and their various manifestations in different civilizational settings), and the different themes, dilemmas, and problems typical of each, rather than "society," institutions, or the individual's "rational choices." In certain epochs, such as our own, some domains may fall into relationships of irreconcilable antagonism (for example, the rational economy and the religious ethos of *brotherhood and compassion*). All domains serve as orientational constructs for researchers seeking conceptually to "locate" empirical patterned action. A central organizing concept in Weber's comparative historical sociology.

Specialists. People who develop only one talent or ability. Specialization inevitably takes place in societies characterized by a high division of labor. Following Goethe, this occurs to the detriment of other talents or abilities, Weber emphasizes. His texts frequently contrast the specialist to the "cultivated" person. This individual possesses *Bildung:* a broad and deep education, a wide range of experience, and an integrated personality. The epoch in which *Bildung* flourished will never return, Weber maintains.

Spirit of Capitalism. Synonyms: modern economic ethic, rational economic ethic. Represented in *PE* by Benjamin Franklin, this spirit constitutes a secularized *legacy* of the *Protestant ethic.* An "elective *affinity*" connection exists, according to Weber. This "spirit" refers to a methodical orientation toward profit and competition, work "as an absolute end in itself," and a perceived duty to increase one's wealth (yet the avoidance of its enjoyment). Weber insists that the origin of the spirit of capitalism cannot be located in *utilitarian economic activity* or *practical rationalism;* rather, a set of religious values and the quest among *ascetic Protestant* believers for certainty of their salvation constitutes the source of this *frame of mind.* To Weber, this "spirit" played a part at the birth of *modern capitalism.* See *Puritanism* and *the Protestant ethic.*

The State. An organization that monopolizes the legitimate use of force within specified territorial boundaries. Under certain empirical circumstances, its laws, statutes, and legal procedures endow the state with autonomy, even vis-à-vis a *modern capitalist* economy.

Status (status group). Status groups appear where social action is patterned and oriented to social honor, social esteem, and a shared style of life and consumption patterns. Against Marx, Weber argues that inequality arises not only from property ownership; status differences also constitute an important cause.

Status Naturae. The "natural state" of the human species. Human nature is not tamed, channeled, sublimated, or organized. For example, *Puritanism,* in rigorously *organizing the lives* of believers according to a set of values, accomplished just this, Weber argues—indeed in an extremely methodical manner.

Steel-Hard Casing ("iron cage"; *stahlhartes Gehäuse*). Once "in the saddle," *modern capitalism* no longer requires a set of values—a *spirit of capitalism*—as a supporting pillar. Rather, this *grinding mechanism* now sustains itself entirely on the basis of adherence to the laws of the market. Widespread *impersonal* calculation, *practical rationality,* and mechanisms to maximize efficient production characterize this steel-hard casing. *Formal, practical,* and *theoretical types of rationality* become dominant. *Brotherhood and compassion,* as well as *ethical action,* generally are defined as "irrational" and pushed to the margins, and pulsating emotions become restricted to the private sphere.

Stereotypization. A custom, convention, or law may become viewed as permeated by magical forces. It becomes then "stereotyped" and, as a consequence, extremely difficult to change.

Subjective Meaning. Weber's sociology never aspires to establish that which may be said to be objectively valid. Rather, it seeks interpretively to understand the subjective meaningfulness of particular patterned action by persons in specific groups (for example, *churches, sects, bureaucracies, status groups,* etc.). Throughout his sociology, Weber attempts to comprehend how persons lend their action meaning (no matter how odd it may appear to the observer). He wishes in *PE,* for example, to understand why continuous work and a systematic search for profit constitute a subjectively meaningful endeavor for *ascetic Protestants.* And why, for Buddhist monks, is a *flight from the world* meaningful? *Ideal types* capture subjective meaning.

Substantive Rationality. A constellation of internally consistent values. If patterned *social action* is oriented to it, people are uprooted from *traditional action* and the random flow of interests typical of everyday life. Weber fears that the dominance under *modern Western rationalism* of *formal, theoretical,* and *practical types of rationality* will weaken all substantive rationalities.

Symbiotic Dualism. Weber sees an unusual synthesis in the American political culture—namely, an activity-oriented, *world-mastery* individualism became juxtaposed with an orientation of persons to the values of a viable *civic sphere.* A mutually sustaining relationship congealed. He discovers the original manifestation of this dualism in 17th- and 18th-century *Puritan sects* and its later—secular—manifestation in 19th-century *civic associations.*

Testify (*Bewährung*). This central notion for *Puritanism* (and for all striving for salvation) implies both an outward demonstration visible to others (one's conduct, demeanor, and bearing) and a psychological element: the devout understand their strength to "prove" their belief through righteous conduct as emanating from God's Hand. Hence, they feel an inner confidence regarding their salvation status.

Testify Before People. "Qualities of a certain kind" were indispensable to become a *sect* member and devout conduct must be maintained continuously. Owing to the sect's close monitoring of the behavior of all members, the faithful were required to "*hold their own* before people," Weber argues, to sustain self-esteem and respectability. He saw "no stronger means of breeding traits than through the necessity of holding one's own in the circle of one's associates." See *sects.*

Theocracy. A society in which the influence of religious doctrine, sincere belief, and religious figures are dominant in all societal spheres.

Theocratic State. A state in which the influence of religious doctrine, sincere belief, and religious figures are dominant.

Theodicy, the Problem of. When an anthropomorphic God is omnipotent and omniscient, the search to comprehend the reasons behind evil, suffering, and injustice in the world becomes urgent. Just the continuous confrontation with this dilemma by Christian theologians and ministers, and their continuous formulation of "answers" that nonetheless failed to reduce worldly evil and injustice, itself placed into motion repeated alterations of religious doctrines, Weber holds. This conundrum also called forth perpetual transformations of thinking regarding the types of ethical action that would be pleasing to God and thereby reduce or eliminate human suffering. He describes this "religious development" as involving a *theoretical rationalization* process and as following, to a significant extent, "its own internal laws" (*Eigengesetzlichkeit*) independent of economic and political influences.

Theoretical Rationality. The mastering of reality, which is undertaken alike by theologians in search of solutions to the problem of theodicy and modern-day scientists, here occurs through systematic thought and conceptual schemes. Reality is confronted cognitively rather than through values, interests, or traditions, although for theologians this confrontation (unlike for modern scientists) ultimately aims to introduce new values and to banish suffering.

This-Worldly Asceticism (*innerweltliche Askese; diesseitig*). This term implies methodical activity "in" the world in contrast to the activity of monks "outside" the world in monasteries (*other-worldly asceticism*). With Puritanism, Weber argues, asceticism not only organized comprehensively the life of the devout, but also moved out of the monastery and "into" the world. Remarkably, the intense activity of Puritans was *in* the world but not *of* the world: their major orientation was not to this-worldly goods or interests but to, despite the world's various temptations, salvation in the next life. See *Puritanism*.

The Track (*Gleis*). Each *civilizational rationalism* possesses distinct contours and a unique developmental pathway. As Weber notes: "Not ideas, but material and ideal interests directly govern men's conduct. Yet very frequently the 'world views' (*Weltbilder*) that have been created by 'ideas' have, like switchmen, determined the tracks along which action has been pushed by the dynamic of interest. 'From what' and 'for what' one wished to be redeemed . . . depended upon one's image of the world" (1946c, p. 280).

Traditional Action. This action involves "habitual stimuli" and follows an accustomed course. It is "determined by ingrained habituation." One of Weber's *four types of social action*.

Traditional Economic Ethic. See *economic traditionalism*. A *frame of mind* in respect to work. Labor is viewed as a necessary evil and as an arena of life no more important than the arenas of leisure, family, and friends. Static "traditional needs" are implied; when fulfilled, then work ceases. This frame of mind stands in opposition to the development of *modern capitalism*. ("Traditionalism," in Weber's time, referred to the conduct of activities in an accustomed, habitual fashion.)

Traditional Rulership. See *rulership*. Obedience results from an established belief in the sanctity of immemorial traditions and the legitimacy of those exercising rulership under them (for example, clan patriarchs). Three subtypes belong to this type of rulership: patriarchal, feudal, and *patrimonial* rulership. Traditional rulership has been far more widespread throughout history than the other two types of rulership identified by Weber: *charismatic* and *bureaucratic* rulership. Unlike bureaucratic rule, a personal bond exists under traditional rulership between ruler and ruled. Hence, an *ethical* appeal can be made directly to the ruler in the event of abuse.

The Universal Organizations. The family and the clan (*Sippe*). Weber sees the family since Antiquity as weakened in Europe, and strengthened in China. A central life-sphere.

Utilitarian Adaptation to the World. The orientation of action to the world's "pragmatic morality" rather than to a surpassing of this morality on the basis of a rigorous orientation to God's laws, to a constellation of religious values, and to a search for salvation.

Value-Freedom, Freedom from Values (*Wertfreiheit*). Weber insisted that all social science research must be "value-free." Once investigators have selected their theme of inquiry (see *objectivity* and *value-relevance*), personal values, preferences, and prejudices must not be allowed to interfere with the collection of empirical data and its evaluation. An intermixing of the researcher's values with those of the groups under investigation must be avoided. This axiom also implies a strict division between that which exists (the subject of scientific analysis) and that which should be (the realm of personal values and preferences). Social scientists must also uphold this ideal in the classroom, Weber maintains. *See ethical neutrality.*

Value-Judgment (*Werturteil*). An insertion of one's personal values (whether rooted in political, religious, or philosophical positions) into the lecture hall or the collection and evaluation of empirical data. Weber's methodology prohibits both. See *value-freedom* and *objectivity.*

Value-Rational Action. One of Weber's *four types of social action*. People may orient their conduct to values sincerely and to a significant extent, Weber contends, indeed even to the degree that they become obligatory, or "binding." He often contrasts this type of meaningful action to *means-end rational action*. Unlike many sociologists today, Weber perceives value-rational action as capable of, if facilitating contexts of action and strong social *carriers* appear, contesting and then banishing the other three types of action.

Value-Relevance (*Wert-relevanz*). The themes chosen to be researched are selected, Weber maintains, by reference to the investigator's values. For example, researchers who value equality across groups will be inclined to examine aspects of civil rights movements. See *objectivity.*

Virtuoso Believers. These persons possess unusual "religious qualifications." They are focused systematically on religious questions generally and salvation in particular. In contrast to lay believers.

Vocational Calling (*Beruf*). See *calling.*

"The Weber Thesis." Weber's view that values—and, in particular, a constellation of values called the "spirit of capitalism"—played a significant role (however "unquantifiable") in calling forth modern capitalism. More generally, this thesis emphasizes that explanations for economic development must acknowledge facilitating cultural—especially religion-based—patterns of action as playing a significant causal role. See *spirit of capitalism.*

Western Rationalism. A specific configuration of *ideal types, societal domains* and historical developments quite distinct from those in *Chinese rationalism* and *Indian rationalism*. See *civilizational rationalism*. Formulated in reference to the ancient city, ancient Roman law, the monotheism and value constellations of ancient Judaism and ancient Christianity, and the comparative weakening of magic and the sib group in these *world religions,* Western rationalism placed a development into motion along a *track* quite different from the tracks laid down in ancient China and ancient India. This track would eventually, especially in the Western Middle Age and High Middle Age, call forth configurations of *patterned action* that facilitated the expansion of *capitalism* and *modern capitalism*. Definition of the major features of Western rationalism allowed Weber to take a large step toward the isolation of the causes behind its origin and development.

World Mastery. The *frame of mind* of *Puritan* believers. They seek to "master" obstacles, randomness, and injustice to create for their God an orderly, just, and affluent kingdom. Because in accord with their God's commandments, it will glorify His majesty. Considered irrational when viewed from the perspective of the world-fleeing Buddhist monk. See *flight from the world*.

World and Religion. Weber's shorthand phrase to indicate his mode of causal analysis. For him, a narrow focus on "one side of the causal equation" is avoided (except in *PE*). He seeks instead to undertake multicausal investigations and assumes that motivations behind action range broadly across several types of social action, several ideal types, and several societal domains.

World Religions. Religions that, according to Weber, exercised a widespread influence: Judaism, Islam, Christianity, Hinduism, Buddhism, and Confucianism.

World View (*Weltbild*). World views vary distinctly across the great civilizations: China, India, and the West. Each world view is constituted mainly from the values of a *world religion;* each sets a *track* for a civilization's pathway of development. See *track*.

A Chronology of Max Weber's Life

April 21, 1864 Born in Erfurt, Thuringia: eldest of six children.

1866 The child becomes ill with meningitis; sister Anna dies in infancy.

1868 Brother Alfred, who will become a prominent economist and sociologist, is born.

1869 The family moves to Berlin.

1872–1882 Attends the Königliche Kaiserin-Augusta-Gymnasium (elite German high school) in the Berlin suburb of Charlottenburg.

1876 Four-year-old sister Helene dies.

1877–1881 School papers on ancient history and letters on Homer, Herodotus, Virgil, Cicero, Goethe, Kant, Hegel, and Schopenhauer.

1882 Attends the University of Heidelberg; joins the Alemannia dueling fraternity; studies law, economic history, philosophy, and history of late antiquity.

1883–1884 One year of military service at Strasbourg; occasional attendance at the University of Strasbourg.

1884–1884 Continuation of studies, now at the University of Berlin.

1885 Officer training in Strasburg; studies in Berlin for the bar exam.

1885–1886 Completion of law studies at the University of Göttingen.

1886 Passes the bar exam in Berlin; returns to parental home and remains there (except for military duty) until 1893; studies commercial law and ancient rural history.

1887–1888 Military service in Strasbourg and Posen.

1889 Doctoral dissertation on the development of joint liability in medieval trading companies.

1890 Participates with mother in the first Evangelical Social Congress.

1891 Finishes his second academic dissertation (on the agrarian history of Rome), thus becoming qualified to teach at a German university (*Habilitation*).

1891–1882 Study of farmworkers in East Elbia region (East and West Prussia); publication in 1892.

1893 Engagement to Marianne Schnitger in March; marriage in September; wedding trip to London; moves out of parental home; substitutes for his teacher Levin Goldschmidt at the University of Berlin; Associate Professor of Commercial and German Law.

1894 Military exercises in Posen (spring); appointed Professor of Economics, University of Freiburg; moves to Freiburg (fall); participates in the Evangelical Social Congress in Frankfurt (report on farmworkers); publishes study on the stock exchange.

1895 Second trip to England, Scotland, and Ireland (August–October); inaugural academic lecture, University of Freiburg.

1896 Participates in Evangelical Social Congress; appointed Professor of Economics at the University of Heidelberg.

1897 Declines to run for election to the Reichstag; father dies in summer; trip to Spain in fall.

1897–1903 Prolonged incapacity.

1898 Travel to Geneva; first sanatorium visit (Lake Constance); further breakdown at Christmas.

1899 Excused from teaching in the spring semester; resumes teaching in the fall but suffers another breakdown; offers his resignation to University of Heidelberg (declined); trip to Venice.

1900 Leaves Heidelberg in July; sanatorium residence until November (Urach); fall and winter in Corsica.

1901 Resides in Rome and southern Italy in spring; summer in Switzerland; fall and winter in Rome.

1902 Lives in Florence; again submits his resignation; returns in April to Heidelberg and begins to write on social science methodology questions; travels in winter to the French Riviera; reads Georg Simmel's *Philosophy of Money*.

1903 Trips to Rome, Holland, Belgium, and northern Germany; resigns his position at the University of Heidelberg and becomes *Honorarprofessor*; publishes "Roscher and Knies" and begins intense work on *The Protestant Ethic and the Spirit of Capitalism.*

1904 August–December travels widely in the United States; publication of half of *PE* in November and "'Objectivity' in Social Science and Social Policy" (1949), both in a journal Weber begins to co-edit, *Archiv fur Socialwissenschaft und Sozialpolitik.*

1905 Publication of second half of *PE* in *Archive* in spring; debates with the economist Schmoller on value-judgments; studies Russian before breakfast.

1906 Attends the Social Democracy Party Convention; travels to southern Italy in the fall; publication of "'Churches' and 'Sects' in North America" (1985) and "Prospects for Liberal Democracy in Tsarist Russia" (1978).

1907 Relapse of illness; travels to Italy, Holland, and western Germany; publishes a further essay on methodology questions.

1908 Trip to Provence and Florence in spring; travel to Westphalia in the fall to study the psycho-physics of work in his relatives' textile factory; publication of *The Agrarian Sociology of Ancient Civilizations* (1976); attacks in a newspaper article the practice in German universities of refusing to promote Social Democrats.

1909 Travel in southern Germany in spring; summer in the Black Forest after a relapse; attends meeting of the Association for Welfare Politics in Vienna; attacks bureaucratization together with brother Alfred; cofounds the German Sociological Association; assumes editorial leadership of the multivolume *Outline of Social Economics*, a task that eventually leads to *Economy and Society (E&S).*

1910 Trips to Berlin, Italy, and England; Georg Lukacs and Ernest Bloch begin regular visits to Weber's home; the poet Stefan George attends the *jour fixe* twice; speaks against "race biology" at the first German Sociological Association Convention.

1911 Travels to Italy in the spring and Munich and Paris in the summer; criticisms of higher education policies in Germany and fraternity practices in schools of business lead to intense newspaper controversies; begins his Economic Ethics of the World Religions (EEWR) series and continues work on *E&S.*

1912 Spring in Provence; trips to Bayreuth for the Richard Wagner Festival with Marianne and the pianist Mina Tobler, and to further regions in Bavaria in summer; defends a value-free definition of the nation at the German Sociological Association conference in Berlin; resigns from the Association.

1913 Italy in spring and fall (Ascona, Assisi, Siena, Perugia, and Rome); resides for several months in the counter-culture community in Ascona; publishes an early version of *E&S*'s "Basic Concepts" (Chapter 1); continues to work on *E&S*.

1914 Travels in spring to Ascona and Zurich to defend Frieda Gross in a child custody case; after outbreak of war in August commissioned as reserve officer to establish and manage nine military hospitals around Heidelberg; participation in further debates on value-judgments.

1915 Youngest brother Karl dies on the Russian Front; returns to research on EEWR; political activity in Berlin against German annexation policy; honorably retired in fall as hospital administrator.

1916 Trip to East Prussia with sister Lili in spring to visit Karl's grave; further trips to Vienna and Budapest; summer travel to Lake Constance; first public lecture in Germany given in 19 years; newspaper articles opposing intensified German submarine warfare against English and American ships; participates in a study group focusing on the Polish problem and the creation of a European-wide free trade zone and economic community; publishes *The Religion of China* and *The Religion of India* in the *Archiv*.

1917 *Ancient Judaism* published in the *Archiv*; lectures in Munich on science as a vocation; extensive advocacy in newspapers for electoral and parliamentary reform, and argues against censorship; alienates, despite adulation, younger generation at conferences in May and October at Lauenstein Castle in Thuringia; professorship (Economics) offered by the University of Vienna; reads Stefan George's poetry while vacationing in summer in western Germany; publishes essay on value-judgments.

1918 Begins teaching after a 19-year hiatus; two courses in Vienna offered in the university's largest lecture hall: "A Positive Critique of the Materialist View of History" and "Sociology of the State"; 25th wedding anniversary; supports a British-style constitutional monarchy for Germany; member of the founding committee of a new liberal party (the German Democratic Party); gives several election campaign speeches; encourages the Kaiser to abdicate; fails to gain a seat at the Constitutional Convention.

1919 Continues speeches on behalf of the German Democratic Party and is elected to its executive committee; lectures in Munich on "politics as a vocation"; member of the German peace delegation to Versailles charged with drafting a reply to the Allies' war guilt memorandum; in May tried to persuade General Ludendorff in Berlin to voluntarily surrender to the Allies; appointed Professor of Economics at the University of Munich; lecture courses on "General Categories in Sociology" spring/summer and "Outline of a Universal Social and Economic History" in fall/winter; moves to Munich; farewell party in Heidelberg; mother dies in October.

1920 Writes "Prefatory Remarks" to *Collected Essays on the Sociology of Religion*; revises first volume (*PE*, "Sects," 1946b, 1946c, *Religion of China*) of this three-volume project; Part I of *E&S* goes to press; "Political Science" and "Socialism" lecture courses offered in Munich; suicide of youngest sister in April; marriage crisis leads to practical separation; flu develops into pneumonia at the beginning of June; dies on June 14 in Munich.

References

Albrow, M. (1990). *Max Weber's construction of social theory*. New York, NY: St. Martin's Press.

Arnason, J. P. (2003). Max Weber: The comparative history of civilizations. In *Civilizations in dispute* (pp. 86–104). Leiden, The Netherlands: Brill.

Beetham, D. (1974). *Max Weber and the theory of modern politics*. London, UK: George Allen & Unwin.

Bell, D. (1996). *The cultural contradictions of capitalism*. New York, NY: Basic.

Bellah, R. N. (Ed.). (2006). Max Weber and world-denying love. In R. N. Bellah & S. M. Tipton (Eds.), *The Robert Bellah reader* (pp. 123–149). Durham, NC: Duke University Press.

Bendix, R. (1962). *Max Weber: An intellectual portrait*. Berkeley: University of California Press.

Bendix, R., & Roth, G. (1971). *Scholarship and partisanship*. Berkeley: University of California Press.

Burger, T. (1976). *Max Weber's theory of construct formation*. Durham, NC: Duke University Press.

Buss, A. (2003). *The Russian-Orthodox tradition and modernity*. Leiden, The Netherlands: Brill.

Buss, A. (2015). *The economic ethics of world religions and their laws*. Frankfurt, Germany: Nomos Verlag.

Camic, C., Gorski, P. S., & Trubek, D. M. (Eds.). (2005). *Max Weber's economy and society: A critical companion*. Stanford, CA: Stanford University Press.

Campbell, C. (1987). *The romantic ethic and the spirit of modern consumerism*. Oxford, UK: Blackwell.

Chalcraft, D. J., & Whimster, S. (Eds.) (2001). Issues of translation. *Max Weber Studies, 2*(November), 15–64.

Collins, R. (1986). *Weberian sociological theory*. New York, NY: Cambridge University Press.

Collins, R. (1999). *Macrohistory: Essays in sociology of the long run*. Stanford, CA: Stanford University Press.

Coser, L. A. (1971). *Masters of sociological thought*. New York, NY: Harcourt Brace Jovanovich.

Derman, J. (2013). *Max Weber on politics and social thought*. New York, NY: Cambridge University Press.

Eisenstadt, S. N. (Ed.). (1968). *The Protestant ethic and modernization*. New York, NY: Basic.

Ertman, T. (Ed.). (2016). *Max Weber's economic ethos of the world religions*. New York, NY: Cambridge University Press.

Fuchs, M. (2016). India in comparison: Max Weber's analytical agenda. In T. Ertman (Ed.), *Max Weber's economic ethos of the world religions* (pp. 235–256). New York, NY: Cambridge University Press.

Fuchs, M. (2017). Sociological entanglements: Max Weber's comparative engagement with India. In H. Harder & D. Raina (Eds.), *Disciplinary conversations in the sciences and social sciences, technology and the humanities* (pp. 346–375). London, UK: Orient Longman.

Fulbrook, M. (1978). Max Weber's "Interpretive Sociology." *British Journal of Sociology, 29*(1), 71–82.

Fulbrook, M. (1983). *Piety and politics: Religion and the rise of absolutism in England, Württemberg and Prussia*. New York, NY: Cambridge University Press.

Gerth, H. H., & Mills, C. W. (1946). Introduction. In H. H. Gerth & C. W. Mills (Eds.), *From Max Weber* (pp. 3–74). New York, NY: Oxford.

Giddens, A. (1972). *Politics and sociology in the thought of Max Weber*. London, UK: Macmillan.

Gorski, P. S. (2003). *The disciplinary revolution: Calvinism and the rise of the state in early modern Europe*. Chicago, IL: University of Chicago Press.

Henretta, J. (1993). The Protestant ethic and the reality of capitalism in colonial America. In H. Lehmann & G. Roth (Eds.), *Weber's "Protestant ethic"* (pp. 327–346). New York, NY: Cambridge University Press.

Holton, R. J. (1985). *The transition from feudalism to capitalism*. New York, NY: St. Martin's Press.

Honigsheim, P. (1968). *On Max Weber*. New York, NY: Free Press.

Huff, T. E., & Schluchter, W. (Eds.). (1999). *Max Weber and Islam*. New Brunswick, NJ: Transaction.

Hughes, H. S. (1958). *Consciousness and society: The reorientation of European social thought 1890–1930*. New York, NY: Vintage Books.

Jacob, M. C., & Kadane, M. (2003). Missing, now found in the eighteenth century: Weber's Protestant capitalist. *American Historical Review, 108*, 20–40.

Kaelber, L. (1998). *Schools of asceticism*. University Park: Pennsylvania State University Press.

Kaelber, L. (2005). Rational capitalism, traditionalism, and adventure capitalism: New research on the Weber thesis. In W. H. Swatos, Jr. & L. Kaelber (Eds.), *The Protestant ethic turns 100* (pp. 139–164). Boulder, CO: Paradigm Press.

Kalberg, S. (1983). Max Weber's universal-historical architectonic of economically-oriented action: A preliminary reconstruction. In S. G. McNall (Ed.), *Current perspectives in social theory* (pp. 253–288). Greenwood, CT: JAI Press.

Kalberg, S. (1990). The rationalization of action in Max Weber's sociology of religion. *Sociological Theory, 8*(Spring), 58–84.

Kalberg, S. (1994). *Max Weber's comparative-historical sociology*. Chicago, IL: University of Chicago Press.

Kalberg, S. (1996). On the neglect of Weber's Protestant ethic as a theoretical treatise: Demarcating the parameters of post-war American sociological theory. *Sociological Theory, 14*, 49–70.

Kalberg, S. (1997). Tocqueville and Weber on the sociological origins of citizenship: The political culture of American democracy. *Citizenship Studies, 1*(2), 199–222.

Kalberg, S. (1998). Max Weber's sociology: Research strategies and modes of analysis. In C. Camic (Ed.), *Reclaiming the argument of the founders* (pp. 208–41). Cambridge, MA: Blackwell.

Kalberg, S. (2011). Introduction to the Protestant ethic (S. Kalberg, Trans.). In Max Weber, *The Protestant Ethic and the Spirit of Capitalism* (pp. 7–59). New York, NY: Oxford.

Kalberg, S. (2012). *Max Weber's comparative-historical sociology today*. London, UK: Routledge.

Kalberg, S. (2014a). Max Weber's sociology of civilizations: The five major themes. *Max Weber Studies, 14*(2), 205–232.

Kalberg, S. (2014b). *Searching for the spirit of American democracy: Max Weber's analysis of a unique political culture, past, present, and future*. London, UK: Routledge.

Kalberg, S. (2017). Max Weber's Sociology of Civilizations: A preliminary investigation into its methodological concepts. In A. Sica (Ed.) *The Anthem Companion to Max Weber* (pp. 162–191) London, UK. New Anthem Press.

Kalberg, S. (forthcoming). *Max Weber's sociology of civilizations*.

Kim, S. H. (2004). *Max Weber's politics of civil society*. New York, NY: Cambridge University Press.

Knowles, A. K. (1997). *Calvinists incorporated: Welsh immigrants on Ohio's industrial frontier*. Chicago, IL: University of Chicago Press.

Krieger, L. (1973). *The German idea of freedom*. Chicago, IL: University of Chicago Press.

Landes, D. S. (1999). *The wealth and poverty of nations*. New York, NY: Norton.

Lehmann, H., & Roth, G. (Eds.). (1993). *Weber's Protestant ethic: Origins, evidence, contexts*. New York, NY: Cambridge University Press.

Little, D. (1969). *Religion, order and law*. Chicago, IL: University of Chicago Press.

Loewenstein, K. (1966). *Max Weber's political ideas in the perspective of our time*. Amherst: University of Massachusetts Press.

Löwith, K. (1970). Weber's interpretation of the bourgeois-capitalistic world in terms of the guiding principle of 'rationalization.' In D. Wrong (Ed.), *Max Weber* (pp. 101–123). Englewood Cliffs, NJ: Prentice-Hall.

Löwith, K. (1982), *Max Weber and Karl Marx*. London, UK: Allen & Unwin.

Maley, T. (2011). *Democracy and the political in Max Weber's thought*. Toronto, Canada: University of Toronto Press.

Marshall, G. (1980). *Presbyteries and Profits: Calvinism and the Development of Capitalism in Scotland, 1560–1707*. Oxford, UK: Clarendon Press.

Marshall, G. (1982). *In search of the spirit of capitalism*. London, UK: Hutchinson.

Mayer, J. P. (1956). *Max Weber and German politics*. New York, NY: Faber and Faber.

Molloy, S. (1980). Max Weber and the religions of China. *British Journal of Sociology, 31*(3), 377–400.

Mommsen, W. (1970). Max Weber's political sociology and his philosophy of world history. In D. Wrong (Ed.), *Max Weber* (pp. 101–123). Englewood Cliffs, NJ: Prentice-Hall.

Mommsen, W. (1974). *Max Weber: Gesellschaft, politik und geschichte*. Frankfurt, Germany: Suhrkamp.

Mommsen, W. (1985). *Max Weber and German politics, 1890–1920*. Chicago, IL: University of Chicago Press.

Mommsen, W. (1989). *The political and social theory of Max Weber*. Chicago, IL: University of Chicago Press.

Mommsen, W. (2000). Max Weber in America. *American Scholar, 69*(3), 103–112.

Mommsen, W., & Osterhammel, J. (Eds.). (1987). *Max Weber and his contemporaries*. London, UK: Unwin Hyman.

Mosse, G. (1964). *The crisis of German ideology*. New York, NY: Grosset & Dunlap.

Nelson, B. (1973). Weber's Protestant ethic: Its origins, wanderings, and foreseeable futures. In C. Y. Glock & P. R. Hammond (Eds.), *Beyond the Classics?* (pp. 71–130). New York, NY: Harper and Row.

Nelson, B. (1974). Max Weber's 'Author's introduction' (1920): A master clue to his main aims. *Sociological Inquiry, 44*(4), 269–278.

Nelson, B. (2011). *On the roads to modernity*, T. E. Huff (Ed.). Totowa, NJ: Rowman & Littlefield.

Nielsen, D. A. (2005). The Protestant ethic and the "spirit" of capitalism as grand narrative: Max Weber's philosophy of history. In W. H. Swatos, Jr. & L. Kaelber (Eds.), *The Protestant Ethic Turns 100* (pp. 53–76). Boulder, CO: Paradigm Press.

Outhwaite, W. (1975). *Understanding social life: The method called verstehen*. London, UK: Allen & Unwin.

Ringer, F. (1969). *The decline of the German mandarins*. Cambridge, MA: Harvard University Press.

Ringer, F. (1997). *Max Weber's methodology*. Cambridge, MA: Harvard University Press.

Roth, G. (1968). Introduction. In G. Roth & C. Wittich (Eds. & Trans.), Max Weber, *Economy and Society* (pp. xxvii–ciii). New York, NY: Bedminster Press.

Roth, G. (1971a). The genesis of the typological approach. In R. Bendix & G. Roth, *Scholarship and partisanship* (pp. 253–265). Berkeley: University of California Press.

Roth, G. (1971b). Sociological typology and historical explanation. In R. Bendix & G. Roth (Eds.), *Scholarship and partisanship* (pp. 109–128). Berkeley: The University of California Press.

Roth, G. (1971c). Max Weber's comparative approach and historical typology. In I. Vallier, *Comparative methods in sociology* (pp. 75–93). Berkeley: University of California Press.

Roth, G. (1976). History and sociology in the works of Max Weber. *British Journal of Sociology, 27*(3), 306–318.

Roth, G. (1993). Weber the would-be Englishman: Anglophilia and family history. In H. Lehmann & G. Roth (Eds.), *Weber's Protestant ethic: Origins, evidence, contexts* (pp. 83–122). New York, NY: Cambridge University Press.

Roth, G. (1997). The young Max Weber: Anglo-American religious influences and Protestant social reform in Germany. *International Journal of Politics, Culture and Society, 10*, 659–671.

Roth, G. (2001). *Max Webers deutsch-englische Familiengeschichte 1800–1950.* Tübingen, Germany: Mohr Siebeck.

Roth, G. (2005). Transatlantic connections: A cosmopolitan context for Max and Marianne Weber's New York visit 1904. *Max Weber Studies, 5*(January), 81–112.

Salomon, A. (1934). Max Weber's methodology. *Social Research, 1*(May), 147–168.

Salomon, A. (1935). Max Weber's political ideas. *Social Research, 2*(February), 369–384.

Scaff, L. (1998). The 'cool objectivity of sociation': Max Weber and Marianne Weber in America. *History of the Human Sciences, 11*(2), 61–82.

Scaff, L. (2011). *Max Weber in America.* Princeton, NJ: Princeton University Press.

Scaff, L. (2014). *Weber and the Weberians.* London, UK: Palgrave Macmillan.

Schluchter, W. (1981). *The rise of Western rationalism.* Berkeley: University of California Press.

Schluchter, W. (1996). *Paradoxes of modernity.* Palo Alto, CA: Stanford University Press.

Schroeder, R. (Ed.). (1998). *Max Weber, democracy and modernization.* New York, NY: St. Martin's Press.

Sica, A. (Ed.). (2017). *The anthem companion to Max Weber.* London: UK: New Anthem Press.

Silber, I. F. (1995). *Virtuosity, charisma, and social order: A comparative sociological study of monasticism in Theravada Buddhism and medieval Catholicism.* New York, NY: Cambridge University Press.

Smelser, N. (1976). *Comparative methods in the social sciences.* Englewood Cliffs, NJ: Prentice-Hall.

Swatos, W., & Kaelber, L. (Eds.). (2005). *The Protestant ethic turns 100.* Boulder, CO: Paradigm Press.

Swedberg, R. (Ed.). (2004). *The Max Weber dictionary.* Stanford, CA: Stanford University Press.

Tenbruck, F. H. (1980/1975). The problem of thematic unity in the works of Max Weber (Sam Whimster, Trans.). *British Journal of Sociology, 31*(3), 316–351.

Turner, B. S. (1974). *Weber and Islam.* London, UK: Routledge & Kegan Paul.

Turner, B. S. (1992). *Max Weber: From history to modernity.* London, UK: Routledge.

Walliman, I., Rosenbaum, H., Tatsis, N., & Zito, G. (1980). Misreading Weber: The concept of 'Macht.' *Sociology, 14*(2), 261–275.

Walzer, M. (1965). *The revolution of the saints: A study in the origins of radical politics.* Cambridge, MA: Harvard University Press.

Warner, S. (1970). The role of religious ideas and the use of models in Max Weber's comparative studies of non-capitalist societies. *Journal of Economic History,* *30*(1), 74–99.

Weber, M. (1966/1891). *Die Römische Agrargeschichte in Ihrer Bedeutung für das Staats- und Privatrecht* [The Significance of Roman Agrarian History for Civil and Private Law]. Amsterdam, The Netherlands: Verlag P. Schippers.

Weber, M. (1914). Vorwort. In K. Buecher, J. Schumpeter, & Fr. Freiherr von Wieser (Eds.), *Grundriss der Sozialökonomik, 1. Abt. Wirtschaft und Wirtschaftswissenschaft* (pp. vii–ix). Tübingen, Germany: Mohr.

Weber, M. (1927/1923). *General economic history* (F. H. Knight, Trans.). Glencoe, IL: Free Press.

Weber, M. (1946). *From Max Weber* (H. H. Gerth & C. Wright Mills, Eds. & Trans.). London, UK: Oxford.

Weber, M. (1946a/1919). Politics as a vocation. In H. H. Gerth & C. Wright Mills (Eds. & Trans.), *From Max Weber* (pp. 77–128). London, UK: Oxford.

Weber, M. (1946b/1920). Religious rejections of the world. In H. H. Gerth & C. Wright Mills (Eds. & Trans.), *From Max Weber* (pp. 323–359). London, UK: Oxford.

Weber, M. (1946c/1920). The social psychology of the world religions. In H. H. Gerth & C. Wright Mills (Eds. & Trans.), *From Max Weber* (pp. 267–301). London, UK: Oxford.

Weber, M. (1949/1922). *The methodology of the social sciences* (E. A. Shils & H. A. Finch, Eds. & Trans.). New York, NY: Free Press.

Weber, M. (1951/1920). *The religion of China* (H. H. Gerth, Ed. & Trans.). New York, NY: Free Press.

Weber, M. (1952/1920). *Ancient Judaism* (H. H. Gerth & D. Martindale, Eds. & Trans.). New York, NY: Free Press.

Weber, M. (1956/1909). Some consequences of bureaucratization. In J. P. Mayer (Trans.), *Max Weber and German Politics* (pp. 126–128). New York, NY: Faber and Faber.

Weber, M. (1958/1920). *The religion of India* (H. H. Gerth & D. Martindale, Eds. & Trans.). New York, NY: Free Press.

Weber, M. (1968/1921). *Economy and society* (G. Roth & C. Wittich, Eds.; Roth, Wittich, et al., Trans.). Berkeley: University of California Press.

Weber, M. (1975). *Max Weber: A biography* (H. Zohn, Trans.). New York, NY: Wiley.

Weber, M. (1976/1909). *The agrarian sociology of ancient civilizations* (R. I. Frank, Trans.). London, UK: New Left Books.

Weber, M. (1978). *Weber: Selections in translation* (W. G. Runciman, Ed.; E. Matthews, Trans.). Cambridge, UK: Cambridge University Press.

Weber, M. (1985/1906). 'Churches' and 'sects' in North America: An ecclesiastical socio-political sketch (C. Loader, Trans.). *Sociological Theory, 3,* 7–13.

Weber, M. (1988/1894). Entwicklungstendenzen in der Lage der ostelbischen Landarbeiter. In Marianne Weber (Ed.), *Gesammelte Aufsätze zur Sozial- und Wirtschaftsgeschichte* (pp. 470–507). Tübingen, Germany: Mohr.

Weber, M. (1992). *Wissenschaft als Beruf, Politik als Beruf* (W. J. Mommsen and Wolfgang Schluchter, Eds.). *Max Weber Gesamtausgabe I/17*. Tübingen, Germany: J.C.B. Mohr.

Weber, M. (1994). *Weber: Political writings* (P. Lassman & R. Speirs, Eds.; R. Speirs, Trans.). Cambridge, UK: Cambridge University Press.

Weber, M. (2001/1907–1910). *The Protestant ethic debate: Max Weber's replies to his critics, 1907–1910*. D. Chalcraft & A. Harrington, Eds.; A. Harrington & M. Shields, Trans.). Liverpool: Liverpool University Press.

Weber, M. (2004). *The essential Weber: A reader* (S. Whimster, Ed.). London, UK: Routledge.

Weber, M. (2005). *Max Weber: Readings and commentary on modernity* (S. Kalberg, Ed.). New York, NY: Wiley-Blackwell.

Weber, M. (2009). *The Protestant ethic and the spirit of capitalism with other writings on the rise of the West* (S. Kalberg, Ed., Trans., & Intro.). New York, NY: Oxford.

Weber, M. (2011/1920). *The Protestant ethic and the spirit of capitalism* (S. Kalberg, Trans. & Intro.). New York, NY: Oxford.

Weber, M. (2012). *Max Weber: Collected methodological writings* (H. H. Bruun & S. Whimster, Eds.; H. H. Bruun, Trans.). London, UK: Routledge.

Whimster, S., & Lash, S. (Eds.). (1987). *Max Weber, rationality and modernity*. London, UK: Routledge.

Zaret, D. (1985). *The heavenly contract: Ideology and organization in pre-revolutionary Puritanism*. Chicago, IL: University of Chicago Press.

Index

About the Author

Stephen Kalberg teaches classical and contemporary theory, comparative political cultures, and comparative-historical sociology at Boston University. He is the author of *Max Weber's Comparative-Historical Sociology* (1994), translator of Max Weber's *The Protestant Ethic and the Spirit of Capitalism* (2011), and editor of *Max Weber: Readings and Commentary on Modernity* (2005) and *The Protestant Ethic and the Spirit of Capitalism with Other Writings on the Rise of the West* (2009). An earlier introduction to Max Weber was translated into German, Spanish, Italian, Portuguese, and Turkish. He is the author more recently of *Max Weber's Comparative-Historical Sociology Today* (2012) and *Searching for the Spirit of American Democracy: Max Weber's Analysis of a Unique Political Culture Past, Present, and Future* (2014b). His *Max Weber's Sociology of Civilizations* is forthcoming. In addition, he has written numerous studies that compare German and American societies.